THE ACTOR

T H E **A** C T O R
A PRACTICAL GUIDE TO A PROFESSIONAL CAREER

By Eve Brandstein
with Joanna Lipari

DONALD I. FINE, INC.
New York

Library of Congress Cataloging-in-Publication Data

Brandstein, Eve.
  The actor: a practical guide to a professional career.

  Bibliography: p.
  Includes index.
  1. Acting—Vocational guidance.   I. Lipari, Joanna.
II. Title.
PN2055.B73   1987   792'028'023   86-82380
ISBN 1-55611-003-0 (pbk.: alk. paper)

Manufactured in the United States of America
10 9 8 7 6 5 4 3 2

In memory of my sister and brother,
Ruth and Oscar

IN APPRECIATION:
*to Harold Clurman, Sanford Meisner and Darryl Hickman;
to J. Remi Aubuchon and Leigh Skinner;
to Dawn Dreiling, Rochelle Linker;
to Richard Pine;
to George Coleman;
to Norman Lear;
to all those who love the "work."*

FOREWORD

I'M crazy about actors. To the dramatist, the actor is often more than just the interpreter of the character; a well-known actor can inspire a character before the writer puts the first word on paper.

Even with a good script in hand, the writer, producer and director may think they know exactly what the piece and the character is all about, only to find that when a good actor inhabits the role, something new, something different, something better may evolve.

We are talking, of course, about working actors. But for every one of them, there may be a hundred banging on the door. The business of being an actor is often mired down with frustration and confusion because they don't understand the realities of the business. Most actors are afraid of the realities. I understand their problem, but I also know how important it is that they overcome it in order to succeed. Actors need information, along with talent and training. They need the tools to understand how to achieve their career goals. Eve Brandstein shows the actor how to do just that.

I've known Eve for ten years. I've watched her work with

actors, helping them to develop their skills, encouraging them and counseling them through their fears and frustrations. With her guidance, I've seen actors put their careers together, learning the business skills they need to implement their craft. Eve Brandstein tells the truth about "careering."

Beyond her background in casting, Eve has been a creative artist—a producer, director and poet. Her sensitivity to the actors' creative needs, coupled with her acute knowledge and sense of the business, makes her a unique career guide for anyone interested in this profession. This book can help the actor form a strategy for success.

—Norman Lear
1987

CONTENTS

Foreword   ix

Introduction   xiii

SECTION A:
GETTING TO KNOW THE ACTOR IN YOU
1. Knowing What You Want—and Why   3
2. The Actor's Personality   20
3. Question-and-Answer Seminar   38

SECTION B:
LEARNING THE RULES OF THE GAME
4. Your Next Move   43
5. The Nuts and Bolts of Show Biz   55
6. Interviews, Auditions and Callbacks   74
7. Rejection   88
8. Question-and-Answer Seminar   96

SECTION C:
CAREER-WINNING STRATEGIES
9. Opportunity!   101
10. The Luck Factor: How to Create It!   108
11. The "Who-You-Know" Game: Networking and Nepotism   129
12. Sex and Your Career   143
13. The X Factor   154
14. The Confident Style   165

15. Making the Most of Your Looks   177
16. The Ultimate Strategy:
       Self-Appreciation   187
17. Question-and-Answer Seminar   193

SECTION D:

STAYING ON TOP OF YOUR CAREER

18. How to Pay Your Rent   199
19. How to Stay Sane in a Crazy Business   209
20. Why Careers Stop and How to Get
       Them to Go   220
21. When to Quit   242
22. Don't Be Your Own Worst Enemy   253
23. The Working Actor   261
24. A Daily Work Plan   270
25. A Final Note   276
26. Question-and-Answer Seminar   278

Suggested Reading and Resource Index   280

INTRODUCTION

THROUGH many years of experience as a casting director, a stage director and, now, a producer, I have observed a startling aspect in the actor—some of the most talented have failed to succeed in the professional arena. Why does this happen? Why do so many talented people fail while others, perhaps less talented, succeed? In many cases, the answer is shockingly simple: they have no *career skills*. They fail to realize that the performer must master skills that will help him advance in show business. Time and again, I see actors frustrated and confused because they simply don't have the right information on the workings of the industry. Often these talented people lose work or find the process unduly difficult because of this lack of simple, yet important, information.

This business is not fair, nor is there a checklist for success. Unlike medical or law school, the curriculum is uncertain, often controversial, and the job outcome capricious. One does not advance on merit alone: the actor must concentrate on constructing an awareness and execution of his career as if it were an enterprise—a business.

Don't misunderstand: exploring your talent and studying your craft are essential elements in creating the professional actor. However, it is only half of what it takes to be a success in this industry. The other half is the development of the skills and strategies necessary to become, maintain and advance as a *pro*. That is what *this* book is about.

I have watched hundreds of acting careers develop—some well, some not. I've seen newcomers without any training or special ability swept into stardom in a few minutes. I've also seen talented performers continuously plug away without much tangible success. That's the curse of this profession and, in fact, the curse of *anyone* who desires success in the entertainment industry, whether actor, director, writer, producer or studio executive. Whether overnight star or well-seasoned pro, an actor must work hard on his career. That's it—plain and simple. Anyone who thinks this career is easy is an absolute fool. An actor probably spends, at best, only 10 percent of his time actually performing. The rest of the time, the artist looks for work, rehearses when he gets work, continues study to augment his craft and, in between, looks for future jobs. When the performer steps up to receive an Academy Award, those few precious minutes at the podium represent years of continuous effort.

In this book, I will share with you the knowledge and discoveries I've acquired. I will be your "coach" and assist you in developing your career. I'll help you develop and actualize your talent, create a winning strategy and shape your career for maximum satisfaction. This isn't just a "how to" book with interesting information; we will investigate the psychology of the actor's career mind. The interactive approach requires you, the actor, to participate.

If you're just beginning in this profession, read through the entire book first, then go back to those sections you need to concentrate on. If you already have a professional career, I suggest you use this book a bit differently. Use the first two sections as a refresher course in career basics. The third and fourth sections are specifically geared to someone needing a catalyst to move their career forward.

Let's get your career headed in a winning direction.

Eve Brandstein
January 1987

Getting to Know
the Actor in You

SO YOU'VE GOT THE ACTING BUG? Great, but how do you break in? Perhaps you've already embarked on an acting career but find that most of your performing is done while waiting on tables in a restaurant. You need help: not airy cliches on luck and perseverance, but cold, hard information to get you on the fast track.

As a veteran casting director and producer, I'm going to give you the information—*the inside information*—you need to get your career going. As your personal "coach" and confidante, I'll help you develop and actualize your talent, create a winning strategy and shape your career for maximum satisfaction.

Where to begin? With *you,* the actor*! This section focuses on *you:* what you want and why, what location would help you actualize your goals and most importantly *who you are.* We'll take a look at your strengths and weaknesses. In-depth surveys and exercises will help guide you on the most constructive path, molding and shaping you for success. This book requires you to be an *active participant.* You can maximize the information

---

*The term actor is used throughout the book to mean both male and female.

in this and subsequent sections if you approach it with an open mind, a positive outlook and an enthusiasm for work and success. We will work together to make the most of your professional potential!

Knowing What
You Want—and Why $\textbf{I}$

*Acting has to be a religion. It should be sacred and yet not
be taken too seriously. It should be self-evident. It takes
discipline and hard work. Some actors have gregarious
personalities—I'm not like that. But I have a career and it's
the only one I can live with. It allows me to realize the
business of acting isn't everything, but the craft is.*

—Aidan Quinn, *Early Frost*,
All My Sons, Reckless,
The Mission

YOU have a burning desire to be an actor. Now what? Attend
classes, have pictures taken, send out résumés? First things first:
what do you want and why? Do you want to be a star on
Broadway, a regular on a soap opera, a stand-up comic with a
talk show? What is your dream—your focus? Without a focus,
an individual is lost. Can you imagine yourself going to the
airport and getting a plane ticket without knowing where
you're going? Absurd, isn't it? Yet I often see actors trying to
do this exact thing with their careers. They are "along for the
ride," so to speak, with no clear idea where they are going and
what they want to do when they get there. It's a terrible way
to run your career and *your life*. Having an acting career requires
discipline, consciousness and dedication to your goals.

For the beginner just starting out—take the time to consider
your goals and motivation. Exploring these issues will help
build the strong foundation that allows your career to survive
the ups and downs of this variable profession. If your career is

already underway, but seems at a standstill, it may be that you've never addressed these vital topics—or perhaps you have only given them a cursory review. Generalizations and vague yearnings rarely materialize anything. Maybe your goals and motivations have been clearly delineated and it's now time to take the next step: reevaluating your priorities. Maybe you have accomplished some of your earlier goals and it's time to raise the stakes a bit; maybe your goals are no longer sufficiently motivating for you. The fact remains that the first step to career success is to define clearly what "success" means to you in terms of setting tangible goals and determining concrete motivation.

If you don't invest a meaningful amount of commitment to your art, your talent won't develop. Similarly, you need commitment to the career side of acting. Seems simple, but surprisingly, most actors have no idea what they want. Oh, they say things like "I want to be a star" or "I want the respect of my peers" or "I want to be rich and famous." But what do they *really mean?* My experience has shown me that the most successful performers are the ones who *know what they want* and *why they want it.*

I always have had the need to express myself. Whether it's photography or painting. I have to be creating something. I felt actors were special people. More in touch and open with their feelings. That attracted me. Acting is creating with your body and soul, and that's a great challenge.

—Elizabeth Bracco,
Color of Money,
Stake Out, Crime Story

Goals and motivation. That's where we'll begin. The answers to these two questions—*what do you want* and *why do you want it*—shape a working strategy for achievement!

INVESTIGATING THE "WHAT AND WHY"

Setting solid goals and utilizing powerful motivations—it's not easy to know exactly what you want from something, whether it be your career or your mate. We hear people talk about wanting to "fall in love," but though it's a very real desire, they find it hard to explain what they mean. Some goal/motivation duos are stronger than others. Consider the following:

EXAMPLE 1:

I love my home. It's the one I've always wanted. I need to make money to pay for it.

EXAMPLE 2:

Someday I'd like to have my own home. And when I can afford it, I'll start looking.

The difference between the two is obvious. In Example 1, the goal is real and immediate (the speaker is already living there), and the motivation is strong. If you don't pay the mortgage, you lose the home. Whereas the other is not very immediate nor highly motivating. That doesn't mean that you can't be motivated by a goal in the future. You can. But your goal must be clear and specific and the motivation strong.

Let's go back to Example 2 again. What if the person expressed this goal and motivation in another way?

My dream is to someday have my own home. It's what I really want, and I'm working hard to make that a reality. I even put money away to start saving for the down payment.

See? Now the goal, though possibly far off in the future, is nonetheless real and highly motivating for this person. This is what you must do—formulate solid, specific and highly motivating goals.

Exercise # 1: Dreaming Is Planning

What do you want from your career? Try this exercise. Sit in a chair, hands relaxed on your lap, feet resting on the floor. Relax your neck and face. Push aside your worries and the lists of things you have to do. And now, fantasize . . . That's right—*dream!* Go on. Run a little movie in your head. The movie's about *you* and what you want from your career. The plot is simple, and the lead character, *you,* is captivating. What pictures do you see? Make your "dream" as real as possible. Add to it. How do you become a success? Where do you see yourself? On a Broadway stage taking a curtain call? Or accepting an Academy Award? If so, what kind of play or movie were you in? Let your mind explore this fantasy freely and in as much detail as possible. (Later on in the book, we'll use this same exercise to help you accomplish your goals.)

Well, what happened? How much of your dream had to do with the actual art and craft of acting and how much had to do with trappings like fame and money? Are your goals actually extraneous to the work itself? If so, can you achieve your goals in another way? For example, if becoming very wealthy is a major goal for you, you might want to investigate other avenues of making money rather than being an actor. Although major stars may make millions of dollars per film, most actors, 80 percent in fact, make under three thousand dollars per year! Many people are drawn to the idea of quick money as a ticket out of poverty, not realizing—or wanting to deal with—what the odds really are.

What I'm suggesting is that you take a look at your goals. If they are full of the trappings and not the actual work itself, it might be wise to reevaluate. Successful actors who have careers that last the test of time are invariably people who for one reason or another are drawn to the work itself, to the creativity, to the process. It's this sense of vocation, the fact that they've set their sights on this particular career and not just on what this career might bring as a result, that makes them professionals. These people are able to withstand the rigors of the career because they have the type of goals and motivation that can carry them through the tough times. And trust me, no matter who you are, there will be tough times. Honest. Even for the biggest stars.

> *I was going to be a doctor for my family, but acting was for me. So I kept it a secret. When I started out I was very different from the sleek, slim black women who were on television and films. I was heavier and I had frizzy hair. I knew I was overweight and I looked different. Roger Corman believed in me, inspired me and told me I could do anything. By the time I went out for readings, I was told I was good, but my hair was too radical (though they were accepting afros, mine was full and wilder). I lost weight and began running. I studied the classics and was filled with integrity. I always play true to myself, and I've been accepted for who I am. I respect acting, and I applied that to my sense of this business. If I'm accepted, fine. If not, it will happen with someone else. It always did and it always will.*

> —Pam Greer,
> IMAGE AWARD WINNER for
> *Fool for Love, Fort
> Apache, The Bronx,
> Crime Story, Miami Vice*

If your only goal is to be a "personality" or a "celebrity," acting may not be the right choice for you. I'm not saying that you can't be successful with those goals. There are numerous examples of just such people. I am saying that with these goals, you limit your chance for fulfillment and satisfaction in your career as well as your chance for a successful life. There's a difference between a shallow goal and a solid one. It's the solid ones that I want you to focus on. It's the solid ones that will give you the strength to grow, succeed, flourish and be satisfied. I want nothing less for you.

If it sounds like I'm trying to discourage you from this career, you're absolutely right. This is not an occupation for the faint-hearted. I don't care who or what kind of actor we're talking about—whether a brilliant Shakespearean actor or an ex-model in a TV series, all actors who have professional careers work very hard for them! Remember: *working hard may not be hard work.* We don't generally think someone's working hard if they look like they're enjoying themselves. It's true. When we think of working hard, we think of working long hours, foregoing other, usually more pleasurable, activities and, in general, sacrificing and "slaving" away. Hard work is the buck private of the army. It's drudgery, a drag, a bore. But that's not necessarily true! Working hard is devoting a good deal of time and energy to accomplishing a goal. You are giving of yourself. Rehearsing and working on a character part for ten hours a day is working hard, but the actor playing the part may not think of it as anything but sheer delight.

Digging a ditch is hard work—and probably not very enjoyable. Practicing scenes, watching plays and movies, taking acting and singing lessons, going on auditions, keeping up your appearance and meeting people—all of that takes dedication, drive and high-level motivation, but if you love acting, it's fun! And hardly hard work! Forget the suffering artist in the garret. Sure, you'll make sacrifices—because you want to—to accomplish your dream. Successful people understand that mental framework. Ask Lee Iacocca if he works hard and he'll say yes and immediately tell you how much he enjoys it. Doesn't sound like the ditch-digging definition of hard work, does it?

Let's go back again to that first exercise. Take your dream and expand on it a little. Try and see yourself doing the work. What are you doing? Picture yourself in the *process.* Imagine different work aspects of your career—performing a play, singing, acting in a film or television show, auditioning for parts. Now what do you see? Where are the images vague? Where are they strongly delineated? Remember: odds are, when the images are vague it might be because you don't have enough information to be able to create detailed images. Or the images may be vague because you have no particularly strong feeling or need for that aspect of your career. Is that true? What do you really want and why? It all comes back to that.

A CLOSER LOOK AT THE "WHY" COMPONENT

Now let's dig into the *why*—your motivation for this career. Ask yourself *why*. Not "what" got you started or "who" said what about your talent, but *why* you want to be an actor. Investigate. Chances are there are a number of reasons. Think it through. Go back to the dream exercise. Try again. What fantasies carry you through? What can motivate you about being successful as an actor? Try jotting down any and all ideas about the why of it. Don't edit yourself. It may take you several trys before you start zeroing in, or it might come out in seconds. What's there? Money? Approval? Possibly revenge—the "I'll show them" punch? Try to be specific. There may be one motivation, but more likely there are several. Get in contact with them. In a most practical, behavioral way, the why—your motivation—can be especially helpful when you understand its function in your career. It can feed you energy and support. On the other hand, it can also turn against you.

For example: say you discover your motivation is to prove to your crabby Aunt Betty that you can sing. Then suddenly one day, Aunt Betty admits that you've got a terrific voice. Now what happens to your motivation? Maybe it crumbles. Or maybe Aunt Betty is no longer important—it's all the other "Aunt Bettys" out there who don't applaud you. In fact, maybe you're doing very well as a singer but still feel a failure because you know of an "Aunt Betty" who doesn't like your voice. See what I mean? Investigating the *why* can lead you to all sorts of life notions and decisions by which you live. For the actor, these ideas can translate into powerful motivations for success—or failure.

Over the years, I have heard a wide range of motivational reasons. It's said that famed actor/director John Cassavetes became an actor just to meet girls! Seems he had a buddy who was an actor and accompanied his friend to an audition. When he saw all the beautiful girls waiting to read, he decided to take up acting. Obviously, his motivation worked for him.

On the other hand, I've known many actors who describe a "profound knowing" that acting is what they must do. It's almost a mission—and one that they are willing to pursue despite obstacles. I've seen a lot of actors succeed only after a long period of hard work and continual disappointment. Yet, through all the doubts and hardship, these actors remain dedicated to their mission. Why? Because it makes them happy! Sounds trite, but it's true. It is the ultimate goal in life.

These actors are motivated because they enjoy the process. Success, pleasure, the challenge of obstacles: that's only part of their life—or rather, their way of life. The real core is the work—the creativity, growth, psychological understanding and almost spiritual development. It's the person who loves the art of the theater versus someone who yearns to be a celebrity. I've talked to dozens of actors who have an authentic desire for the profession. Of course, they want to be successful, wealthy and recognized. But their desire goes beyond that. They desire the artistic work for itself. Often they must deal with hardship, setbacks and insecurity—both financial and emotional—yet when they talk about acting, it is clear that it makes them feel good. When the work itself starts "feeling bad," it may be time to look in other directions. I'm not suggesting ditching your career when the going gets rough. What I am talking about is putting your life—and the quality of that life—ahead of some made-up goal that has lost its value and enjoyment. I'm talking about searching for happiness in your life, rather than fulfilling a childhood quest for fame and fortune. Throughout this book, we'll keep looking at the ultimate goal—and how to help you achieve it.

Are you ready to harness that motivational power to work for you? Why do *you* want this career? The *why* helps you keep your eye on your goal and travel through obstacles as they appear. Sometimes it is only the sheer force of your motivation that will keep you going despite hopeless odds.

To be a professional actor, you have to speak with your heart, not with your head. Stop thinking of it as just a business but as a way of life.

—Perry Lang, *1941,*
Tales from the Darkside,
The Big Red One, Body and
Soul

It is that power that elevates your acting career from a mere job to a life vocation. Most of all, it is the spirit that allows you to enjoy the process of your career as well as the results. But more about that later. Right now, let's get to work on discovering your motivational power.

Exercise 2: Goal/Motivation Clusters

This exercise was originally designed to help writers free up their creativity. Perhaps clarifying your goals will help your creativity—to know what you mean by "success," "getting the job" or "being the star." It can also give you clues to what your powerful motivators are.

Here's how it works:

1. Pick a word or short phrase that represents a goal you would like to achieve as an actor. It doesn't matter if the word is general, for example, *success,* or specific, for example, *Academy Award* or *movie star.*

2. Write down the word or phrase in the center of a blank piece of paper. Draw a circle around it.

3. Now get ready to play. From this nucleus, develop clusters of ideas, words, images that are sparked when you think about that nucleus word or phrase. For example, *star* might lead to *movie roles.*

4. For each new word or phrase, note it down on the page, draw an arrow to show where it came from and circle it. You can continue adding circles emanating from your original nucleus, or another circle can become the nucleus for a new cluster.

5. When you've finished brainstorming, take a moment's rest, come back and look at what you've written. Often, there amid the circles lie your real and specific "wants." Think about them. Which are important to you now? Which will be important in the future? Which can you begin work on *now?*

The following are two examples, step-by-step, of cluster exercises done by two different actors. Do the cluster exercises as many times as you like. You can use the same nucleus word or another. Below are a list of nucleus words and phrases which might be helpful.

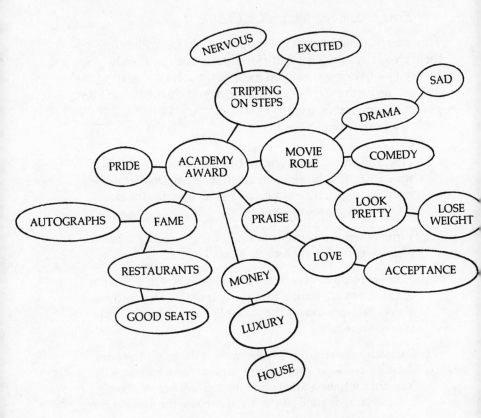

NUCLEUS WORDS AND PHRASES

movie star
respect of your peers
auditions
acting classes
singing

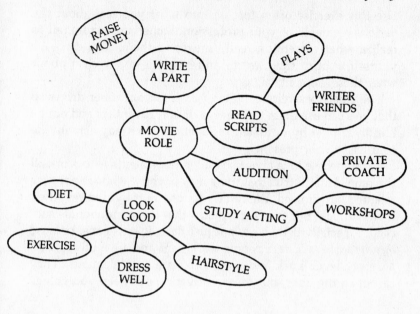

NUCLEUS WORDS AND PHRASES

Academy Award
vocation
career
success
leading role
pictures and resumes
theater
popularity
plays
Broadway
television
comedy
TV series
drama
Shakespeare
fame
interviews

Use this exercise often to clue into what you feel about the various elements of your profession. Sometimes actors fail to realize what something really means to them. You can save yourself a lot of time, worry and hassle if you're clear about what these elements signify.

The cluster exercise can clue you into your inner drives so that you can use them to your maximum advantage and not be blindly driven by outdated motivations that may actually be counter to your present goals.

Many people joke about so-called non-talents who work all the time. And it's true that there may be those who are not very talented but succeed. We can try to toss it off by crediting their looks or luck, but the fact remains that these individuals succeed, especially if they are not just flash-in-the-pans, because *they are driven to.* These people work hard and are motivated on a deeper level. Luck and good looks are only elements. They can open the door, but only motivation can keep you going.

ATTENTION AND ACCEPTANCE

One of the most common motivations for actors is getting attention and acceptance from the public and fellow actors. We all want attention. And the rule of thumb is *The More You Can Get, The Better It Is.* It starts young. A little girl twirls around in front of Mommy, who's delighted at her child's dancing ability. Mom smiles and hugs the little girl, and the quest for attention begins.

It's the same with acceptance. Who doesn't understand the need to be accepted by people? I don't think it's possible for any of us to pass through puberty without knowing the joy of acceptance or the pain of rejection. It's human nature. Mix that with some creative talent, an empathetic sensibility and a desire for the limelight and you have yourself one fully zestful—and motivated—actor. In fact, I don't think it's possible for an actor to succeed unless acceptance and attention are part of his motivational makeup. Now, what this means to you personally might be different from what it means to other actors. To get close to these motivational forces, ask yourself: do I crave attention and acceptance? From whom? Is it a goal I'm moving towards, for example, "People will like my work and heap love and kindness on me"? Or is it a goal I'm moving away from, for example, "Nobody pays any attention to me or likes me. If I can become a star, then things will be better"?

Motivation away from something or some consequence is not as powerful as motivation toward something. It's only logical. When you're moving *toward* something, you look ahead with expectation, your attitude is positive and your thoughts are filled with the wonderful goal and how happy you will be when you achieve it. When you're motivated *away* from something, the process is reversed. You back away, concentrating on putting distance between you and your feared result. You can't see the future because you're *backing up* into it. There's no positive expectation or delight in fantasy, only hope that you can get away and fear that you'll fail. Motivations away from goals may work for you. However, the likelihood that you can sustain a satisfying, fulfilling career is doubtful if you are consistently motivated *away* from a situation rather than motivated *toward* a goal.

Take a look at your motivations. Start with general ones like *acceptance* and *attention*. Are they *forward* motivations or *avoidance* motivations? What other things motivate you? Money? Power? Sex? Fame? Love? Again, are these motivations *toward* something? If not, how do these *negative* motivations work for you? Do they help you accomplish your goals and improve your life? Or are these motivations draining you? Are they tied up with maintaining the status quo in fear that your life condition will worsen? I've seen a goodly number of actors put all their attention into "treading water," hoping against hope that their condition won't worsen and cause them to "drown." Not a terrific mental environment for engendering success!

If you discover that many of your motivations are *away* from situations, take a look and see how you might change them from the negative to the positive. For example, say your financial condition is in the pits. You're behind on the rent, you can't afford your acting classes nor would you have the time if you could. Your financial picture looks pretty bleak. Now, you can choose to motivate yourself by worrying what will happen if you don't get this acting job or that commercial. This is valid but won't give you a tenth of the mileage you'll get if you focus on what you want. You might choose to look at your financial condition as an excellent opportunity to take on an extra job that earns money while you research a role or gather character insights.

I've seen many actors do that. I've seen middle-class, college-educated male actors work as construction workers. Not only do they earn money and keep their bodies in shape, but in addition, they have the opportunity to investigate a way of life that otherwise would be unknown to them. There are millions of jobs in unfamiliar areas where you not only can earn that much-needed income, but also expand your life experiences to use later in your acting. One actor took a job as a floor reporter on the Stock Exchange. Her rationale was that it exposed her to the world of business and high finance, earned her some money and would come in handy later as a source of both character material and investment expertise when she made her first million! These people have transformed a negative necessity into a positive adventure. How to survive while looking for work is one of the actor's toughest challenges.

In another section we'll discuss possible ways to earn money on the "outside" and how to get the most out of it. For now, what I want you to see is that the *quality* of your *goals* and *motivations* can affect your attitude, desire, stamina and consequently your career! I'm not looking to urge an army of beatific thespians to handle rejection and poverty with a song in their hearts and a smile on their lips. It's just fine to be angry, upset, frightened and everything else when faced with obstacles. It's just that it's better to use all this energy to *get somewhere* than to *back away from something*.

There is one more vital element to goal-setting—organizing your priorities. As you've probably already noticed from the first two exercises, there is no paucity of goals in your clusters! That's wonderful—the more goals you have, the more motivation. But there is a catch: if you haven't ordered your priorities, your plan of action will suffer from trying to accomplish too many things at once. I see actors making this mistake time and again. When you ask them what their goals are they usually have quite a complete list, ranging from movie roles, TV commercials and TV guest appearances to stand-up comedy and nightclub singing. . . . The list is inexhaustable. Then I ask which of these goals are top priorities. At this point I get a rather glazed stare and the response "All of them." It seems that actors proceed on a shotgun theory—they throw out as much as they can in as many directions as they can and hope something hits. Well, I'm here to tell you that *the shotgun theory doesn't work.*

It can't work. Stand in the center of the room, and take one step in every direction at once. What happens? Not much. And that's exactly what happens when actors do not order their priorities. It's one of the most elemental mistakes in managing a career—any career, not just one in this business. You need to order those items, errands or projects according to their importance. You simply can't do everything. You need to focus, hone your options and concentrate on the most important ones. It's an incredibly simple concept. Yet time after time, I see actors suffering from this lack of priority organization.

Where does that leave us? Actually, right back at the beginning of this chapter—*what do you want* and *why do you want it?* It's time for us to seriously sit down, take pen in hand, and figure out where you're headed.

Exercise #3: Priority Goal-Setting

This next exercise helps you delineate and prioritize your goals and link them up to your powerful motivational forces.

Take the time to do this exercise completely. This is your career. No one else's. And frankly, few, if any, will give a fig about it. So take the time now. Start exploring. It can only make you stronger. Being *specific* about what you want in a career, or in life, is no easy task. Many people cling to vague, dreamlike visions of what they want their lives to be like. Going nowhere, these folks bemoan their fates and the cruel industry that has kept them from success. True, there are no guarantees—except this one: *If you don't know where you're going, you probably won't get there.*

On a piece of paper, list the most important goals or values in your life *now.* Are you interested in theater? Do you want to break into television? Films? What immediate goals do you want to concentrate on? Don't limit yourself just to acting goals. Include *all* life goals. Do you want a family? Is there a specific place you want to live? After you've made a complete list, go back over it and pick out the top *ten* goals. (If you have less than ten, don't worry. Many very directed people have only one single goal that motivates them to accomplishment. However, check your goals and make sure they are not too general, such as "successful actor" rather than "a leading role in a dramatic play.")

Next, look over your ten goals. Which one is the most important to you? That is, if you could pick only *one*, which would it be? When you've made a choice, write it down as your number one goal. Now go back over your list and find the second most important, then the third and so on. When you're done, you should have your goals listed from one to ten, according to their importance. This is called setting priorities. But you're not finished yet. How do you know that these are really the goals that are most important to you? You don't until you've thoroughly investigated and explored them.

Take ten sheets of 8" × 11" paper. On top of each page, put a different goal from your list. Now go page by page through your goals. On each page, write what that goal means to you, what steps you would have to take to accomplish it, what you are willing to sacrifice to accomplish it, and what you hope to get from this goal. Why is this goal important to you at this time in your life? Write a complete page. If you discover that you can only scribble a couple of sentences that are too vague or general, put that page aside, go on to the rest and return to it later.

Once you've organized your goals according to their priority in your life and have written one entire page of "details" per goal, review the ten goal choices you've made.

You might discover that a goal you thought was vital is actually not as important as something else in your life. Also, you must take into consideration that this is what you want *now*. Those goals may change in six months, a year, five years. In fact, part of effective goal-setting is the regular reviewing of priorities and adjusting them according to changing life needs.

Repeat this exercise until you feel absolutely certain of your immediate goals. Remember: this is where you are today. This doesn't mean your goals won't change. It is a starting point—a plan of action. Reviewing the detail pages for each goal will give you ideas on what steps to take first. Concentrate on your number one goal. What should you do to make it a reality? Formulate a plan of action and go for it. If this means that some of your other goals must wait because they are lower on your priority list, then so be it. Don't throw the goal away; just realize that you can't head in too many directions at once. Begin now to go after goal number one. Then, if you have more time, add goal number two. This is effective time management. Concentrate your energies. Stay focused, and go for the goal.

Don't be discouraged if, at first, it seems impossible to really know what you want and why. If it were all that easy, you would have done it ages ago. Sorting out what we really want to accomplish with our lives is one of life's challenges. Just remember: being an artist does not excuse you from the responsibility of handling the "business" side of your life. It actually doesn't matter *what* it is you want. If it's truly important to you, it will be a good motivator. Notice how others set priorities. Do you know some efficient goal-setters? Do you know others who are floundering? It's up to you. Take the time to really think these things through. After all, it's not only your career— it's your life. And the only one you've got.

The Actor's Personality 2

*Life is a never-ending process of falling in and out of touch
with oneself. As an actor, I can only hope for perfect timing.
I think "Honest John" from Walt Disney's Pinocchio
says it best: "Hi diddle dee, an actor's life for me."*

—Bobby DiCicco, *Night Shift,*
The Big Red One, 1941.

"KEEP your chin up and keep trying." "You gotta get out there
and hustle." "You need to be more confident (or ambitious,
diplomatic, outgoing, etc.)." Every struggling performer gets
advice. At best, it's confusing. More often it sends you off into
a depressing "self-evaluation" wherein you become painfully
aware of all your foibles and feel even less secure about succeeding. The questions you need to ask yourself are very simple: What are the strong points of my personality style, what
are the weak points and how can I maximize the former and
minimize the latter? Do I have the right personality to be a
successful actor? Is there such a thing? There are so many
different kinds of personalities that wind up in the acting profession. There are nice actors, selfish ones, happy ones, cynical
ones. Some actors have moved their careers forward because
they have great personalities. They sell themselves well with
charm, appeal and focus. Some actors (brilliant talents) turn
people off. Their personalities are negative. How does this
apply to you?

ACTOR PERSONALITY PROFILE QUIZ

Let's start with what kind of personality *you are* compared to what kind of personality you think *an actor should have.*

Read the adjectives and phrases below. Put a check in the first column labeled "I Am" for each word or phrase that describes you as you see yourself. Then cover the first column.

Now go back and read through the list again. This time, you are discerning what traits you think an actor should have to be successful. This time place a check in the second column labeled "A Successful Actor Would Be" for each word or phrase that describes the way someone should be to become a successful actor.

I AM		A SUCCESSFUL ACTOR WOULD BE
	emotional	
	shy	
	aggressive	
	opinionated	
	sensitive	
	hustler	
	independent	
	ambitious	
	relaxed	
	impulsive	
	rational	
	resilient	
	average	
	enthusiastic	
	handles stress well	
	considerate	
	expressive	
	energetic	
	cynical	
	humorous	
	business-minded	

_____ apathetic _____
_____ goal-oriented _____
_____ attractive _____
_____ craves attention _____
_____ honest _____
_____ retiring _____
_____ intelligent _____
_____ bossy _____
_____ likes privacy _____
_____ clever _____
_____ self-centered _____
_____ interesting _____
_____ lucky _____
_____ forceful _____
_____ success comes easily _____
_____ sincere _____
_____ fragile _____
_____ vain _____
_____ large ego _____
_____ dedicated _____
_____ nervous _____

INTERPRETING YOUR TEST RESULTS

Take a look at your columns. How many matches do you have—that is, how many times did you either have BOTH columns checked or *neither* column checked with regard to a single trait? How many *did not* match? Is there a big gap between your concept of your own personality and your concept of the personality required to succeed as an actor?

The most important lesson to learn from this quiz is that there is no such thing as an actor's personality! Traits like outgoing, emotional and aggressive are often thought to be necessary to the actor out there hustling jobs. The reality is actually *any* trait—if used positively—is exactly the right trait to help with your career. There isn't one trait listed on this quiz that doesn't have both an up and a down side to it. A plus or minus aspect. Don't discredit the various aspects of your personality before you look at the potentially positive side of these traits. Likewise, look at those traits that seem unilaterally beneficial and see if they too can have their minus aspect if taken too far.

The most valuable lesson I've learned is that no matter how hard you try, not everyone is going to like you. Be the most real you you are. If you're real, you get work. But remember: you can't please everybody.

—Mindy Cohn, *Facts of Life,*
The Boy Who Could Fly

There is no "right" kind of personality that is necessary for an actor to be successful. The one you've got is just fine. It might need some fine-tuning and perhaps some self-exploration, but overall, your personality has as much chance of working for you as against you. Most personality traits can operate as an asset or a liability, depending on how you utilize them. What is important is how *you view your personality traits.* Look over the checklist. How many mismatches did you have? And what do they mean?

Use this quiz as a barometer to learn about yourself. It helps identify your *persona*—both the one you think you have naturally, and the one you think you ought to have.

This *isn't* a test to help you determine what to change in your personality in order to succeed as an actor. First of all, there is no such definable personality. And secondly, forcing yourself to be something that you think you should be and that you actually aren't can only backfire in the long run. No one likes a phony. Neither the industry insiders nor the general public. And finally, being a phony simply isn't a lot of fun! You constantly have to watch your behavior to make sure it matches the image you've created. On a day-to-day basis, it can be terribly draining.

Rather, I'm suggesting that the personality you have now can be enhanced and understood so that it can work for you in *all situations.* Of course, there may be instances when you're in a social situation and meet someone you take an instant dislike to but cannot offend since they might be in a position to give you a job. Is withholding your negative feelings about this person tantamount to being a phony? Many actors worry about this. The fact is that you don't have to insult the person nor reveal your true negative feelings in order to maintain the integrity of your personality. You can remain truthful to your real feelings yet avoid cutting off a viable employment source. It's a matter of adapting to the needs of the situation. Let's say at a party you meet Johnny X., a casting executive you feel negative toward. To be truthful, you need not run up to him, call him "scum," throw your glass of wine in his face and proclaim your negative opinion. Conversely, you are not required to ignore your true feelings, put on a happy face and give the man a giant hug and kiss on first sight. There is a middle ground. You can be civil and noncommittal, say hello if it is awkward not to do so and move on to chat with the other guests. You haven't *lied* about your true feelings. Rather, you've simply exercised judgment, business acumen and restraint to handle an unpleasant encounter. And most importantly, you haven't eliminated a potentially fruitful source of employment!

Never Confuse Business Acquaintances with Personal Friends!

Sometimes you will have close friends with whom you also have a business relationship. But more often, you're likely to have an array of business people in your life that have nothing to do with your private life. It's an important distinction to make.

TAKING A LOOK AT THE MISMATCHES

The mismatches on this test are the most important element of the checklist. They break down into two categories:

1. Those qualities you think an actor *must have* that you don't have

2. Those qualities you have that you don't consider *USEFUL*
   as an actor

Looking at these discrepancies can save you a lot of personal
grief. I have found that many actors assume that there are
certain qualities that they *must* have or *must not* have. The fact
is that there isn't one trait on that list that is a "bad" trait—only
the bad use of it!

Let's take a look at a few of those traits that many actors feel
are setbacks to a successful actor's personality.

SHYNESS CAN BE A PLUS

Take shyness for example. Many people think that it would be
difficult to be an actor if you are shy. The irony of that misconception is that *a lot* of truly successful people are shy both on
and off stage. For many of these timid souls, acting was the one
profession that could allow them to break out of their shyness.
Perhaps it's just the act of playing pretend, of being someone
else. Many shy actors become emotionally expressive, outgoing
individuals when playing a character.

Though some "shy lambs" become "outgoing lions" during
a performance, there are others who feel they are consistently
shy. Does that portend a doomed career? Not if you know how
to use it. Being shy can be an enormously attractive trait to
many of us. Who doesn't remember the shy person in the
corner of a room during a wild, crowded party? There's a certain sweetness and attractiveness about them. Perhaps it's only
because it enlists our protective instinct, but many socially shy
people do quite well just allowing themselves to be shy.

The same is true for performers. Many outgoing performers
are actually rather shy in real life. They find it difficult meeting
people, going on interviews, being talked about in the media,
attending social functions, etc. These talented people often use
their shyness in their work. The excellent dramatic actor David
Morse, of tv's *St. Elsewhere* series, is quite shy in real life. When
I directed him in the play *How I Got That Story,* I was fascinated
with the way he used his shyness to investigate the role. Rather

than view this personality trait as a weakness, he probed the character like a shy man probes a new friendship. Relaxed with himself, David brought a gentleness and compassion to the role that was astounding. Certainly in David's case, shyness gave him a unique way of approaching his work.

There is a down side, however, to shyness—it's looking "cold." Sometimes when people are shy, they withdraw and assume a "cold" persona as a defensive. How many times have you met someone who on first impression seemed to be a snob, only to learn that the person is actually shy—and scared of meeting people? In many instances such as auditions, interviews and social functions, the shy person may only have one opportunity to meet someone who is in the position to advance his career. If this person comes off "snobby," it can be a turnoff, and suddenly a perfectly okay personality trait—one that might even be appealing at times—becomes a liability. Look at your own shyness: do you act defensively in social situations where you feel shy? Is your shyness often interpreted as coldness? If you think you respond defensively to your own shyness, ask yourself why. Do you think being shy is a weakness? Some people do. Instead of criticizing yourself for a shy tendency, why not delve in a bit to the "whys" and "wherefores" and how you might use shyness to an advantage. Ask other people, especially your friends who give you truthful insight. Especially ask outgoing folk. Many outgoing people actually wish they *were shy!* Why? Because every personality trait has its appealing side. Find out from your more sociable colleagues what is appealing about this trait and try to work from that *positive* perspective.

BEING NERVOUS IS OKAY

Let's also take a look at nervousness. Every actor has been nervous at some time, whether in real life, at auditions or in performance. Actors are notoriously nervous—a lot—in many situations. Some let their nerves cripple them. Others use the nervous energy, translating it from a minus to a plus. How? Did you know that nervous energy and a state of excitement have the same physiological characteristics? That means that determining whether you're excited or nervous is a purely psychological decision. If you think you're nervous, you will be nervous. Conversely, if you choose to think you're excited, you will be excited.

Nervousness or anxiety can help spur you forward into action. Akin to the "fight or flight" rush of adrenaline in times of danger, your body gets infused with energy when you feel nervous. Trying to deny that you're nervous is silly and totally counterproductive. What you can do instead is concentrate on having this extra energy and directing it into your work. (In the section on auditioning, we'll discuss this more fully.)

BOSSY

"Bossy" conjures up the bullies from grammar school and the irritating teachers, the obnoxious kids who run for student government and the employers who think they're always right. No one likes to be bossed around, and thus no one likes a bossy person. But there *is* an upside to this trait. It's called *leadership ability*. We all look up to leaders—those among us who assume responsibility for themselves and, often, for others. Being a leader is a sign of maturity, wisdom and strength. If you think you're bossy, take a look at how you might convert that to the more positive context of being a leader. Apply your energy to getting things done from a positive stance. Sometimes people are called "bossy" because they insist that people do things a certain way not out of strength, but out of fear. Think about the bossy people you know. Could they possibly use that same personality force to project instead the more positive aspect of leadership? Could you?

VAIN

We think of vain people as being terribly preoccupied with themselves—how they look, what they are doing, what they want, etc We especially don't like it when a vain person insists on focusing on himself at the expense of others—especially *us*. But let's look at vanity in another light. An actor *needs to be vain* to a certain extent in order to be successful. Attention to how you look and what you want, close attention to incidents that affect your future, concentration on your own personal development and the development of your craft—these are all necessary aspects of being an actor. In other words, you need to have a certain *vanity* in order to pay the proper attention needed to succeed in this business. Here again, it's a matter of degree and perspective. When we think of vain people, we don't like it because it's self-attention at our expense. However, perhaps a certain amount of self-attention—as described above—is actually a positive trait and a skill that leads to success. In my experience, those actors who tend to themselves and pay close attention to events and situations that affect them can be very strong and stable personalities. Their self-awareness incites self-confidence. Their attention to the slightest detail makes them very knowledgeable about their personalities and sensitive to their own strengths and weaknesses. In a proper amount, being vain can actually build confidence and self-esteem. Taken too far, it's a turnoff. This is true of any personality trait—even those qualities considered positive.

Beware the "career-killers"

Most personality traits have both good and bad aspects. However, some have only a downside—especially in this business. Some examples:

1. A "chip-on-your-shoulder" attitude

2. A pessimistic world view

3. Pretense

4. Laziness

THE "CHIP-ON-YOUR-SHOULDER" ATTITUDE

Anger permeates the room. When you walk in with anger, everyone feels it. Lose the anger and you may win the part.

—Alan Rich,
ACTOR/DIRECTOR/TEACHER

It's amazing how many actors translate their own fears of failure and rejection into anger against those that can actually *give* them the jobs, namely, casting directors, producers and directors. I can guarantee that you will sink your career hopes if you operate with this attitude. Sure, some things are unfair, and you have a right to get angry. But some actors decide to adopt this angry persona in every situation—and it's very self-defeating.

There are insensitive casting directors. None of us is even remotely perfect. But for the most part, we try to do our job as well as possible. I love actors. I love meeting them. I love nurturing them and finding them work. Most casting people feel as I do. That's why we're casting—because we enjoy it. There may be a few rare exceptions, but don't let them color your dealings with the rest. It simply isn't to your advantage. No one—I repeat, *no one*—wants to deal with an actor who is consistently hostile, negative and insulting. Life's too short to be faced with such unpleasantness. Sometimes an actor might get away with it for a short time. Perhaps he's cast as the "angry young man" or in some other way that suits his character. However, eventually, this kind of attitude turns against you. Sometimes an actor develops this attitude after becoming a star. And for a while, nothing happens. But remember: this is a people business, pure and simple. And one day, that actor will need to work with these people again and they are not going to forget being treated badly. There's a show biz maxim that counsels: "Be nice to those you meet as you climb the ladder of success. They are the same ones you'll meet coming down." It's true. That doesn't imply that you should be a flattery wimp.

uggesting is that you take a look at what you do
ar, anxiety, anger and frustration. Do you flaunt
the guise of "creativity?" More importantly, do you
tyrannize others with it? Some actors are so terrified of rejection that they feel compelled to "reject" those that they believe are in control and sitting in judgment. It's bad business.

Check your own personality and approach. Do you go to auditions or similar situations looking for a potential insult? Are you vigilantly defending yourself in business situations? One of the reasons this sort of attitude is so self-defeating is that often actors aren't even *aware* that they are dealing with such anger and hurt. This attitude is insidious. Sometimes one justifiable wrong—a casting person keeps you waiting an unusually long period of time—sets off a chronic attitude problem.

There are definitely going to be situations where you are treated badly. I wish it were not so, but it is. Sometimes it is just bad timing. You arrive for your audition on time and ready to do your reading. The casting director carefully scheduled the appointments so each actor would have plenty of time. However, at the last minute, a meeting is called due to a crisis—the script's changed, a star dropped out or is now in, the producer is down with the flu and the staff is bordering on hysteria. The casting director behind the door is living out a life—events, circumstances and situations you know nothing about. And unfortunately, these situations often demand immediate attention—and you, and your audition, fall lower on the priority list. It's a shame—and a situation every casting director tries to avoid—but it does happen. It's simply the nature of this business where minute-to-minute crises are commonplace. You don't have to like waiting. But you should understand that it isn't an intentional slam against you or an indication of the casting person's disrespect for actors. Realize that being made to wait is a hazard of the profession.

When you're out working on your career—whether it's general interviews, auditions, taking classes—check your attitude. Do you "cop" a posture of hostility? How do you deal with tough, uncomfortable situations? Do you often rely on hostility to get your point across or to stick up for your rights? Again, remember: there may be times when it is entirely appropriate to get angry. But as an overall attitude, it's definitely a self-defeating proposition.

A PESSIMISTIC WORLD VIEW

The next career-killer is a pessimistic outlook. This is another self-defeating attitude. And like the "chip-on-your-shoulder" attitude, pessimism is often insidious and destructive. If your outlook is pervasively negative, how can anything good happen to you and to your career? Comments like "Why perform in this acting showcase? No one ever comes anyway," or "I'm going to miss acting class for a few weeks. I won't need it for TV." With this kind of an attitude, you can't attract, notice or take advantage of opportunity.

Time and again, I observe actors setting themselves up for failure. Most common is the "nothing-ever-turns-out-for-me" attitude. Actors bring this defeatist attitude right into auditions. They overlook the positive aspects of their life and only focus on the negative. Many times I've heard actors discuss themselves in the most degrading terms. Women constantly focus on physical flaws such as weight or looks. Of course, you have to attend to these issues; physical appearance is part of an actor's trade. Yet there is no reason to focus on your flaws to the exclusion of everything else! Too many actors do precisely that.

A pessimistic outlook only serves to concentrate on what is wrong or lacking. It doesn't leave any room for praise, triumph or, most of all, happiness. Unless you can enjoy your career, this profession can break you. It's tough enough already. Underneath it all, I think a pessimistic attitude results from fear —of life, failure, disappointment. For some of us, the only way to handle this fear is to never expect anything in the first place. It then becomes easier, and even necessary, to look for what's negative in a situation. It's an odd form of control: if you are certain that things will turn out badly, you can never be surprised or disappointed. This attitude costs dearly. Many times, an individual who persists in this kind of negativity actually works *hard* developing this attitude and languishing in it. After awhile, it becomes a self-fulfilling prophecy: You expect things to turn out badly, and with continual and concentrated focus in that direction, eventually the "bad news" is spotted and the individual's belief that life "sucks" is confirmed. A sad way to live.

You have to make a choice. Right now. How do *you* intend to look at life's events and situations? Are you willing to be courageous and expectant? If you are, then starting *today*, focus on the positive—on the constructive—on what life *offers* and not what life *withholds*. You don't need to be a "cock-eyed optimist" to be a person with a positive outlook. Recognizing and dealing with obstacles is an important component for personal growth and career advancement. You also don't need to like everyone nor look at any job situation with rose-colored glasses. That would be foolish—and perhaps, even detrimental to your career. What you do need to do is examine your personality, interests, career and life goals to find those areas that offer the most growth. For example, you get cast in an off-off-Broadway play. The part is solid and the play is good, but after one rehearsal, you see that the director wouldn't do well with traffic, much less a play. In addition, you're not getting paid because it's a showcase. How do you look at this situation? For the pessimist, this type of situation is just typical of the screwed-up way things are in this business. Angry and frustrated, the actor righteously tells off the director, leaves the play and complains to everyone he knows. Or worse, he *stays* in the play, quibbling, arguing and generally being unpleasant until he's either fired or has driven the rest of the cast insane. The upshot? By the time the situation is over, the actor has actually lost ground by making enemies with the cast and crew and, most likely, by irritating friends and colleagues with his constant carping.

In contrast, the person who is optimistic doesn't ignore the drawbacks such as not getting paid or having a monster for a director. However, this person also looks at the advantages of working and perhaps being seen in performance. Then, weighing the pros and cons, the actor makes a decision depending on which choice affords the most benefit. It's really not important in this situation whether the actor stays with the show. What matters is that the decision will be based on a realistic and optimistic view of life in general, and the actor's career in particular. One of the most striking aspects of optimistic professionals is that there is a noticeable absence of griping. If the actor with a positive world view chooses to leave the play, he puts the incident aside and goes on to the next opportunity. If, however, the actor chooses to stay, he does everything possible to make the work as pleasant as possible and focuses on the positive benefits.

Everyone has doubts. It's only natural. It's how you deal with these doubts that makes the difference. Do you recognize these doubts and then let them pass? Or do you focus on them, reinforce them and turn them into self-defeating behavior? Actors who choose this route will come into auditions with a "I-know-no-one's-gonna-like-me" attitude and you know what? They're right!

In short, a pessimistic attitude in this kind of a career is *nowhere*. This career *demands* optimism, energy, a sense of innocence, an ability to survive and an incessant talent for rejuvenation. A pessimistic attitude is antithetical to *all of these things*. Pessimism and an acting career are mutually exclusive. Don't let your fear and doubt become a pessimistic view! Instead, look at a more constructive outlet for your doubts. Use them as provocative thoughts that can help you focus and learn more about yourself, your goals and your priorities. For the actor, pessimism is certain death.

PRETENSE

Pretense. Phony. Lying. I'd love to tell you this negative quality is never rewarded, but the reality is that people often get far lying. Whether it's "creative accounting," falsifying a résumé, or Watergate, the fact remains that dishonesty is fairly common in our society. Morality aside, does pretense or dishonesty get you ahead as an actor? Over the long run, no. People don't like being taken or conned, and ultimately, that's what pretense and lies do. As I've said before, this is a people's business. And if you're in the habit of lying to people to advance your career, you eventually will be discovered, and believe me, it will not be forgotten!

There are all sorts of pretense ranging from downright dishonesty to putting forth a phony persona. Some actors seem to feel that being upbeat means coming off like a Pollyanna. That couldn't be farther from the truth. When I meet an actor in an interview or audition, I'm interested in getting a feel for who this performer is as a *person*. I'm not interested in how well they can put over a phony image. Insincerity has a way of sticking out like a sore thumb. You can tell that the person isn't being "real." It's really uncomfortable watching these people put on their acts. Be yourself whatever that is. There's nothing wrong in trying to change personality traits; however, true change is slow and often internal. Trying to be some particular way by falsifying your behavior will do you little good and, more often than not, a good deal of harm. Again, it's a matter of learning to adapt your true personality to a situation rather than utilizing pretense. What's important here is to understand why and what you feel you need to hide about your true personality, attitudes, work background, etc. Is pretense really necessary, or even helpful, in these situations? I believe you can remain true to yourself and still feel comfortable and effective. Social effectiveness and operating a career are discussed in Section C. Instead of being a phony, you can be an honest and sought-after person.

Lying on a résumé is incredibly commonplace. Actors just starting out will try to up their chances of getting a job by putting lots of made-up credits on the résumé. Ironically, it often goes *against them*. Casting people are always on the lookout for new talent. When you come in with a résumé that indicates you've been working for years, it actually makes the casting person question your honesty. Instead, when confronted with a résumé that honestly delineates experience, the casting director is cued to the fact that although shy of experience, this actor is a fresh face in the talent pool. In the next section, I'll show you how to construct a full, yet honest, résumé even if you haven't a long list of professional credits.

There are many reasons why you should avoid dishonesty—some moral, others practical. The bottom line is that pretense only works for a while. It's simply the law of averages: at some point, you're going to be found out. And when you are, you'll be turned away. Pretense is a turnoff. And in the long run—even if you can fool people for a time—it will eventually hurt your career.

LAZINESS

Personally, I'm not crazy about lazy people. These actors wish for the world, but on a day-to-day basis they do nothing to advance their own cause. I've seen many a talented performer fail to have a working career through no fault other than their own laziness. Why? Well, it's easier not to do anything. There isn't a soul alive who wouldn't prefer sitting around a swimming pool, waiting for the jobs to come rolling in. But that simply doesn't happen—to anyone. The most successful actors are people who work hard for what they want.

We are all a bit lazy. It's difficult not to procrastinate, especially when the activity seems more of a chore than a delight. But ambitious, successful people realize it is simply a matter of discipline and ambition. In seminars, auditions and conversations, I've heard lots of actors ask about ways to break into the business. They feel stymied and frustrated—and not without good reason, I might add. It's hard sending out pictures and résumés that you think will probably end up in the trash; or to attend an acting seminar taught by a series of casting directors, in the hope of getting noticed. A lot of an actor's promotion of his own career is difficult and riddled with potential rejection. Nevertheless, it is part of the profession.

Sometimes it is necessary to "lay back" and stop trying so hard; but don't confuse this with laziness. The difference? Laziness is waiting for other people to *do* what you should do yourself. Lazy people waste their time trying to justify their lack of courage and effort. They lanquish in idleness. Watching television becomes a substitute for doing something. (To make matters worse, often these idlers will try to convince you that they are doing "research" while spending the day in front of the tube.) Don't be fooled—either by others or by your self. If you're concerned that perhaps you've been too lazy about your career, take stock now. What is it that gives you those gnawing doubts about your discipline and industriousness? Ask a friend or someone close to you. Listen to what they have to say. Most importantly, be your own judge. Truthfully, are you doing all you can to advance your career? If not, what's holding you back? Can you formulate a more active approach? Be courageous. Give it a try. Get up and out there and work for what you want.

I am interested in knowing and working with those people who do something *every day* to further their career and improve themselves. Whether it's staying on a diet or reading a play or making phone calls, each day is utilized to work toward their goals. There's simply no other way to accomplish them.

I'm often surprised by the number of actors who don't even show up for auditions. I've been in social situations with actors who have an afternoon appointment that they ignore because they are having a "good time." It's amazing. Also, there are many actors who are chronically late for auditions or come unprepared. I've heard numerous tales from agents about unreachable clients—those actors who forget to put on their answering machines, or worse, forget to check in. It's a terrific way to miss a giant opportunity or turning point in your career.

Laziness gives you no control of your career. While you are waiting for things to come to you, you miss the opportunities your more energetic colleagues enjoy. Ultimately, if you are lazy and neglectful about your career you will find success a difficult commodity to come by. Without work, there are rarely any rewards. So, you can relax around the pool catching the rays and fail, or you can get out there and work to make your dream a reality.

The above are some examples of "career-killers." There are others. Negative traits and attitudes are often potent self-sabotoge techniques because people can sometimes be unconsciously uncomfortable with success. Thus, when put in a potential career-advancing position, they tend to find a way to mess up the opportunity. Don't minimize the psychology here. Afraid of the unknown, it's sometimes easier to *fail* rather than to risk *succeeding* and a subsequent advance into new territories and responsibilities. You might hear people talking about fear of failure, but actually they are afraid of success. Otherwise, why wouldn't they avoid failure at any cost if they are so afraid of it? Rather, these folks *know* how to *fail*. And they know how to deal with defeat. In fact, they are quite comfortable in that condition and have quite a bit of control.

Do you know what negative attitudes you employ? Take a look. Refer back to the test. Do you use certain traits as fully and positively as possible? Or do you allow your own negativity to get in the way? If you do, be aware that you are slowly, perhaps unconsciously squeezing the lifeblood from your career.

Question-and-Answer Seminar for Section A 3

HERE are some questions actors have asked about the material covered in this first section:

1. I'm cast as a young ingenue, but I feel so much more experienced in life than the parts I play. What should I do?

Be grateful that you are able to play younger roles, because eventually they will be unavailable to you. If you are getting noticed because of these roles, it is a tremendous advantage. You can use that career movement to help you shift your image later. For now, be happy you have the work. Invest the money wisely so you will be economically free to take parts because they are interesting even if the pay isn't that terrific. You don't have to give up on your own notion of who you are.

2. Is it bad to want to be an actor to prove that you're better than others?

It is not that it is "bad." In fact, negative motivators such as revenge or anger can be powerful and effective. Unfortunately, a negative motivator will fail you as an ultimate goal, nor will it help when your career demands endurance. Positive passion is about the strongest motivator you can find and it also allows you to enjoy your successes.

3. How do I know if my goal is something I really want and not something that just seems like fun?

This is not a career for someone who wants to have fun. Even though performing is childlike and joyous, this is a profession. That doesn't mean that the actor shouldn't have fun. In fact, it is that particular energy—the ability to take pleasure and give pleasure—that an audience looks for in an actor. Just know that the actor's career takes a tremendous amount of hard work, and a lot of it isn't pleasant, easy or even enjoyable. Those who love to act are willing to forge through all the un-fun stuff to get to their moment on stage or screen. This focus and determination doesn't leave room for an actor to be a "baby."

4. Can you list some of the personality traits and attitudes that turn you off when meeting new actors.

Bitterness, resentment, hostility—these are the major ones. Obviously they are very negative attitudes. The actor with a chip on his shoulder turns off not only *me,* but also anyone in a position to assist his career. In principle, the people in this industry are not your friends or your family. They are not interested in your bad attitude. No one wants to see how angry you are with the realities of the business.

In contrast, the "too sweet, too nice" actor can also be a turn-off. This type never seems authentic; he sounds and acts like a little robot. It's terrible and irritating. I want to meet actors who are real, who have lives and dreams and ambitions. I like to talk to actors who are in touch with themselves and aware of the world around them.

SECTION B

Learning the Rules of the Game

IF YOU HOPE TO WIN IN THE ACTING GAME, you've got to know the rules. There are only a few, but they can be tricky. The Catch-22 of show-biz regulations can make you crazy if you're not prepared. This section gives you the facts—plain and simple—about the business of show business.

Your Next Move 4

THERE are certain steps you have to take to begin a career in acting. In the next chapter, "Nuts and Bolts of Show Biz," we'll review the tools you'll need to make a career a reality. However, before you can begin formulating your career, you must decide *where* you want to start out.

CONSTRUCTING THE FOUNDATION

Where should you go? The best way to answer that is to look at where you are now and consider how much experience you have. For example, if you live in a small town in Mississippi, you might first wish to begin by investigating the theater around your home. Community theaters provide an excellent introduction to the new professional. Professional regional companies usually have a program for apprentices, where you can learn a great deal about acting and stagecraft. In any case, first explore the market you are in before you rush to move on.

TAKE A LOOK AT WHERE YOU ARE

When I say market, I mean precisely that. As an actor, you are a salesperson. You are selling your talent and skill. You are selling yourself. Like any wise salesperson, you should go to the marketplace where you think you can sell your product the best. In large urban centers like Los Angeles, Chicago or New York, your competition will be fierce and might knock you down before you ever get a chance. It's like wanting to be a professional baseball player. You start out in the minor leagues, and with experience and talent you work your way up to the big leagues. If you haven't studied acting or worked on stage, take this opportunity to check out the opportunities right there in your community. Also, don't forget to investigate your local TV and radio stations—they often make their own commercials using local talent. If there are clubs or organizations that involve acting, check them out. Not everything will be to your liking, but you just might get some experience and knowledge that will help later on.

CHOOSE YOUR FIRST MARKETPLACE

Generally speaking, urban centers will hold more potential for your burgeoning career than rural ones. That doesn't mean you have to immediately set your sights on Los Angeles or New York. Of course, if you have a burning desire to go to the two largest markets, then by all means go. However, it might be wiser to take a more gradual step. It would probably be better to go to the next closest and larger marketplace. Cities such as San Francisco, Louisville, Nashville, Seattle, Atlanta, Denver, San Diego, Dallas, Boston or Houston, to name but a few, are all fine places for a new actor to begin to shape a career. Continuing our example, the actor from Mississippi who outgrows the confines of his community might choose to go to Nashville, Atlanta or New Orleans. All of these places have good theaters and produce local television and radio commercials and industrial programs. These cities have regional offices of the acting unions, and since competition isn't as stiff, it is often the best and easiest way to earn your union card. (More on that in the next chapter.) In addition, you are likely to find more challenging training in larger urban areas.

There is also the advantage that these cities are not going to be as alien to the actor from Mississippi as New York might be. Starting out to build an acting career—one of the hardest—is a tall order in itself. To add to that a confrontation with a totally different geographical area and lifestyle may be putting unnecessary strain on yourself.

THE INDUSTRY IS NATIONWIDE

At one time, if you wanted to be an actor you had to move to New York or Hollywood. In fact, it was even more specific than that: You went to New York for the stage and to Hollywood for the movies. That is no longer true. Films are cast and filmed all over the nation and the world. Stage isn't limited to Broadway but is alive and well in professional regional theaters all over the country. Casting directors routinely visit these large cities to find new talent. All of us in the industry know that these cities are seeding beds for new artistic genius to flower.

A WORD ABOUT THE WINDY CITY

One of the most fascinating cities for a new actor is Chicago. My professional experience has made me aware of just how great the city of Chicago truly is. It has all the advantages of a large marketplace, but the feeling of a small community. Excellent schools like Northwestern University and the University of Illinois offer the actor solid training. In addition, this city is just teeming with a vital theater community that has done more than its share of supplying professional actors to the industry. The famous Second City group began in Chicago in

1960 and is still going strong today. A quick perusal of Second City actors reads like a star-studded ball. Steppenwolf originated in Chicago. The theater is very active, and the audiences very supportive. Also the film and television industries are quite active. Film companies know the talent is there, and it is also a popular location. Chicago is a major advertising center, so there is a lot of work in commercials and industrials. I think this city should be a serious consideration for any new or seasoned actor.

THE BIG TIME: NEW YORK AND LOS ANGELES

Eventually, whether you're discovered in another city and brought to the big time or go on your own, you will have to come to one of the main centers for the industry—Los Angeles or New York. This is the Big Time. The two cities are vastly different, but anyone serious about a full-scale career spanning all the media will have to become acquainted with these two places.

NEW YORK

Now the question becomes, which one to go to first? There are many considerations, the first of which is lifestyle. New York is a teeming metropolis, crowded and intense. The struggling artist in New York conjurs a romantic image. The city is expensive, fast-paced and very competitive—a city unlike any other. A truly international metropolis, New York City is akin to other cosmopolitan areas like Paris, London or Rome. It is actually less an "American" city than a sophisticated blend of international influences in one very small area. One need only walk a few blocks in New York to be struck by the amazing diversity of its citizens. With museums, art galleries and libraries, the cultural assets of the city are rich and unbelievably accessible. New York's enthusiasm for life is so colorful and evident that the city can even, at times, be overwhelming. New Yorkers are among the most devoted and loyal dwellers of any geographical area. In fact, some maintain that you can become *addicted* to this city in such a way that anywhere else pales by comparison. From Radio City Music Hall to the Metropolitan Museum of Art, from Carnegie Hall to a Greenwich Village jazz club, anything and everything that you can imagine exists in New York. Yet, with all this sophistication and excitement and expensive living costs, New York is surprisingly unimpressed by material splendor and display. There is very little social pressure for an actor to live like a "star," making possible a lifestyle for those desiring a low profile with little show.

There is an incredible amount of work available here in television and radio commercials, television daytime soaps, industrials and film. It is also common in New York for an actor to freelance with a number of different agents before signing with one. This gives the actor access to all the major auditions going on in the city. Furthermore, New York is considered to be the premiere city for theater in this country. Some feel that the actor professionally trained in New York is a more respected and serious artist. This may or may not be true; there *are* fantastic acting teachers of enormous reputation here. But perhaps New York's greatest asset to its new actors is the existence of a tight and vital community feeling among artists. The stage actor in New York is taken seriously as an artist because the New York audiences take theater seriously as an art form. As an actor in New York begins to become part of the theater community, he meets other actors, writers and directors, who get together and discuss work, classes, the state of theater and the allied arts and, of course, the development of their own careers. They discuss these topics with fervor and a kind of modern "angst" that suits the artist as he is permitted to air feelings and ideas. Different hangouts, restaurants and bars serve as regular meeting places for the community.

New York has soul.

LOS ANGELES

Los Angeles is a cool town. The romantic image here is a life of leisure. The weather and the minutes-away availability of the ocean and mountains make L.A. a place where being healthy and living the good life are prime goals. Housing, food and entertainment are all far less expensive, but do remember you will need a car. In general, with little effort, living in L.A. can be quite comfortable.

Los Angeles is heavily populated but far more spread out than almost any other modern urban center. Some actors complain that there is no theater community here, that the only time they have an opportunity to get together and chat with other actors is while on the set. It is a more isolating city than New York. In contrast to New York, with its incredible, ongoing stimuli and drive, Los Angeles is "laid back"—slow and more insular; you must supply your own stimuli and momentum. In New York, the energy of the city itself can seem to carry you along, but this energy is also stressful. In Los Angeles, it is easier to focus on your work without distraction, enabling an actor to concentrate on himself and to take care of all those elements necessary to a career without having to buck the continual flow of input from the city.

There is just as much theater in Los Angeles as in New York—perhaps even more—but it is not given the same status. Nonetheless, anyone wishing to work on the stage will not find a lack of opportunity on the west coast. There are plenty of acting classes and fine teachers.

Lifestyle aside, Los Angeles' biggest draw is that there is simply more work there. L.A. is the center for the television and the feature film industries. If you are interested in a continuing career in these mediums, it will be necessary for you at some point to become acquainted with L.A. This does not mean that you won't get cast in New York or another city for film and television roles, just that the majority of the work is cast in Los Angeles only. However, having an agent in L.A. is a must. Practically all auditions are done through agent submission. Access to the studio lots to meet casting executives can be difficult and getting a good agent might be a long process.

BI-COASTAL PROS

Ultimately, most performers become "bi-coastal," moving regularly between both cities as their careers or lifestyles demand. There are many famous film personalities—Paul Newman, Al Pacino, Dustin Hoffman, Diane Keaton, Meryl Streep, to name a few—who work almost exclusively in feature films but prefer to permanently have residence on the east coast. There are also Los Angeles residents who will return to New York to work in theater, film or the soap operas for years at a time.

Basically, actors must prepare for the reality that they will probably have to do a lot of traveling during the course of their professional career. This industry has truly become a global enterprise, with projects being produced around the world in television, film and theater.

Your decision whether you should make a move or not depends on what you are trying to accomplish both professionally *and* personally. Erin Gray, star of TV's *Silver Spoons* and *Buck Rogers* as well as over 50 nationwide television commercials explains:

> *The seeds of my career were in New York through my modeling career. Soon I was doing television commercials—my first break into acting. After some successful ones like the L'Oreal "I'm worth it" and "All my men wear English Leather" campaigns, more people began to take me seriously—a model who also could talk! I knew my chances of getting acting work were better in California—there was more work in California and I would be less likely to be typed as just a fashion model, so I moved to Los Angeles. For a while my husband stayed in New York making us a bi-coastal couple. It was hard at first, but we were certain that this was the place for me to be to advance my career. Then I got* Buck Rogers. *Moving to Los Angeles was the right decision for us because of where we were in our careers, and wanting to raise a family. Everybody has a unique position and a unique set of needs. You have to take them into consideration if you wish to make the right career choices for you.*

How to decide

In deciding between New York and Los Angeles, you should first assemble what information you know about each city and the way the industry works there. To do this, you will need to gather information from books such as this and, more importantly, to begin to talk to people who have experienced these cities. Also, take note of which place you can start off knowing some people. Perhaps your third cousin moved to Los Angeles a few years back and is willing to help orient you to the city. Consult your acting teachers and others in your peer group. A good way to start off in a new place is with a friend with a similar interest. Check to see if any of your peers are contemplating such a move. That way you can join forces and have some company while trying to establish yourself.

There is no right or wrong decision here. If you don't like one place, you can always try another. I've known some actors who flourished in New York, only to feel their career stagnate in Los Angeles, and vice versa. Also keep in mind that you may be more suited to one city than another. In a few years, your needs might change and another location will be your destiny.

For your interest, here is the latest breakdown of Screen Actors' Guild members by geographical branch:

BRANCH	MEMBERS
Hollywood	24,693
New York	19,646
Chicago	1,855
Florida	1,443
San Francisco	1,303
Washington, D.C.	508
Arizona	479
Detroit	476
Philadelphia	451
Texas	443
Georgia	396
Boston	385
Colorado	351
Hawaii	303
Nevada	265
San Diego	260

Utah	175
New Mexico	85
Other states	500
TOTAL	54,017

—Source: Screen Actors' Guild

THE FOLLOW-THROUGH OF YOUR DECISION

Whichever city you choose, you should be prepared. You will need to have some money saved, a "stake," in order to get set up. You should take this into consideration *before* you make your move. You will need to find housing, which can be very expensive. Also, as soon as you arrive in your chosen city, you should immediately get a post office box where you can receive mail, and an answering service or machine so you can get your calls. These are three absolute necessities from day one. Save money, research your chosen area and prepare as much groundwork as possible, such as contacting friends or relatives, inquiring about transportation and the average cost of things. The more groundwork you can lay before you actually make the move, the faster you will be able to get things going in your new location.

CLASSES

The new actor or the veteran returning to a career will no doubt want to study the craft of acting. Not only are classes helpful in developing your talent, classes are where you will begin to construct a network of contacts. Participating in a professional class can be one of the cornerstones of an actor's career.

There are all types of classes and all kinds of teachers, many of whom don't know the first thing about teaching acting. Anyone can hang out a sign and say they teach acting, so it is absolutely crucial to check out their reputation and references. Who have they taught? Some schools advertise a list of famous students, but when you check on it, you realize the star came for a week and then quit. Don't be too ready to believe the teacher's own press packet. Instead, ask around. If you had a teacher in another area that you respected, ask for a recommendation in your new city. Also, check the biography section in play programs. Actors often list their teachers or the schools they attended. If you like an actor's performance, look to see where the person studied.

When researching a school or teacher, find out how long they have been teaching. The longer the school or teacher has been in business, the better your chances that the instruction is good. Also ask your prospective instructors about their own background. How seriously did they study? And with whom?

It would take another complete book to discuss the various acting techniques and courses of instruction that are available. Browsing through any theatrical bookstore will give you an indication of the thousands of pages of material on acting techniques. It can be overwhelming. Not only are there classes available in basic acting craft but in such specialty subjects as voiceovers, commercial acting, camera technique, audition technique . . . The bottom line is that the best way to find a good class is through recommendations from people you respect. Ultimately, however, only *you* can decide whether or not a class is right for you.

AUDITION YOUR PROSPECTIVE CLASS

Many factors determine whether an acting class will work for an individual. When you search for classes, ask your prospective teacher if you can audit a class before making your decision. Don't be put off if some teachers tell you they do not allow this type of auditing; this is fairly common. In some classes, the teacher might feel that a continual influx of observers will be disturbing to the students already in the class. Still, from speaking with the teacher and checking into his/her background and that of the school's, you will be able to ascertain whether these classes might appeal to you. The only way you'll know for certain is to take the class.

Once you choose a class, allow yourself a little time to get used to it before you evaluate it. Usually after a month or so, you will have an idea if the class is really helping you. You can be in class with one of the most famous acting teachers of all time, but if the chemistry isn't right, you should leave. I've heard of quite a few instances of an actor doing badly in one class just to switch and have his technique leap forward. So don't be discouraged if you have to shop around a bit before finding the right class for yourself. Also remember that there are different classes for different levels of actors. If this is your first class, try to find a teacher whose reputation is in dealing with new talents rather than getting into a workshop geared to seasoned professionals.

MAKING THE MOST OF YOUR CLASS

A good class with a solid instructor can make your work grow in delightfully unexpected ways. It should be a safe environment for you in which to grow and stretch no matter how many years you have been performing. This chance to experiment and go beyond your own artistic limitations is one of the reasons pros like Anne Bancroft and Jon Voight consistently return to a class. I know of one actor who hadn't worked for a long time and found that by returning to class, she was not only stimulated creatively but was developing new confidence, new contacts and most of all, a conviction toward "making it" that she hadn't had in years.

Be patient. You can't grow a plant overnight. Likewise, you need *time* in class before your craft can really begin to develop. As noted actor/director/teacher/producer Darryl Hickman points out:

> *The biggest enemy I see amongst young actors is impatience. They are compulsive about getting results rather than experiencing a process.*
>
> *One needs to continue practicing his/her craft and stretching in order to grow. Many actors are not prepared to work on the stage—they are just*

not equipped. They can get by in film and on TV. It is a problem that American actors suffer because they don't keep growing.

The best way to use an acting class is as a laboratory. As a place to experiment.

Learning to live in the moment. That's the basis of a good process and a good life. Learn to live fully in this moment and not try to force the next one. Letting it happen, not making it happen. That is the greatest wisdom.

The Nuts and Bolts of Show Biz 5

YOU'VE made your move. You're in classes and workshops and beginning to meet people. The next step is to get professional work, which means that at some point you will have to deal with getting admission into one or more of the acting unions and choosing an agent and possibly a manager.

THE ACTING UNIONS

Getting into the unions is a frustrating experience for the new actor. It's the classic Catch-22: You can't get in the union until you have a job, and you can't get a job unless you're in the union! So how do you do it? There are many ways, none easy, but with diligence and persistence the break will come.

There are three actors unions:

AMERICAN FEDERATION OF TELEVISION AND RADIO ARTISTS (AFTRA)

Jurisdiction: This union is responsible for any work in which audio and/or video tape is used. Thus, all radio work is under this union as well as television shows and TV commercials that use tape as opposed to film. AFTRA television shows include a majority of situation comedies, plus daytime soap operas, news programs and many variety and news-oriented productions; AFTRA is also responsible for phonograph, tape and disc recordings.

Eligibility: Anyone can join AFTRA by simply paying the current initiation fee and maintaining a membership in good standing, paying dues as required. Because there is no eligibility requirements, membership in AFTRA is not necessarily helpful in getting an agent or casting director interested in you. However, should you work as a *principal performer* in any AFTRA show, you will be eligible to join the Screen Actors' Guild after a one-year waiting period. This is called "crossing over," and for some actors this has been a good way to enter the film union.

SCREEN ACTORS' GUILD (SAG)

Jurisdiction: This guild is responsible for all work performed on film. This includes theatrical and television films, the majority of prime-time television, commercials, industrial and educational films, student and experimental films and music videos shot on film.

Eligibility: An actor may become eligible by getting a part in a motion picture or television production that is signatory to the guild. One can also join if a member of an affiliated guild for at least one year and has worked as a *principal performer* under that guild ("crossing over").

ACTORS' EQUITY ASSOCIATION (AEA)

Jurisdiction: Equity governs actors and stage managers in live stage productions. This includes Broadway, off-Broadway, regional theaters and small theater groups. (Note: An easy way to remember which union has jurisdiction over what is that the jurisdiction is determined by the medium in which the work is done. Thus, tape is under AFTRA, film is under SAG and live theatrical performance is under AEA.)

Eligibility: The most common way to become eligible is by getting a job in an Equity production. You can also join the Equity Membership Candidate Program at participating regional theaters. In this program, you work with Equity actors as you earn points toward union admission.

AGVA, AGMA AND SEG

In addition to these three actors' unions, there are three other unions for performers: The American Guild of Variety Artists, which covers a wide variety of live performers such as nightclub artists; the American Guild of Musical Artists, which has jurisdiction over singers and dancers; and the Screen Extras' Guild, which has jurisdiction over extras and atmosphere players in film and television. While membership in these unions might not enable you to join either SAG or AEA, they will be there for your assistance when searching for work in those various fields.

WHAT THE UNIONS MEAN AND HOW TO BREAK IN

The two most difficult unions in which to become a member are Equity and SAG. Here is where you run into the famous Catch-22. In many cases, nonunion actors are barred from even auditioning. In Equity theater productions in most states, you must show your Equity union card before being allowed to sign up for an audition. For television and film roles, most casting directors will not accept auditions unless they are from actors submitted by franchised agents and the actors are union members. (We'll discuss "franchised agents" later.)

There are exceptions to even the most ironclad rules. Agents who are franchised by the unions can act on behalf of their clients to obtain auditions for union projects even if the actor/client is not a union member. The problem here is that it is often difficult to convince an agent to take you on as a client if you are not in the unions. I told you it could be a Catch-22!

Some actors find that entrance to the unions is easier if they first pursue a job in commercials. In this field, there is a lot of work and a constant demand for new faces. Whether a television or radio commercial, many casting directors are willing to see nonunion talent, and a job in this field will either get you into SAG or give you the work record to cross over. Along these same lines, finding work in industrial and educational productions can accomplish the same objective.

WHAT THE UNIONS CAN DO

The unions are there to help and protect you. If you are on a job and there is a problem, you can notify the union with that jurisdiction and they will send a representative to work out the problems. There are health, pension and welfare plans providing care for the members and their families.

To help you find work, there are bulletin boards in local offices informing members of upcoming auditions and projects in which they can participate. In some cities, Equity has a "hotline"—a telephone number with daily updates of casting information for its members. There are also special seminars and information services that help advise actors on various aspects of their career from figuring IRS returns to finding roommates, from car sales to special career related instruction. For more complete information and details about the various unions, call or write the nearest local chapter. If you do not know where it is, you can always contact the offices in New York.

AGENTS AND MANAGERS

An agent and a bunch of other passengers are on a boat in dangerous waters and the agent falls overboard, and before anyone can do anything this giant shark comes swimming up, and when the shark is six feet away he veers off and swims in the other direction, and one of the passengers says, "Did you see that, did you see what just happened, it's an act of God," and another passenger answers, "That wasn't an act of God, it was professional courtesy."

—from *Adventures in the Screen Trade*

AGENTS

Agents have always gotten a bad rap. Almost all actors complain about agents—they can't find one, the one they have doesn't have "clout," they don't work hard enough, they never listen, they aren't concentrating on them, etc. There are tons of agent jokes. I think this all stems from the fact that agents *do* have power. They can make the difference in a career. They can find out about opportunities and connect an actor with the right people to move a career from a struggling phase to a starring one. In Los Angeles, having an agent is especially important. Most auditions for television and film roles are limited to those actors who have come through agent submissions.

WHAT DOES AN AGENT DO?

In order to be considered a professional, you must get professional work. An agent is someone who helps you find work, gets you auditions and interviews, advises you about career choices and is your business consultant and negotiator. If your agent is a good one, he will be able to get you in to see the casting, network and studio executives that can help you get work. The agent regularly makes the "rounds" for clients, visits casting directors, makes phone calls, sets up interviews and auditions and recommends clients for various projects. This person acts on your behalf. Thus, it is imperative that you are sure this person has a good reputation for honesty and forthrightness, that he is respected in his territory and that he is truly interested in your career and advancing it. For his services, the actor pays the agent a 10 percent commission on the gross amount for each acting job. (If any agent suggests you pay more than this 10 percent of your gross, or asks for any "fees" up front, you are not dealing with a bona fide agent and should terminate your relationship immediately and inform the unions of this situation.)

Good agents work very hard for their clients. As witness to that fact, there's an old story about two famous agents lunching at the studio, when a famous star enters the dining room. One of the agents says, "That's my client, that bum. He takes 90 percent of everything I make!"

YOUR AGENT IS NOT YOUR MOTHER

The agent is *not* your mother—there to "take care" of you. You still must take responsibility for yourself *and* your career, including the *business* side of things. Because it is a difficult process to get an agent and because having one is so important to career development, actors sometimes mistakenly believe that once they have one, they no longer have to attend to the business of their career: that they no longer have to hustle for work, actively seek out opportunities, listen for tips on casting or continue their networking. They erroneously believe that their agent will do all that for them. *They are wrong!* The truth is that even with the best agent in town,

You Are Responsible for the Development of Your Career!

You and only you. Your agent is part of your *support* staff. Not your alter ego. Even when you are a star, you must continue to work hard to develop your contacts, keeping your ear to the ground for new, exciting projects and continually seeking out and developing your business and artistic relationships. Working on your career never stops. And you must never depend on your agent to do the work *you* should be doing.

You Act From the Child, You Do Business From the Adult.

A good actor must be able to call upon that child's sense of "let's pretend" to practice his craft. Unfortunately, an actor sometimes tries to run his business from that "child" position rather than from the "adult" side of his personality. He makes his agent the "adult authority" in his life. I think this is a mistake. There is no reason why an actor can't be capable of taking control of his own career development. Perhaps because finding a good agent is so difficult, an actor sometimes forgets that the agent works *for* him. Your agent doesn't want to run your life, nor should the agent be expected to do so. If you look at all the biggest stars, each is fully responsible for his own dealings. Many big stars don't even have agents at certain times, relying instead on a support staff to seek out and/or develop material for the actor and on a lawyer to negotiate contracts. These professionals understand that having support does not mean their job is over. It is the wise performer who understands this. Professionals also understand that like any employer, they must continue to develop their relationship with their agent, helping and guiding him to a better understanding of their career needs and the directions they desire to go.

HOW TO KNOW WHICH AGENTS TO CONTACT

First, you must be clear on which agents are for real and which are bogus rip-off artists. Legitimate agents are those that are *franchised* by the acting unions, which means the agents have agreed to follow union regulations. They apply for their franchise directly from the unions and are licensed by whatever state they are in, after they take an eligibility licensing test.

An agent can be franchised by one or all three of the acting unions. Most agents are franchised by all three since most actors work in all three jurisdictions. However, there are some specialty agents that may actually be franchised by only one or two guilds.

To find out which agents are franchised and by what unions, all you have to do is stop by the local union office and ask for their roster of franchised agents. Most lists delineate each franchise so that you will know if the agent you are thinking of contacting actually concentrates on the area you are interested in. If you have made contact with an agent who *is not franchised,* run for the hills! This person/organization is not legitimate and will only try to take whatever money you might have.

RESEARCH THE AGENTS

Once you have a list of bona fide agents, the next step is to do some research. Sure, you can blindly send out hundreds of pictures and resumes and hope that one hits. But I think it is better to know at least something about the people you are contacting.

A good place to start is with the clients they already represent. All franchised agents keep a client list on file at the Screen

Actors' Guild. You can go there and look over the list. (If your agent is *not* franchised with the guild, he is *not legitimate* and you don't want him.)

What kind of clients does the agent represent? Young, old, male, female—what is the mix of his client list? Does he handle mostly established names? If you are just starting out and the agent you want represents nothing but stars, chances are you'll have a difficult time getting this agent interested in you. However, that is no reason for you to forget about the agent. I have known actors who have set their sights on certain agents and kept pursuing them until they had enough credits to get signed. Conversely, I have seen many actors go with a smaller, less well-known agent because they felt this person would really work hard *for them.* Ultimately, as one agent pointed out, "If you're good, it doesn't matter who you go with. You'll rise to the top."

You can also look at an agent's clients by browsing through the two directories of actors. These directories have the actor's picture, name and the name and contact number of his agent. These volumes are used by casting directors and executives for referrals and to refresh their memory of an actor. In Los Angeles, this guide is called *The Academy Players' Directory.* In New York, the guide is called *The Players' Guide.* (See reference guide at the end of this book for information on placing your picture in either of these directories, or on obtaining copies of them.)

Another terrific source of information is other actors. Ask them about various agents, what they have heard, if they've known anyone who was represented by them, etc. Questions like these help you to piece together an image of what this agent might be looking for. For example, agencies that began in New York and expanded to the West Coast are usually very interested in stage actors. They are used to representing them in New York. They are familiar with the demands of the stage and the different types of training that most stage actors in the East acquire. This type of agent might be more open to seeing you do an audition scene and/or monologue. Do your homework. Find out as much as you can. You should make this kind of research a habit as you develop your career. Whether knowing a director's credits before a meeting, or doing some preliminary scouting for agents, being informed is an asset and helps to crystallize your goals by making them more real and tangible.

HOW TO GET AN AGENT

There are sixty thousand members of the Screen Actors' Guild and only a few hundred agents. With odds like these, it is very difficult for an actor to find a good agent—one who can make a difference and who is "right" for the actor.

There are a number of ways to get an agent, from mass-mailing your picture and resume to being recommended by a friend. Some ways are more reliable than others, but you should try *everything* because you never know exactly what will hit.

Here are some suggestions on how to get an agent:

1. *Being seen in plays and showcases.* Having an agent see your work is the soundest way to get an agent interested in you. It shows the agent what you do best—act. You can meet an agent other ways, but ultimately the agent must know and like what the agent is going to sell—and that is your acting ability! For this reason, it is important for you to constantly be in plays and showcases. That way when you make contact with an agent, casting director or producer, you can invite him to see you perform. The more people that become familiar with your work, the better. That's how an actor's reputation begins. When you are in a show, contact the agents that interest you.

2. *Recommendations.* As your work begins to get known, you will be meeting people who can help you get representation. Ask these people to help by recommending you to some agents. Just be aware that the people you are asking should be familiar with your work. It is difficult for someone who might only know you socially to feel comfortable recommending you to an agent contact. In addition, if people have seen you act, their recommendations will mean more to the agents they contact.

3. *Ask other actors for agent recommendations.* Actors are a wonderful source of information in this area. Discuss agents with your actor friends. They can give you insight into what a certain agent will or will not do for you. For example, some agents are terrific for male actors but aren't quite as strong representing women. Or perhaps the agency has a reputation for representing "beautiful people" and you're a character actor. To spend time going after an agent who is not right for you can be a waste of effort and terribly discouraging. Another actor can sometimes arrange for you to meet his agent. Your colleagues can be a wonderful source of information and assistance.

4. *Send out your picture and resume to those agents that you might be interested in.* When you know which agents might be right for you, send them a picture and resume with a note saying you'll call. Then, follow up. This way of getting an agent is definitely a long shot, but it *is* a possibility and you should always follow up on *all* possibilities. You can never tell when a lucky break will appear.

5. *Be persistent, polite and resourceful.* Don't give up after one rejection. When you are playing a role that you think might interest the agents you're trying for, let them know about it. You can be persistent without being pushy. Sending a nice note or postcard telling them of your new show isn't pushy. Letting them know of your interest and your career progress isn't pushy. Also, be resourceful. If a connection pops up that can give you access to the desired agents, make concrete use of it. Develop a relationship with someone in the office—a secretary, or sub-agent. These people are on the rise and perhaps can help your cause. Above all, be polite to everyone. You don't have to fawn all over someone to be well-mannered. Remember that each time you are out in the business world, you are creating an impression. A bad reputation can follow you for years, ruining the opportunities and relationships you most want to cultivate.

AVOID THE BAD AGENT

A bad agent is someone who never returns your phone calls. A bad agent is someone who doesn't respond to your suggestions. A bad agent is someone with a bad reputation—either for attitude or bad behavior. A bad agent is discouraging or debilitating to you in some way. If you get a bad agent, leave. If you don't feel a positive, constructive business relationship with your agent, leave. At certain times, it is better to have *no* agent than one who might be harmful or discouraging to you and your career. Again, remember: your agent works for you and represents you to the industry. Make sure he is representing you the way you want to be seen.

IS A BAD AGENT SOMEONE WHO DOESN'T GET YOU WORK?

Not necessarily. Your agent can be the best in the world, but without *your* assistance, work and drive, your career isn't going to go anywhere. Most actors, from bit players to major stars, will tell you they get a lot of their own work.

I want you to understand this because too many actors think that they can rest once they've signed with a reputable agent. That isn't true. In fact, you have to work harder. Now that you have representation, you must concentrate on putting yourself in the arena, which means you have to constantly update your audition material, your picture and résumé, and keep in touch with what's going on in town and what parts might be coming up that you'd be right for.

If your agent hasn't sent you out in months, you have to make a choice to stay or to go it alone. For some actors, having someone to negotiate salaries is worth the 10 percent even if the agent does little else to initiate work for the client. If you understand that's how it is, then fine. However, if you feel you could negotiate your own deals, then try it alone for awhile. When I was casting, I often discovered that those actors who were not represented by agents were more focused on getting themselves out. They were fully aware that they were relying on themselves and put a lot of effort into making the rounds. Many of these actors worked on my shows consistently over the years. They were responsible and dedicated people who knew how to run their businesses and they always followed through. For them, "having an agent" wasn't enough unless that agent was really out there for them.

On the other hand, there are actors who are more motivated when they feel they have someone who can represent them in business negotiations. Maybe it's just a feeling of security— knowing that they "belong" to an agency's family. In any case, for these actors, having an agent allows them to go out and hustle. Whichever you are, the ultimate result is still the same:

> *With or Without an Agent,*
> *Your Career Is Up to You!*

Getting an agent is a process. Some actors may switch agents every few years while others may have only one agent for their entire careers. It is a very special relationship with very few ironclad rules. You must judge for yourself. The only *must* is to make sure that the agent you choose is a reputable representative acknowledged by the unions, and not some fly-by-night huckster who's out to take you for a ride.

In the resource and reading-list supplement at the back of this book, you will find listings of books and materials with additional information about agents, plus some useful addresses and references. If you are about to embark on your search for representation, remember that you are looking for an associate. An agent-client relationship is a lot like a marriage, so choose your partner well. Allow yourself some time: Most actors don't land agents within a few months. It sometimes can take years. Be patient and look upon it as a game. That way you may even have fun!

MANAGERS

When actors just starting out ask if they should get a manager, many professionals would reply, "No, get a dog instead. It's better company." Actually, there are a lot of fantastic managers. These dynamic wheeler-dealers can shape an ongoing career by close attention to specific goals and future planning. However, the many new actors will not be able to attract a fantastic manager. The ones he will attract might not be the help the actor hopes for.

Actors sometimes have the misconception that the more people that are working for them, the faster the breaks will come. This isn't necessarily true and can be a tremendous emotional and financial drain. Unlike agents, managers are not governed by any actors' union or organization whose purpose it is to regulate and oversee them on behalf of the actor.

Managers take approximately 15–20 percent of the gross from your acting work. I say "approximately" because there are managers that do charge more, but 15 to 20 percent is considered the standard. For this percentage, it is the manager's role to help guide and watch your career, and often your personal life, with far more detail than an agent. Whereas agents may have as many as a hundred clients, managers limit themselves to many less. A manager will involve himself in everything from setting up auditions and interviews to overseeing an image change or switch in personal style. Your manager will work closely with you every step of the way. Sound terrific? It can be. Unfortunately, there are a lot of charlatans out there, ready to take you for a ride. Be wary. As with agents, it is imperative that you check out a manager's reputation before signing anything. There is nothing worse than to be represented badly to the business community. If you don't know the person's reputation, ask around. If no one has ever heard of the person or the management firm, I would question the manager's usefulness to you. Even if the firm is legitimate, if no one readily recognizes them, how can they really help advance your career?

WHEN TO GET A MANAGER

It is my personal opinion that, with few exceptions, the actor starting out does not need a manager. Management is appealing to actors because it can be an ego stroke. It also can give you the illusion of security, that your career has significance. But don't let illusion confuse your business sense. In addition, the only manager I think someone should take on is someone with proven, solid business contacts and a strong reputation. Chances are this type of manager will not be interested in representing a new career. If you can't get a well-respected manager, it may not make sense to sign a contract giving away such a large portion of your income. Contracts with managers can run from one year on up. If your manager doesn't really have the contacts to help, you may be carrying him for years should you get a break and hit it big. (Managers can also be detrimental when they are involved with a career and lack the necessary skills or respect from industry.)

Of course, if a recognized, well-known manager wishes to take you on as a client, it could be a break. This manager is willing to invest in your career. This means spending time, and often money, putting together your professional image and getting you out to meet the industry executives.

I got a manager, Pat McQueeny, after I did American Graffiti. *Pat represented Harrison Ford, Mackenzie Phillips, Candy Clark, Cindy Williams as well as Frederic Forrest and Teri Garr long before* Graffiti. *On the set, Cindy would tell me how wonderful Pat was, and finally, Pat and I got together. I stayed with her right up until she stopped managing. She was a terrific businesswoman and a terrific friend as well. But if someone asks me if you really* need *a manager, I'd have to say that I don't think it's necessary. Pat was remarkable and we "clicked." I was young and didn't know much about the business, nor how to handle my career once* Graffiti *took off. I needed someone to help guide me at this point and was lucky enough to find Pat.*

—Charles Martin Smith,
*American Graffiti, Never
Cry Wolf, Starman,
The Untouchables*

Obviously, taking on a manager is a personal choice involving many factors. As a general rule, though, I think the best time for an actor to get a manager is when there is a career in progress—when there is something to manage. When your career begins to take off is the time to start pushing national publicity, to consider a variety of game plans and to build for a long-term vital career. That is when you could really use the contacts, help and advice a good manager can provide.

PICTURES AND RESUMES

The actor's calling card is his picture and resume. When you are being submitted for roles, it is your picture and resume the casting director will request. A professional picture and resume are an absolute requirement for the professional actor. Snapshots and sloppily thrown-together resumes are the signs of an amateur.

PICTURES

There are two kinds of pictures that actors use professionally. First and foremost is the headshot, which is an 8" × 10" black-and-white photograph of just your head and face. This is the most common type of picture used, and every actor must have one. The other is called a composite. It is a double sided picture: on one side is the head shot, on the other a group of photos showing various aspects of the same actor. There is usually a full-length shot combined with other shots in different types of situations to show a range of "looks." The composite is used generally for television commercials. Many agents prefer to have a hand in choosing the photographs for the composite so it might be wise to wait until you have a commercial agent before spending the money on creating a composite.

WHAT MAKES A GOOD PICTURE?

Unfortunately, most actors, even many veterans, don't know how to get the *best* picture for themselves. It may be because they choose bad photographers. Sometimes they don't know how to go after the *right* look. A good picture is *one that looks like you.* By that I mean it portrays how you look, not how you wish you looked, or how you look sometimes after four hours of hair and makeup, but how you look *most* of the time. The first time I met Michael Keaton, star of *Night Shift, Mr. Mom, Gung Ho* and *Johnny Dangerously,* he walked into my office holding his 8″ × 10″ glossy, black-and-white photo over his face. It was terrific. Not only a cute, humorous entrance, when he took the picture away, you realized that the picture really looked like him— how he looks on a day-to-day basis. Keaton had *a good head shot.* Unless you are interested in very "character-y" parts, you should avoid any bizarre or outlandish costumes. Don't wear a hat. Arrange your hair as you normally wear it. Don't appear too glamorous because it limits your image.

HOW TO GET A GOOD PICTURE

You have to find the right photographer. The best way? Ask for referrals from agents, other actors, teachers. Look at the photographer's work before deciding. Is the photographer good with women, or with men? Young or old? Is this person's photography fairly straightforward or is their style perhaps more "fashion" or glamour oriented. You don't want a fashion photographer who is expert at making clothes look great doing your head shot. Instead, you want a specialist. You want someone who specializes in shooting this kind of picture. Once you pick someone, go over your look—makeup, hair and clothes. In a head shot, all that will be seen will be, at best, from the shoulders up, so collars can take on new meanings. Also, remember when planning your options that this is a black-and-white photograph, so choose clothes and makeup with that consideration in mind.

When you finally get your picture, you will need to have it reproduced in mass quantity. There are a number of photo reproduction houses in almost any city. They will take your photo, make a negative from it and then run off copies from that. Most actors run off about a hundred at a time because it becomes more cost effective.

RÉSUMÉS

A good résumé may help you get an interview, but a bad one can hurt you. A young actress once came to meet me on a general interview and brought a "bad" résumé. I glanced at her résumé and saw listed as one of her credits a dramatic production that I had directed in New York. Clearly, this was a lie—and I felt embarrassed for her—but I never said anything about it. Almost every casting director can tell tales of this sort. Needless to say, you won't win any points with casting and studio executives, directors or producers with this sort of deception.

There is No Need to Lie on Your Résumé; Nobody Expects You to be Born With Credits.

There's a way to compose a résumé that is both truthful and provocative: an effective résumé, one that consistently helps get you work and tells the truth, the whole truth—or almost.

WHEN YOU HAVE NO PROFESSIONAL CREDITS

When you are just starting out and haven't amassed any professional credits, you can still have a professional résumé. First, make a list of all the roles that you have played—anywhere—in high school drama clubs, professional workshops, community theaters, etc. Pull from this list the parts that are the most significant and which you enjoyed the most. These roles and the plays they are from can be put on your résumé. All you need do is list them with the heading "Representative Roles." This will give the casting director an idea of what type of roles you like, have worked on and feel right for. It also tells the truth without submitting a blank page.

WHAT SHOULD BE ON YOUR RÉSUMÉ

There are certain essential pieces of information that should be on everyone's résumé whether they are just beginning or not:

- *Name, address and telephone number.* Your address and telephone number need not be your home address and telephone. If you have a post office box and/or answering service, you can give those. Later on, when you have an agent, you can use his address and number. But it's essential that there be some way for people to contact you both by mail and by telephone.

· *Union affiliations.* Put this information directly under your name, using abbreviations for the unions, i.e. SAG, AEA, AFTRA.

· *Height and weight.* This information helps give a casting director a picture of what you'll look like so that he can better judge your appropriateness for various roles.

· *Color of hair and eyes.* Again, this is for the purpose of visualizing what you look like.

· *Credits.* The best way to organize these is by medium, dividing your experience according to STAGE, FILM and TELEVISION. On most résumés, actors do not list the commercials they have done but rather have a separate listing that they can attach for a commercial audition. On the résumé, they might note they have that list by indicating "Commercial list upon request."

· *Training.* This should include your acting classes as well as related areas such as singing, dancing, speech, etc.

· *Special skills.* If you are an expert fencer, you will want to note that in this section. It could help you when auditioning for a production of Shakespeare. Special skills can include anything from horseback riding, skiing, all physical activities and sports, to dialects, proficiency on a musical instrument or in a foreign language. In other words, this section is where you can list any other skill that might be of use to you and make you more qualified for a specific role.

WHAT SHOULD NOT BE ON YOUR RÉSUMÉ

Some actors make the mistake of following business résumé formats when making up their acting résumés. Corporate résumés serve a different function than the actor's résumé and there is some information that, if included, can even be a detriment to an actor. Some examples:

- *Age or age range.* Unless you are under eighteen (because of child-labor laws), it is not necessary to put down your age. You will be cast on how old *you look,* not how old you really are. There are some actors who play ingenues well into their thirties and others who play middle age before they're thirty. Each actor has an age range based on how they look. However, it is not for you to decide what that range is. Casting directors may differ in their opinion of an actor, but it is still up to them to decide if you look right for a certain character of a certain age. Putting your age or what you think is your age range on your resume can actually hurt you at times. Let's say a casting director thinks you look twenty-one and is considering you for a character of that age, but your resume notes that you are actually thirty-four. This could give the casting director pause and he might question his own initial impression, or worse, eliminate you from the running because he assumes you have too much life experience to play someone of twenty-one. Instead, let the casting execs and others decide how old you can play.

- *Character Type or Range.* This is really inappropriate on your résumé. Some actors feel the need to *tell* you how they would cast themselves. Again, your image of yourself may actually be too narrow, so why risk limiting your chances. On the other hand, I've seen résumés that boast an amazing range in age and type that is absolutely physically impossible. This just looks silly and amateurish. Leave this type of judgment to the people who'll be interviewing you.

Your résumé represents you. It should be typed, neat and only one page long. List credits and information. Do not write your resume like a biography. Finally, remember not to lie. If you want to check form, look at other actors' résumés or ask your teacher to help. Just remember to keep it simple and direct.

Interviews, Auditions and Callbacks: How to Be Spectacular 6

For Clue, they requested a 19-year-old, sexy, bimbo type who was also a great comedienne. I wanted to do this part but everybody said I was wrong. I believed I could do it, and with the help of my manager, I got to audition. I put together a costume, put on a French accent and got the part. Don't take "no" for an answer and trust your instincts.

—Colleen Camp,
*Police Academy 2, They
All Laughed, D.A.R.Y.L.,
Illegally Yours, Clue*

LET'S say it straight out: no one *likes* to audition to get an acting job. Unfortunately, it's still the way most roles are cast. Auditions can be grueling. Some actors may have to audition half a dozen times to get just one part. Others might "talk" with a director only once before capturing the role. As a casting director, I've watched *thousands* of auditions. There are no hard and fast rules for the audition process, but I've seen what consistently works—and what doesn't.

GETTING OUT

There are two types of appointments actors go on: the interview and the audition.

THE INTERVIEW

This is a chance for you to meet casting executives, directors, producers—the people who can give you a job. Rarely does an actor get cast on the basis of an interview. This is just a chat—a way for these people to get to know you a little more personally. Some casting departments schedule regular interviews to get acquainted with new actors. This is called a General Interview.

THE AUDITION

At the audition, you will either perform material you have prepared, such as a scene and/or monologue, or read a role from a script being cast. You might have the material ahead of time, or you might have to do a cold reading, which means having only a few minutes to review the material.

You should audition whenever you can for whatever you can. Don't worry if you're not right for the part, get out there and read for it anyway. Sometimes actors refuse to read for roles because they don't think they are the "right type." In an industry so quick to typecast, it is silly to typecast yourself. One way you will get better at auditions is to practice. Go on everything you can.

HOW TO GET AN INTERVIEW AND/OR AUDITION

How to get an interview or audition? The very best way to have access to a meeting is through a personal contact. This can be your business representative or a friend, colleague or relative. Who you know in this business can determine how well you will do. I am not talking about just getting someone to do you a favor. Rather, I'm talking about requesting assistance because of mutual artistic and professional respect.

Ideally, you have a fabulous agent who knows everyone in town and gets on the phone arranging interviews and auditions for the newest talent on the client list—you. Well, that's the way actors would wish it, but the truth is that even with the best of agents you are going to have to pursue work on your own much of the time. You have to know what's happening in town and be prepared to cash in on opportunities. Even with an agent, you will have to seek out information and tips on new projects and work with your agent to get the meetings. If you don't have an agent, you will have to do it all yourself. And with persistence and patience and hard work it can be done.

CONSULT THE TRADE PAPERS

Most cities publish "trade papers," which are show business publications. Some devote themselves exclusively to the actor and post casting notices.

In New York, the trade papers *Show Business* and *Backstage* come out once a week. They list casting information for both union and non-union stage productions plus information about what is going on in New York in television and feature films. There is also *Variety*, a weekly that gives you general information about the industry, in addition to casting notices.

In Los Angeles, *Drama-logue*, the actor's weekly paper, supplies updates on stage, television and film production, as well as all the city's casting notices. In addition, there are the daily trades, *Variety* and *The Hollywood Reporter*, which will keep you up to date on what's happening in television and film. Once a week there are casting notices and lists of what television and film shows are in production.

If you are not in Los Angeles or New York, check around with other actors or acting schools to find out where local auditions are listed.

The only drawback to this method of auditioning is that many actors complain that the parts have already been cast *before* the auditions. In many instances, this is true. Union regulations require open interview and/or auditions even though the director may already have cast the play. It's unfortunate, of course, but I still think it is worth auditioning. You gain more experience in auditioning and get to meet another new person who might hire you. And you never know what is going to happen. Thomas Hulce, the talented actor who played Mozart in *Amadeus,* got his first big break through an Equity open-call audition for *Equus.* Many actors wouldn't even go to such a "futile" audition, but for Tom Hulce—he wowed the auditioners, who were looking for a replacement for the male lead—the effort more than payed off. The truth about these auditions is that you have to hope for the law of averages. Out of every hundred auditions, perhaps only one will be worthwhile, but if it's the one that gets your career on the winning track, isn't it worth it?

UNION NOTICES

Don't overlook your unions either. Actor's Equity posts notices on its bulletin board in every local office. In some cities, Equity has a hotline number to call for the latest auditions. The other unions from time to time have notices about seminars and workshops plus information about student films, industrials, etc. Consult the local office of each union to find out what opportunities they might have for you.

OTHER WAYS TO GET IN THE DOOR

I've gotten a couple of jobs by calling the casting director and saying I was an agent. Then, I'd recommend myself for the part. Do whatever you have to to get through the door to be seen—within the realm of morals and ethics. You've got to believe in what it is you have to offer.

—Elliott Gould,
E/R, M*A*S*H, Bob and Carol and Ted and Alice, California Split

The ways of getting an audition or interview range from the ridiculous to the sublime. I've had actors wait by my car in the parking lot, sit outside my office all day, send me presents, flowers, funny gags—all to capture some attention and get themselves known. One darling comedienne took such an unorthodox approach to gain my attention. First she sent me a plaster cast of her arm on which was written, "Cast me!" The next week, a rubber hand appeared with a note saying, "Let me lend you a hand." The following week, a rubber finger with "Just want to point out my talent." I couldn't resist. I had to meet her.

Although such ingenuity can work for you, you have to be careful. It can also backfire, making you seem like a bit of a nut or a pest or both. You should reserve these ingenious ideas for auditions that are special—that really count. There is a more traditional way, and though it may seem fruitless and frustrating at first, if you set out your game plan you can accomplish a lot.

MAKING THE ROUNDS

In the golden age of television during the 1950s, most of the casting activity was done in New York City. The traditional way for an actor to find work was to make the rounds, which meant going to each producer's office or casting headquarters. Today it's not as easy or as useful to make the rounds. In Los Angeles, with its guarded studio entrances, it can even be impossible. Still, there is a way to get yourself out there.

WHO DO YOU WANT TO MEET?

The first step toward getting an audition or interview is making a list of who you want to meet and what territory they cover, such as stage, television or film. There are casting-director guides published in most cities. Some examples are *The Ross Reports,* published in New York City, and the weekly production lists in *Variety* and *Hollywood Reporter,* published in Los Angeles.

MAKING CONTACT

Now that you know *who* you want to contact and *why*—for a specific role in a specific project, or a general interview or audition—your next move is to decide the best way to contact them. Your best choice would be through an agent, but if that's not possible, how about through another contact, such as a colleague, another casting director, or a director or producer who might know the person you are trying to reach? If you have no contact, you are going to have to initiate contact yourself. The best way to do this is through the mail. You may be tempted to phone or stop by in person, but I guarantee you will be spending a lot of time for nothing, and you might even irk someone if you barge in on them at a busy time. Instead, send the casting office your picture (which, of course, really looks like you), your résumé and a note requesting a general interview/audition. Ask if there is any set procedure that you should follow. Tell them you will follow up this letter with a phone call in a week or so.

There are two reasons for telling them you will follow up:

1. It relieves them of the responsibility for answering your letter, for which they will be grateful since they barely have enough time to answer the mail they are supposed to answer.

2. It gives you the opportunity to make phone contact with a decisive purpose. In fact, when you call the office and the secretary asks why you are calling, you can say that you are following through on your letter request. It's polite and absolutely proper protocol.

If you do not get an appointment because the casting director is too busy or doesn't hold general interviews or auditions, thank him anyway for responding to your query. And thank him again by mail. The object here is to get your name in front of these people as often as you can without being irritating or pushy. Thank-you notes are a marvelous way to make contact and give a compliment. Even though this casting executive isn't going to see you, you have made at least cursory contact. The next step is to follow through over time. That means sending a note, or an ad or a postcard with your picture, whenever you are in a play or showcase—something the casting director might be able to see to become familiar with your work. Here again, you have to face the harsh reality: it's hard to get casting execs out to showcases. It's not because they don't want to see new actors, but rather the horrific constraints on their time and energy. Still, the more you can contact a casting director with realistic communications like informing him of a play you're in or asking him watch you on a TV episode that's airing, the better your chances of meeting this person.

Even after you have met and/or auditioned for someone, you should continue to remind him of your existence from time to time. Casting is a very hectic process. For a television series, the casting director may have only a few days to cast the entire thing. That means they don't have the time to go through all their casting files for every part that comes up. Sometimes that postcard reminding them of you comes just at the time a role you are right for is coming up. A consistent course of mail contact can help your odds of being in the right place at the right time.

"NO PHONE CALLS OR VISITS, PLEASE"

Most casting offices specifically request that you do not call or arrive in person to try and get an interview or an audition. The reason is they are busy and your arrival or phone call only serves to disrupt an already taut schedule. It may make *you* feel better to actually *see* the office or *hear* the secretary's voice, but in actuality it will do nothing for your chances of getting a meeting with the casting director. And it can backfire. I remember one actor who phoned our office every day for three weeks, requesting an interview with me. My secretary and I were swamped with work setting up auditions and interviews for a piece I was casting. Every day this fellow would call and bug my secretary for an appointment. She tried to explain to him that this wasn't a good time, and would he send a picture and résumé and she would see what could be done. The next day he called again, saying the picture and résumé were in the mail. Then the next day, called to ask if it arrived. Then the next day, wanted to know if she could set up the appointment yet. Then the next day . . . Need I say more. After three weeks of this, my secretary was about to tear her hair out. But the actor did get his wish—his name was brought to my attention, but not in the most positive light.

There may be times when breaking the rules is okay, but remember you have to be pretty sure that something like that won't backfire. My general rule of thumb is save the rule-breaking for something important. As I mentioned earlier, if there's a role-casting for which you would be perfect, you might have to take some risks if the normal channels fail to deliver the opportunity.

How to prepare for an interview

The interview is an opportunity for the people in the entertainment business to get to know you. Sometimes an interview leads to the next step in your career. Therefore, the impression you give at this time may affect your relationship in the future.

There are some actors and agents who believe that interviews are a waste of time. I don't agree. I learn a lot about an actor at the interview and find myself compelled by their individuality. I've learned more about an actor's ability from an interview than I have from some readings. I realize that my sensitivity may be unique, and I have been fairly accurate, but there are other people in this profession who also can see your ability. Ultimately, when it comes to an individual role I still need to have the actor read.

Sometimes this process is very nerve-racking but you can make it an enjoyable experience. You can do it better than almost anybody else because you are an actor. One of your greatest charms is that you are interesting. Instead of concentrating on your fear, put yourself into a positive mind-set. It is also necessary to realize that the person you are meeting with is just that, a person—a live human being who has a life and interests of his/her own.

When you're "taking a meeting," it's important to remember to deal with the person on the other side of the desk as an equal, a peer. You're there to get a job. They're there because they need someone to do a job. If you come in subservient or needy, it will make people nervous. Instead, imagine how you'd behave if your best buddy were introducing you to another of their friends. It's that kind of relaxed, confident behavior you want to bring into the meeting.

—Fran Drescher, *Spinal Tap,
Ragtime, American Hot Wax,
Dr. Detroit*

Before you go into an interview, try to know as much as you can about the individuals you will be meeting. It will help make conversation easier. Ask questions at your meeting so that you have more control of the situation. The interview can also be a chance for you to learn and to expand. It's not just a time for you to be on display.

· Be on time.

· Dress for the occasion. Wear something comfortable but not too casual. Don't costume yourself.

· Be prepared to talk about yourself.

· Be ready to do a short monologue (one or two minutes) of material that you've prepared and which suits your abilities. You probably won't have to do it—but just in case.

· Bring a picture and résumé even if you're sure one was already sent in.

· Treat everyone that you meet with respect and dignity.

· Try to get out of your own way and enjoy this opportunity.

Although the above describes the general interview, it also applies to those interviews that are the preliminary step before auditioning for a specific role or project. If you can find out before the interview what role the casting director has in mind, it might help specific considerations such as dress and conversational topics.

HOW TO PREPARE FOR THE AUDITION

Confidence is preparation. Everything else is beyond your control. I approach an audition like a job I'm ready to shoot. I give the auditors a good product and it's up to them to use that "take" or not. The auditors have a problem; you are the solution. Confidence is enjoying the ride from the audition.

—Richard Kline, *Three's Company,*
New York Shakespeare Festival,
Lincoln Center Repertory Company

The audition is one of the most terrifying processes the actor has to go through. Even after an actor has received great acclaim, an audition is still a nightmare. Someone is judging your ability based on how you handle a piece of material. This is not meant as a trial in which you are the victim; just the opposite. This is an opportunity for you to perform. It might also help you to know that it is uncomfortable for those at the other end. It's a lousy system, but so far, there's no way around it.

The preparation for the audition is not unlike that for the interview. If this is a general audition, you will be performing prepared material, a scene and/or monologue. If the audition is for a specific project, find out in advance what the role consists of. The receptionist or secretary in the department will be able to answer many of your questions. Check to see if the material you will be reading will be available in advance. If you cannot pick it up prior to your audition date, be sure to come to the appointment early so you will have time to read over the scene before you go in.

Reading cold is not the end of the world. If you have a problem with this or any other area of auditioning, there are many valuable workshops that deal precisely with audition techniques. It is not necessary to memorize your audition material. It is far more worthwhile to look over the material, understand it and make choices on how you wish to interpret it. Memorizing the scene may actually work to your disadvantage because the acting will look too "set" and not spontaneous. It also announces a final performance long before you would be able to give one.

It may be necessary to spend a little more time psyching yourself for an audition. Try to find ways to overcome your nervousness. One of the best ways is through breathing exercises. Another is concentrate on something else (your character, listening to the people in the room, etc.) rather than on yourself. Placing your focus outside yourself is a constructive way to get your nerves in control. Vocal and physical exercises will help you release tension and give you more power and control. These are only a few suggestions. Seek out other alternatives. There are many methods available.

> *It's crucial to bring the essence of yourself into an auditin and leave your personality behind. Before my audition for General Hospital, I tried to set aside my past and my fear and get to the essence of who I am and then put the character's personality on top of that. So, I became "her," unencumbered by Gloria and it really grounded me. The "I am" is the essence of ourselves.*

The best auditions I have seen are given by people who come to the process in a good mental frame of mind. They are usually involved in other activities and seem to enjoy themselves. That energy is really captivating and affects how the actor will read.

YOUR AUDITION

Your audition begins the first moment you walk in the door. Impressions are important. Be careful not to blow all your energy demonstrating your personality. Too often I have watched actors use the first moments of their audition to captivate the auditors with their charm. Through the introduction and the first few minutes of polite chatter, these actors completely win you over. However, now that it's time to read the material, guess with whom they compete? That's right—themselves! This is an impossible feat. You can never make a character you've prepared for only minutes leap off the page with as much verve and vitality as your own personality. After all, you've been working on developing that personality for years. Result: the reading can't help but be a disappointment. Save yourself—literally. Be polite and friendly but save your energy for the reading. After that, you can go all out to wow them with how interesting you are.

The casting director, the director, the producer and the writer are often present for your audition. Obviously, one of the rules is, don't be hostile to the people you are meeting. Be polite. Consider the meeting the same way as you would when visiting someone in their home. I'm pointing this out because sometimes an actor thinks he'll win points if he cops a "you're-not-such-a-big-deal" attitude and questions and probes the people in the room as if it were the actor doing the interview. It might make you feel empowered for a few moments, but it will do nothing for your rapport with the people who can hire you.

What are they looking for? For you to be brilliant, that's all. The best way for you to do this is by following your own instincts, rather than trying to figure out what they want. If they knew exactly what they were looking for, they wouldn't have to see so many people. The fact is, they want you to be the one so they can stop casting!

It's perfectly okay for you to ask questions to fine-tune what you have in mind for the reading. One expression that actors use in auditions, which I think works for them, is "Let me show you what I've done with this. If it isn't right, please feel free to stop me, or let me perform it another way when I'm finished." This is a solid strategy because it lets the auditors know that you are flexible and interested in doing the work. It also can buy you a second chance—possibly to read the material a different way. After you read, you can ask if that's what they wanted. If they say yes, believe them. If not, they will tell you what kind of changes they want you to try.

Be alive and be conscious. It's important to extend your humanity to this situation. Allow yourself to really be in the room concentrating on what is going on. Try to notice everything, and then let yourself just "be."

AUDITIONS FOR STAGE, FOR FILM, FOR TELEVISION

STAGE AUDITIONS

Please be aware of two things: being seen and being heard. Too often actors forget that they must speak up to be heard in a theater. Adjust your volume to the size of the house. One way to do that is to really commit to the audition. Even if you're reading with a stage manager who's an expert in monotone recitation, still throw yourself into it. It's your audition. The stage manager already has a job. Don't shortchange yourself because Laurence Olivier isn't your audition partner.

Also, be sure you are in the light and that your auditors can see you. If you are not sure, ask if you can be seen. In television and film auditions, usually set in small rooms, these are not considerations, but on the stage you must always take into account the physicality of the place in which you are reading.

TELEVISION AND FILM AUDITIONS

These differ from stage readings in that they are usually held in offices or small rehearsal spaces. It isn't necessary to worry about volume or light here. But you do have to concentrate on what you are doing if you are not to be distracted by the "living-room" feeling of the audition. Also, film and television cameras notice everything. On stage, there are no close-ups to transmit a special moment. On film and tape, however, your every facial movement can be enlarged and emphasized. Consequently, it isn't necessary for you to act "big" so that it "reads" in the last row. Keep your reading on a more intimate or conversational level. Make your acting truthful—not big.

CALLBACKS

In the process of choosing an actor, callbacks may be necessary for various reasons: having seen so many people, the auditors' memory of you may not be as sharp as they would like it; they can't decide between you and two other people so they want to see you all again; there are additional executives, who are also involved in the decision-making process, who have not seen you; they want to try seeing if you can do the material in different ways; they may add some specific directions they want you to work with; they may want to see how you go with another actor you would be playing with. For all these reasons and more, actors sometimes are called back five or six times for the same role.

By knowing who you are, you don't have to depend on exterior successes to make you feel good. You believe in and enjoy yourself regardless of the results. With believing in oneself comes an inner quietness, a peacefulness. Anxiety is in the mind. So is peace. That's what you have to take into and out of an audition.

—Donna Dixon,
*Spies Like Us, Bosom
Buddies, Dr. Detroit,
Couch Trip*

Each time you return, you must bring to the reading the same energy, assurance and enjoyment. Do not change your interpretation of the role unless you've been specifically requested to do so. Don't change your wardrobe; you are often remembered by what you wear.

Keep in mind you are getting closer with each audition. As you get more comfortable and realize you won't die during the experience, you will probably find yourself more alive.

Rejection: How to Handle It and Love It 7

The difference between success and failure is simple.
Successful people persist beyond their failures.

—Lotus Weinstock, COMEDIENNE

YOU'VE just come out of the audition knowing you were wonderful. It was your third callback for a series regular, and you could tell everybody loved your reading. This was a role you were born to play. And now it's down to you and someone else. You can barely sit still in your apartment, waiting for the phone to ring. In your head you're already spending your new star salary. Deep in your heart, you know the part is yours. The phone rings. You grab it and it's your agent: "Sorry. They went with the other actor. They felt you were not really right for the part."

Disappointment? Of course. But worse, you feel rejected. That's what this business has in spades—rejection. Unlike other occupations, actors are asked to expose themselves to constant judgment and assessment. It doesn't matter whether you are a novice actor, a star or a veteran of twenty-five years, you will have to cope with rejection on a continuing basis.

It's tough when I experience a disappointment because I didn't get the part. But I get over it by realizing it's all absurd. What's meant to be is meant to be, and finally, you have to experience acceptance. These are business decisions, not the thing that I love—acting.

—Aidan Quinn

"Everyone gets rejected at times." "Don't be so thin-skinned." "It's all the law of averages." Well, these are nice platitudes, but they don't help much when you lose that perfect part. Here's the straight scoop: rejection is lousy. That's the truth— but if you want a successful career in this highly competitive business, you're going to have to accept rejection as part of the territory and develop techniques to deal with it. You're not alone. Every well-known actor has a rejection tale to tell.

Consider this one, told to me by the respected comedienne Lotus Weinstock:

It was 1969. The place: Toronto! I was nine months pregnant and I was on a comedy roll! Laughs were coming faster and faster than ever before! Me and my built-in partner were becoming an underground sensation on the performance art scene! Rumor had it that I might give birth on stage!

Five days before my daughter decided to break up the team by being born in a hospital, we had our peak performance at the then famous Riverboat Coffee House. We were on a bill with Richie Havens . . . Mr. Woodstock himself.

He attracted my dream crowd! The type that give standing ovations and applauded insights, one of my favorite things to share!

The biggest concert promoter in Canada at the time was in the audience and after the show he asked me if I'd consider opening for the Byrds in five weeks in a 4,000-seat concert hall!

Maybe I should have consulted my soon-to-be-born baby, but since I had done all the talking for both of us in the nine months we'd been together, I said "yes" with the certainty that only follows a perfect show.

Unaware of the life-changing effects that follow a three-day labor and subsequent cesarean, I viewed my opportunity to perform on the bill with one of America's musical elite as the coronation of my eight-year career in comedy!

Postpartum blues notwithstanding, I was highly anxious when I heard the five-minute curtain call. It was my first time away from the baby since conception and birth and the milk was coming into my breasts as I entered the spotlight. As has always been my policy, I shared my reality with the audience in order to create the intimacy necessary for my brand of humor.

My opening line: "If I rush a little, it's cause the milk just came into my breasts and I have to go home to feed my baby." Since the audience was composed of 4,000 kids on acid who were there to get away from their mothers, their reception of my reality was like a greeting from Hell! Within seconds, the entire audience was repeatedly chanting: "Go home now! Go home now!"

As my life flashed before me, the chanting seemed to me to be a deafening sign from the universe that I should perhaps find out where home really was or not open for rock musicians!

It took me five years to recover fully and as I look back from here, I view the experience as my "Daniel in the Lion's Den."

Imagine standing at the altar with your mate after you've taken your vows, and the rabbi and/or priest asks if anyone objects and the entire world yells, "I Do!"

What that experience did for me was to enable me to ride my adrenaline in the face of death! Ten years later, I talked my way out of an armed assailant's attack, and when a casting director rejects me, it's like a message at a July Fourth picnic!

I am not suggesting that you be booed off stage by 4,000 in order to be glib with a gunman, but rather to use your rejections as an investment in the bank of confidence!

THE BIG REJECTIONS

Losing the role when it comes down to the wire—as in the opening scenario of this chapter—is what I call a "big rejection." You've been working very hard for the part. Your hopes are high. The stakes are high. And then, suddenly, it all crashes down. This type of rejection is quite severe and you have a right to feel deflated. But you can't allow yourself to feel destroyed.

Two reasons you will often hear when you lose a role is that you "are not right" or they "went another way."

YOU'RE NOT RIGHT

It's hard to believe that this is an objective consideration, but there is something to it. Even if you've given a brilliant audition, if you are not the right size, height, look, age or type, you won't get the job. This doesn't mean that after several callbacks, you don't have a right to feel you've been led on. You may believe you're perfect for the part, but often there are considerations that arise that suddenly will knock you out of the running. For example, they decide on a male lead who's six feet four. Now they must find someone to match him. Though you've given a few fabulous readings, the fact is you're too short to look good with this fellow. You've been the right type for three weeks, but now you are no longer right. It's a brutal change in the course of events, but it is not uncommon.

GOING ANOTHER WAY

Sometimes the creative people who are searching for the right actor feel that they might be able to take a chance and change the essence of a character they are casting. For example, when director Mike Nichols originally was casting for *The Graduate*, the lead role was envisioned as a Jimmy Stewart–type character. But Nichols liked a certain odd-looking character actor and wanted to see him for the part. Nichols was looking "to go another way" with this role. The actor captivated Nichols, and suddenly the image of Jimmy Stewart went out the window—the lead in the movie went to Dustin Hoffman. It was the part that made him a star.

This can happen. So you might find yourself the only brunette at an audition filled with blondes. You're the candidate for "going another way." However, be prepared that though the creative forces may entertain this idea, they may stick with their original concept. Conversely, you may read a script that describes you to a tee. Your readings are great, but you don't get the role. Then you discover that the part went to a completely different type! How come? That's right—they decided to go another way. If you can see the absurdity in this business, you will survive, get stronger and go on.

LITTLE REJECTIONS

How to handle the day-to-day rejections is the more common plight of the professional actor. Unless you're at the height of your career, there isn't that much work you'll be offered. Even if you are, you may not be right for the parts you are offered. Dealing with continual feelings of rejection is part of the process of an acting career. The bottom line is that sometimes you will be the chosen one, but more often you won't be.

HOW TO HANDLE REJECTION

The first step in handling rejection is to *detach yourself from the situation*. When you are turned down for an opportunity, you must not take this as a personal rejection. Writers who have fabulous careers still have some of their writing rejected, yet they clearly understand that it is the particular piece being rejected, not themselves as writers. This kind of separation is obviously more difficult for actors to create. After all, you and your "piece of work" are one and the same. Though it's tough to make that separation, it is a must if you want to survive.

When an actor loses a role, he will usually express it by saying, "They hated me" or "They turned me down" or something of that nature. These common expressions indicate how little separation most actors feel between the rejection of themselves as actors and of themselves as human beings.

Instead, I suggest to actors that they think of losing a role in less personal terms. Rather than saying, "They didn't want me," why not express it by saying, "They didn't want my acting services for this part." It may seem only a matter of semantics, but the way we express ourselves has an effect on how we think. Like a writer who says, "They didn't like my script," expressing your rejection with "They didn't like my character choices," instead of "They didn't like me," puts the entire situation in a different perspective.

Detaching your *identity* from the casting process protects you from much hurt and gives you the strength to get back out there. It also forces you to be an adult doing business, rather than the child searching for approval and love.

REJECTION AS AN EMOTIONAL HOOK

If you cannot detach yourself in these situations and make it an impersonal experience, perhaps you are hooked emotionally to other people's opinions of you. This is not part of the professional arena. Perhaps you are falling victim to unresolved issues dealing with self-worth, authority, fear of success and/or failure, or fear of not being loved. If you find you fall apart every time you are turned away, or that you become hostile, angry and have a "chip-on-the-shoulder" attitude, the reality is you are not dealing with rejection in a constructive way. Rather, you are allowing this aspect of the profession to keep you trapped as the needy child constantly demanding approval and adoration.

You must grow up. Become an adult and be responsible for yourself. It is not up to others to approve of you. You must do that for yourself. Don't give away that power to *anyone* ever. Keep auditions and interviews in a proper perspective. You are a salesman selling your acting services, and that's all there is to it. Sometimes others will buy it and sometimes they won't. If they don't, just move on to the next opportunity. If you have a problem with rejection to the extent that it is paralyzing your performance and holding you back, seek guidance or help to overcome the obstacle.

DISAPPOINTMENTS

Instead of focusing on rejection, think of these experiences as disappointments. All artists, business people and professionals experience career disappointments. Life deals out disappointments to all human beings. There is really no way to get around this. The way we get stronger has to do with our resilience after. a disappointment. Because the actor experiences disappointments more frequently, he must acquire the ability to bounce back more quickly.

You Are Allowed to Feel Disappointment.

The degree of your disappointment will be relative to the degree of your expectations. Only you are in control of your expectations—at least on the conscious level. If your attitude is one of "It's great if it happens, but it's okay if doesn't," your disappointment will probably match this easygoing attitude. It's better than thinking in extremes: "If I don't get this job, I'll die." It is better to continually reinforce an easygoing attitude about a job, than to cultivate an attitude of desperation. Eventually, by disciplining your attitude, you will discover that the effects of your career disappointments are less severe.

Sometimes a disappointment calls for emotional release—some self-indulgence and possibly even a trip back to bed and under the covers. Feeling sorry for yourself is okay when the disappointment has been great and your expectations have been high. Why not? You have a right to feel bad. You have a right to cry, scream and carry on. This is a good opportunity to release frustration for all the small rejections also. Go for it. Then, when you've had enough, start all over again.

However, if you find yourself doing this whenever you don't get the job, you are abusing yourself. Don't beat yourself up and be angry with the world because you have lost sight of the reality:

It Is Only a Job—It's Not Your Entire Career

Remember to be objective. You and your work are separate entities.

Another way to lighten disappointment is with a sense of humor. If you put the situation into the context of life's bigger picture, you will see that it isn't such a horrible thing. It's really quite laughable. Remember Puck from Shakespeare's *A Midsummer Night's Dream:*

Ah what fools these mortals be.

Because you did not get the job does not mean you are a bad actor. If this thought goes through your mind, even though you know from past experience that you are a good actor, you are beating yourself up.

Don't decide to quit when you feel rejected. Many actors feel so impotent after a turndown that they need to do something active—something within their control. A negative thought may feel like you have regained power. All that this kind of thinking does is hurt you even more. Know that rejection/disappointment has a positive after-effect.

REJECTION AND CONVICTION

I see rejection as a test of your true conviction. It's the acting profession's own weeding-out process. There's the old adage: "If you can't stand the heat, get out of the kitchen." Every time you audition, every time you are turned down, and every time you try again, you are reinforcing your conviction. You are developing strength through resilience and a committment to your career. You are honoring yourself by believing in yourself. Rejection *is* merely disappointment. Don't distort it into unresolved personal, psychological issues. See rejection as a building block that can reinforce your love of acting and your dedication to the profession. Keep in mind, you may not have gotten the job you wanted because of forces beyond your control. I've heard many stories about great disappointments that made actors available for much bigger and better parts. Trust that there is a greater adventure ahead.

Question-and-Answer Seminar for Section B 8

1. I've heard that some stars don't have either agents or managers. Do they handle all the business things themselves?

Actors who are not represented in the typical fashion usually have a lawyer to assist them in negotiations and a business manager to oversee their financial affairs. Sometimes they put together their own staffs to help them with their careers and develop their own projects. This places a great deal of responsibility on the actor's shoulders. Often, the actor misses out on parts because he is not interconnected properly and does not have the necessary clout. Some actors try this for a while, find that it costs too much to operate this type of enterprise and return to the more traditional form of their careers. Some actors find this autonomous approach successful and challenging, eventually leading them into producing not only for themselves, but for others as well. Some actors do a little bit of everything. It's really up to the individual.

2. How can I be sure that when I'm rejected for a role there isn't something that I should fix?

Listen to your feedback. If the word consistently comes back that you're overweight and your hair's a mess, then clearly you must take steps to fix that. Otherwise, if you felt you did the best you could in your reading/interview, you must trust that it was okay and you lost the part for reasons beyond your control.

3. There are some computer casting services around now. Is this the future for casting? Will it bypass the agent?

For smaller roles, it may eventually become the norm. It is more than likely an excellent form of "bookkeeping" for casting directors and producers. But I do not believe that it will replace the personal-taste element contributed by the agent and/or casting director. So far, it is hard to tell what the future holds for this service, but at the present time, it offers very little to principal roles in stage, film or television.

4. As a black actor, am I more limited then other individuals in getting work on TV commercials, soaps, sitcoms, etc.? Which area affords the best chance for me to get work?

Yes, you are more limited. There simply isn't as much work, and you will have to try twice as hard as everybody else. Just about everything that applies to the actor applies to you, and then some. Not only will you be forging your career, you may be pioneering for future minority performers. The best thing to do is try to educate the people who work for you. Let them know that you don't just play stereotyped "black" characters but that you can play a "teacher," a "doctor," a "policeman," any and all professions. This applies to other minority groups as well. There are community theaters for minority groups, which will always provide a place to perform. Check with the acting unions about their special committees for minority members. Team up and develop projects that will give you and your colleagues visibility. Things have been improving vastly for minority players. In the meantime, just know that when you "make it," you will be the best.

5. I'm having trouble deciding which agent to go with. A well-known agent keeps stalling about whether to sign me. A lesser known agent is enthusiastic to sign me. I like her and the "vibes" seem right. Should I hold out to see if I can get the bigger agent or should I go with the newer one?

As long as the agent that is interested in you is a viable, franchised and well-respected businessperson, there is no reason not to go with somebody who is on your team. A "bigger" agent may do nothing for you. Trust your instincts. This lesser-known agent who believes in you is probably hungry enough to make up for the fact that she is not as powerful at this time.

6. How can I tell if I'm better off in one medium than another? Should I gear myself to one type—film, stage, commercials, TV, etc.?

Work is work, and at the beginning of a career, don't typecast your own abilities. Try everything. It's a misconception that an actor is only going to be "good" in one particular medium. If you look at successful actors, you will see that they travel between film and stage and television with equal ease.

Career-Winning Strategies

IF YOU'VE EVER PLAYED POKER, you know that luck can certainly influence your game. But ultimately, if you want to win—and win big—you've got to have *skill*. The more you play and analyze the way you play, the better skilled you become. You develop your own personal poker style and strategies. From this point on—though talent and luck may influence the outcome—you will improve your chances of winning if you continually improve your skills and strategies. Show business is no different. Talent and luck can certainly get you places, but you don't become a successful, secure actor unless you develop skills and strategies—your personal style!

Opportunity! 9

The failure to recognize an opportunity is the difference between making it and not making it. People don't realize that the "big break" is an accumulative thing. The "big break" comes from small fractures.

—John Kapelos, Second
City, *Breakfast Club,*
Weird Science, Roxanne,
Nothing in Common

OPPORTUNITY. Just the word itself strikes a responsive chord in all who aspire to greatness. One of the greatest career strategies is to learn how to create opportunity, take advantage of it, and make the most of it. Why then do some of us refuse to seek opportunity out and may even turn our backs when it is presented? Perhaps it is a misunderstanding of what opportunity is and isn't. Sometimes opportunity is confused with opportunism.

OPPORTUNISM VS. OPPORTUNITY

There's a crucial difference between the two. And it is this difference that often provides the stumbling block many of us face when we think of promoting ourselves and our careers.

Opportunity is any combination of circumstances favorable for some purpose. It's a "good chance." *Opportunism* is the adapting of one's thoughts, actions, etc., to circumstances, without regard to principles. All too often we think of the hustler as the opportunist par excellence. Again, it sounds like semantics, but the truth is, our conception of something determines our actions. If you think hustling violates your code of decorum and principles, it's likely that you won't do it very well. Thus, if you think taking advantage of an opportunity is the same as opportunism, no wonder you withdraw. Opportunity is simply a good chance.

On the other side—the darker side and some say the unlucky side, lives The Hustler.

THE PARTY HUSTLE: ANYONE CARE TO DANCE?

Two actors are at a party that's studded with important agents, directors and casting directors. It's a dream night for an actor. A job from any one of these individuals could put a career on the winning track. The question is: what should these actors *do* in order to make the most of the situation?

Our first actor, The Mover, assesses the party (who's talking to whom, about what, etc.) and launches into action. This actor knows a lot about these people from reading the trade papers and gossip sheets and, of course, from the industry "grapevine." He knows not only what projects these people are doing, but the state of their marriages, their favorite sports and hobbies and the lowdown on who in town likes them and who doesn't. He knows that he has the advantage, for these executives certainly know less about him! Grabbing a drink, he begins to "work the room," casually inviting himself into conversations where he carefully adjusts his opinions to match the opinions of those present.

Consistency isn't an element here. In one group, the actor may profess an undying hatred for golf, but in the next group, when an important director mentions that he just took up the game, our actor offers some free tips since he played on the pro circuit for a while. The aim is clear: to use this opportunity to get close to some important people. The goal is work and, hopefully, stardom. Not human interaction or friendship. In fact, if some of these industry folk weren't able to help our actor, he wouldn't care to talk to them at all!

The second actor, The Recoiler, is the opposite of the first. He continues sipping his drink and feels paralyzed to act. He wants to meet these people but feels guilty that his interest in them is only professional. He recoils from the "pushy" way actors try to get ahead. It's so undignified, so phony. The very fact that he feels the desire to use this opportunity to advance his career makes him cringe. Unlike our first thespian, this actor decides *not* to make any attempt to meet these people. In fact, he goes to the opposite extreme, making sure that he steers clear of them and their conversations. When the natural flow of party chatter brings him into contact with one of the industry folk, our second actor deliberately avoids the subject of theater and makes sure not to disclose his own professional aspirations. Uncomfortable and self-conscious, this actor leaves the party early. Ashamed at his ambitious yearnings and yet embarrassed at his inability to handle the situation naturally, the actor vows never again to try socializing with industry people. He reminds himself how much he dislikes "hustlers" and trys to comfort himself by self-righteously noting that *he* would never stoop so low as to try and ingratiate himself with people to get work. He's an Artist and will rise or fall solely on the merits of his talent and craft!

If you were at a similar party, which actor would *you* be—The Mover or The Recoiler? Obviously, both actors reacted and acted to the extreme. The Mover is the ultimate opportunist. A Machiavellian nightmare. I personally wouldn't ever want to meet this person, much less help his career once I got wind of his complete insincerity.

On the other hand, the second actor, the Recoiler, just blew a terrific opportunity to meet and converse with some powerful pros who might give him insights into his profession, the industry and life in general, if not a direct line to a job!

The Recoiler's embarrassment at being needy and his self-righteous pride prevented him from making contact. He foolishly wasted a rare lucky opportunity.

BEWARE THE PRIVATE EGO

I call this kind of self-righteous pride the *private ego*. What I mean is that these individuals actually believe secretly that they are *better* than the rest of us lowly mortals. Because they are basically better, because they are superior and more talented, more regal, etc., they refuse to let anyone help them. It's a profound strain of misguided egotism that makes them so self-righteous. Rather than appear as equal or, worse, subordinate and less powerful than someone else, these egoists would prefer to forego the rewards of seeking out an opportunity. Its unfortunate and certainly foolish. Often it disguises a fear of rejection and admission of being in need. Rather than admit you're dying to go up and say hello to Woody Allen at a party, you feign indifference.

A healthy ego allows you to ask for help, as well as to give it. A healthy ego encourages interchange and peerage. It allows an individual to act on his own behalf, not hurting anyone else in the process. False ego that results in self-sabotage is totally counterproductive.

You Need Opportunity to Have a Career!

There is a third type of actor, who would have handled that party in a way that did not sacrifice his sincerity, yet still created valuable contacts. It is this third type of actor I want *you* to be. An actor that's confident and secure and can make the most of the opportunities that life presents. An actor that knows how to hustle—without being a hustler.

> *If you are faced with an opportunity and deny it, try to look at why you turn away. If it's fear—fear of being bad, of failure, of success—I think it's best to confront that fear. In Second City, they say, "Follow the fear."*
>
> —John Kapelos

CAREER SEEDING

If you don't take advantage of opportunity, your career is simply not going to go very far. "But I'm just not like that." "I can't be pushy and aggressive." "I don't like those kind of people." These are some of the comments that I commonly hear from actors. And it's perfectly understandable. We think of a hustler as someone with no moral priorities. Someone who'll stop at nothing to get what he wants. Someone who is "going for the kill." No wonder so many sensitive actors find it hard to "work a room." But there is a way, as an artist, to participate actively and assertively in the advancement of your career. I call this *career seeding,* and it means:

To Participate in the Diplomatic Interconnectedness of Relationships and Opportunities.

It's *not* about being phony or insincere. It's about learning to adjust to situations, recognize opportunity and take action. If the word *hustling* disturbs you, find other words like networking, seeding or careering. Create your own word and your own definition—one that enables you to go out there and seize the opportunities that arise.

> *Timing is everything. You have to be a barometer. Pick your moments. Choose the right time. Don't introduce yourself to someone while they are preoccupied or involved in something or someone else. Act appropriately. It reflects your upbringing. For instance, you don't ask your folks for the car keys when they're arguing. Timing is everything.*
>
> —Michael Hagerty, MEMBER
> OF SECOND CITY AND NUMEROUS
> PLAYS, TELEVISION AND FILM
> APPEARANCES

DIPLOMACY

Tact. Conducting relations between various and sometimes competing elements. Understanding how to express yourself directly and truthfully without sacrificing geniality, acceptance and charisma. In other words, being straightforward without making enemies. It's a matter of learning how to relate and adjust. Everyone needs to adjust—continually and in many situations. When you go to the supermarket and talk to the butcher, you discuss the meat on his terms: "I'd like this or that cut of beef, lamb, whatever . . ." Certainly, you don't try to discuss things in terms of acting. In essence, *you adjust* to the situation, communicating and behaving appropriately.

This Doesn't Mean Compromising Your Principles!

Too often we think of "adjusting" as somehow requiring us to give up some deep personal conviction, idea or behavior. That's patently ridiculous. Adjusting means acting appropriately. If you've been invited to dinner and are served a meal you detest, you don't tell the host that the meal is vile and you refuse to eat it. Instead, you make the best of it, eating those things you do like and bluffing your way through the rest. You do this because you like your host and wouldn't want your truthful evaluation of the meal to unnecessarily cause hurt feelings. Perhaps later you might tell your friend about your personal preferences. But for this evening, you'll delicately make sure that you don't hurt or embarrass your pal. Handling this touchy situation has nothing to do with principles and convictions. It has nothing to do with compromising your morality or beliefs. It has nothing to do with faking your personality. It's simply adjusting to the situation and taking various, perhaps conflicting, elements into consideration.

In potentially career-building situations, there is a way to behave that will enhance your opportunities and still enable you to be true to your inner beliefs and desires—*diplomacy.*

Interconnectedness of Relationships and Opportunities

This is a small business. Honest. There are just a few thousand people in the professional world of show business. And eventually you will discover that every time you connect with another new person, there is an amazing chance that you will know people in common. It's really startling. Many times I have mentioned this to actors and yet they somehow don't think it possible. But I'm here to tell you *it is true.* Every single professional in Hollywood and New York knows it to be the truth. The artistic community is very small, with centers in New York and Los Angeles. But even if you've spent your life in repertory in the Midwest, the likelihood is great that you would have connections if you arrived in L.A.

What this all means is that contacts are, and will continue to be throughout your career, one of your most important assets. Again let me emphasize:

This is a People Business—
and Success in This Business Depends on People.

As you continue to work and develop your career, you will see how interconnected everything is. The projects you work on and those relationships you make along the way are what will help to advance your career later on.

Opportunity Well Used Serves a Career.

Now that you understand the difference between opportunity and opportunism, between hustling and career seeding, we can start to put these ideas into practice to positively boost your chance of success.

The Luck Factor: How to Create It! 10

LUCK is winning two million bucks in the state lottery. Luck is going to the store to buy a stereo and discovering they're having their one and only giant sale. Luck is desperately thinking of an excuse to get out of lunch with your obnoxious fourth cousin and *he* calls to cancel. Everyone is lucky. But some people seem to have a special knack for it.

Luck is getting a gig as an understudy in a Broadway show and going on when the lead actress twists her ankle. And that's precisely how Shirley MacLaine's career took off. Overnight, Shirley became a star. Movies followed. Then, a *third* career as a writer. Is Shirley MacLaine lucky? You bet she is.

LUCK

Human beings like to be in control of their own existence. We formulate goals and strive to attain them. We fret over setbacks and fortify ourselves against potential danger. In short, we like to be in the driver's seat. But there's a force in the universe that, at times, seems to control our lives—sometimes making things go our way, and sometimes foiling our every attempt. Often there appears no logical explanation for the way this force works. This force we call *luck* and its twist of fate can be delightful or devastating.

In the late 1960s after playing on Broadway for 9 months in "The Great White Hope," I segued into a feature role in a film shooting in Spain. When I returned to New York, I was surprised to discover I was back at square one with my career. What a bummer. I thought, 'This profession is not for a grown man. The constant insecurity, groveling, proving you can cut the mustard . . .' I thought about going back to school. As luck would have it, I went on a reading for an off Broadway comedy and won the role. I decided to give my career one last shot. The play was "Steambath." I won the OBIE that year, and this production seriously started my career. There's a Chinese proverb that I think is true: You often find your destiny on the path you take to avoid it.

—Hector Elizondo
Flamingo Kid, TV series Down and Out in Beverly Hills, The Taking of Pelham 123, Young Doctors in Love

THE LUCK FACTOR

We could go on for days, discussing luck. We could talk about the magical moments when the things we've wanted most are suddenly manifested as though by a fairy godmother. We can also remember those times when all goes persistently awry no matter how hard we try to keep on track. When Lady Luck is around, the visit always seems too short. And when she deserts you, those down moments can feel like years.

Though we all have "luck," some people seem to have a special knack for it. For those "lucky" souls, life unfolds in magical opportunities and fantastic breaks without a great deal of effort. But is luck simply a capricious force that touches you or not by some random scheme of fate? Or is there, perhaps, some sort of *luck factor* that a person can create for themselves?

I think there is. Observing successful people from all professions, I've noticed that many "lucky" fast-trackers credit their success to *hard work* and *luck.* However, when you look at their lucky breaks, there are two components consistently present: Lucky people are willing to *take a chance,* and they have the ability to *recognize an opportunity.* And it is this dual ability that I call the *luck factor.*

> *I was playing frisbee on the beach at Santa Monica one Sunday with my friends. On one toss, the frisbee veered off and went crashing into this guy while he was sunbathing. I fetched the frisbee and apologized to the man. We started chatting and he asked me what I did. I told him I was an actor. He told me he was John Crosby, the head of casting for ABC-TV! I couldn't believe my luck, but the best was still to come—he told me to call his office and arrange an appointment for me to bring in an audition scene! I was thrilled. I had been working on a scene in acting class with another actor and we were really ready. I called for an appointment and his secretary told me the scene should be no longer than five minutes and should have no props or require furniture. I didn't know what to do. My scene was fifteen minutes and needed bunk beds! Since I didn't have a choice, I went for it. As politely and with as much charm as I could muster, I arrived for my appointment and when it was my turn signaled my friends waiting outside in the hall with the bunk beds. They marched right into the office over the secretary's protests. We stepped up quickly and began the scene. Crosby liked the scene and put me under contract, starting my career.*

> —George Clooney,
> *Facts of Life*

The very first rule of luck is a simple one:

Take a Chance!

If you want to win a prize, you have to take a chance. Your acting career is no exception. You must take risks. And it might be scary. No one likes looking or feeling foolish at a bad audition, meeting, etc. However, you must remember:

You Always Get Something For a Risk You Take!

You may not get exactly what you expected or wanted. Nonetheless, there *is a reward for each risk taken!* Maybe you'll go out for that audition you dreamed of and flop right on your face. Okay, that hurts, no doubt about it. But you must be of the state of mind that can say, "I'm going to learn from this. I'm not going to run away. Instead, I can use this experience to help me in the future. To help me get lucky the next time around." In many ways, taking risks in your career is like playing a game with yourself. The odds of success are against you, so you try to even the score by taking as many opportunities, as many reasonable risks as possible, in order to win.

All talk, no action

I hear actors professing great desire and ambition—but too often, it's all *talk* and no *action*. These talented individuals simply won't take a risk or put themselves on the line. Maybe it's fear of rejection or failure.

I've seen actors fall into a "failure rut": They work hard at their craft in classes and workshops, struggle with full-time non–show biz jobs to earn a living but *never get out there* in front of the kind of people who can help them create a career. They usually have excellent excuses for not taking risks: they don't have any money and their paying job won't let them out for auditions, or they don't feel quite ready or they need to lose weight, etc. These excuses keep the actor trapped in a web of self-doubt and criticism.

Why do actors sabotage themselves in this way? In some cases it's because they have gotten comfortable with the status of their lives. Comfortable with the security—with the certainty of failure. Comfortable with the *lack of risk taking!* After all, their classes and workshops offer a creative outlet. It offers the respect and approval of their peers. Their lifestyles may be uncomfortable and filled with struggle, but it *is routine.* There are no surprises, no challenges, and certainly there is nothing to lose. It then becomes difficult for these actors to motivate themselves into the professional arena. It's easier instead to continue in the same *safe* way and only dream of a career.

Sometimes a failure addict may actually be afraid of *succeeding.*

The failure addict is afraid of the many changes success will bring into his life. These folks may not be ready for success simply because they don't really want success. Rather than risk upsetting the stasis of their lives, these actors stop themselves at the start by refusing to take risks and instead toss it off to being "unlucky."

The failure addict is right about one thing: when you step out into the professional arena and put yourself on the line, *it is risky!* But if you want a professional career, you've got to get out there and take chances, create and utilize opportunities, see and be seen. You may be the most talented performer to ever grace the earth, but if you do all your performing at home, alone, you can forget about ever having a career. Don't hide your talent. Get out there and take a chance:

Give Luck a Chance To Find You!

If you're not out there performing at every opportunity, you severely limit your chance for success. Maybe it'll be community theater or Equity-waiver showcases—it doesn't matter. You're an actor—*act!* No doubt it might be frustrating. One actor may get a break after only days in the business while another talented soul waits years for his ship to come in. It's not fair—it's life. But you can maximize your chance for success by putting yourself out there in as many different opportunities as you can find and create.

And this brings us to our second rule of "luck":

Recognize Opportunity When it Knocks on Your Door!

That may sound simple and self-evident, but you'd be amazed at how many people pass by fantastic opportunities every day because they don't know how to recognize a "lucky break." Their scope is too narrow. They fail to appreciate an opportunity unless it falls within their restricted expectations. Opportunity is knocking at your door—so answer it!

Mary Kay Place, the charming actress of *The Big Chill* and TV's *Mary Hartman, Mary Hartman,* always wanted to write. To subsidize her writing career, Mary Kay took a secretarial job at Norman Lear's company. She worked hard at her day job and wrote at night. But no one at the company offered her a writing job. So, no lucky break for Mary Kay, right? Wrong. When they were casting *Mary Hartman, Mary Hartman,* someone suggested Mary Kay—as an actress. Voila! An acting career was born. Certainly Mary Kay Place was lucky—but did she possibly have a hand in contributing to that lucky opportunity? She wanted to be a writer, and she did everything she could to help herself move toward that goal. Of course, she couldn't predict that she would first gain recognition and the opportunity to write by becoming an actress—but when the opportunity arose, she certainly noticed it and went all out to make it a success. In fact, you might say that luck is little more than being aware of those random golden opportunities that present themselves.

THERE'S MAGIC IN THE AIR

You prepare for an audition, go and get the part. That's *not luck.* That's *your job.* Luck is being discovered like Mary Kay Place or Shirley Maclaine.

You simply *never* know when a small bit part is going to be your break. You may have only one or two lines, but things *can happen.* Your part is suddenly enlarged, or you meet someone on the set who becomes a good contact. Even if *nothing* happens, you are out there working—and being seen. You can never tell when an ordinary job will turn into a fantastic lucky break. Almost all of the television series that were "spin-offs" of already running shows are good examples of one job leading to "the" job. Bea Arthur, Valerie Harper, Sherman Hemsley— all are examples of professional actors who got their own series after appearing as guests on a show or as minor characters.

There are millions of ways to be "discovered." Some of the opportunities that abound are obvious. You do a local TV commercial and a casting director spots you and puts you in a TV series. A lot of careers are started by such lucky breaks.

LUCKY BREAKS

Consider the career of rock star, Sting. His rock popularity opened the door to his acting career and the opportunity to emerge as a serious film artist. Rock music is only one of many roads to stardom. Voice-overs, commercials, industrials, student films, theater showcases, workshops, print ads—all of these opportunities can lead to your lucky break. You can't know how or when it will happen. You have to trust in yourself, your instincts, and believe that every opportunity leads you closer to your goal.

I have "discovered" actors who came from all phases of the business. Many women and men gain notoriety through their print ads—and not just those who are beautiful. A comic photograph that grabs your attention, an interesting face—print work "advertises" *you.* Once I saw two little girls in an ad, who were adorable. When a part came up for which they were right, I had them audition.

The popularity of singing telegrams can also be a vehicle for the new actor to get known. Recently, I had a "Rambo-gram" arrive at my office. Oddly enough, I was looking for someone whose looks were reminiscent of Sylvester Stallone for a role on *Diff'rent Strokes.* When I saw this actor, I asked him to audition—and he got the part!

Your lucky break may be waiting for you in the comedy cabarets springing up all over the country. In the forties and fifties, young comedians and comedy writers would cut their teeth on the "Borscht Belt," a nickname for a string of resorts in the upper part of New York. It was the training place for anyone interested in a career in comedy. The "Borscht Belt" is long since gone, but now we have a new circuit opening up for those talented folks who desire to make us laugh. Nightclubs like The Improvisation (there's one in New York and one in Los Angeles), N.Y.'s Catch a Rising Star or L.A.'s The Comedy Store are only three examples of clubs springing up coast-to-coast where young talents can get experience in front of an audience, learn and refine their craft and find a lucky break to stardom. The astounding list of stand-up performers who "made it" ranges from David Letterman, Paul Rodriquez and Joan Rivers, to Rodney Dangerfield, Richard Pryor, Steve Martin and Robin Williams.

Many of these comedians not only performed solo acts but were members of improvisation troupes that turned out to be their ticket to stardom. Second City, one of the most well known of these improv groups, began in the late fifties in Chicago and over the next thirty years produced such stars as Alan Arkin, Mike Nichols, Elaine May, Bill Murray, Gilda Radner, Stiller and Meara, John Belushi and Barbara Harris. The list goes on. Other groups sprang up all over. Some, like The Groundlings and Off the Wall in Los Angeles and Warbabies and Cracked Tokens in New York, were created by actors with time on their hands and talents they wanted to utilize. Where others sat at home bemoaning the difficult conditions of obtaining recognition, these people decided to "help" fate along. The result was not only success and recognition, but the opportunity to hone and develop their own unique abilities; learn about themselves as performers, individuals *and* businesspeople. They organized their group, ran it, booked it in clubs, did the advertising, created press—in essence, were involved in every facet of the industry and their own career-making. Lucky? Well, I guess you could say it was luck that so many of them were discovered—but don't you really think that it wasn't luck at all, but the just rewards of hard, self-motivated effort? If you spend most of your time *not* working, *not* "out there" experimenting, motivating and selling yourself, I can guarantee that you will indeed miss the *luck factor*.

Working Hard and Being Seen Brings You Luck!

And one lucky break often leads to another and another . . . and suddenly, you have a career! The best breaks will come out of your visibility. If someone offers you a part in an improv group, better to take that then sit at home twiddling your thumbs. Who knows? You may have a shot at getting noticed.

A lot of industry attention is placed on cabarets looking for those with comedic talent. But perhaps stand-up or improv comedy isn't your forte. What is? What type of work do you want to do? Let your creative interests *lead* you to your *Lucky Break!*

That's exactly what one group of actors did in Chicago. They were interested in creating an ensemble group to do plays. Their talents lent themselves to this type of work environment. But there wasn't enough work for all of them to feel productive. So they decided to form their own theater company, Steppenwolf. Now a well-respected group, these actors created careers for *themselves*, doing the kind of work for which they had a passion. One of their members, John Malkovich, has gone on to tremendous public acclaim, and he has used his success to help focus more attention on the group to make it stronger. This interactive aspect of Steppenwolf is truly wonderful. The group existed for the creative needs of its members, and its members used the "lucky breaks" to strengthen the group.

Again, *remember:*

Work Plus Visibility Brings You Luck.

Maybe you have a one-person show you'd like to perform. Or you and some friends can produce a theatrical piece. Or how about being the most enterprising and putting together a film? It's a question of energy. Working creates energy and this energy force will move you closer to your goal. And, above all, you must maintain a positive outlook and perseverance.

Recently, I was a guest at an actors' seminar being held at the American Film Institute in Los Angeles. I was answering actors' questions about the casting process, when one fellow raised his hand and asked me about the many casting-director workshops that one can attend—at a price—here in town. He explained that he had taken quite a few of them but was stopped now because "nothing ever happened." I looked at this actor for a few moments and could see the frustration and anger he was feeling. Sure, he put himself out there, but in what way? And for how long? There are no *guarantees* in this business. No timetables insuring success. I cannot promise this actor that if he continues with these workshops that something will come of it. I can promise him that if this discouragement results in his staying in his house, bitter against the world, then *nothing can happen.* Only he can decide to change his attitude. Perhaps these workshops aren't for him. Fine, then try something else. Or perhaps his attitude needs adjusting. Or maybe he should just keep at it, hoping the law of averages comes on his side. I don't know. No one can know. But if you want to be lucky, *you have to stay out there working hard and being seen!*

Do what gets you out

There are so many ways to get noticed that to detail them all here would be impossible. The point is to look around at the opportunities that are right under your nose. Events like local beauty and talent contests are often springboards to a career. You have an exceptional talent for athletics? Use it. Join clubs and competitions. Your abilities in one area can help you with this career. Consider the case of Tony Danza, star of the TV series, *Who's the Boss?* and formerly of the cast of the award-winning comedy, *Taxi.* Tony was a professional *boxer,* not an actor. Good-looking and endowed with a charming personality and sense of humor, he was "discovered" when casting executives were looking for an actor to play a boxer on *Taxi.* He was a natural for the part. And his career took off. For Tony, the way to break into television was first to rely on another strong talent and ability.

People who do things well are noticed!

Whether it's waiting on tables or washing cars, whenever you do something well, people will notice you. Remember the old adage "A job worth doing is worth doing well"? Nowhere is that axiom more important than when you are trying to get your career off the ground. Excellence breeds excellence. Operating at your maximum is a habit that must continually be reinforced. When you are in the "habit" of doing things to the utmost of your ability, you are preparing yourself, disciplining yourself, to succeed in your career. In addition, you are allowing yourself to shine and to experience success through your job.

People pay attention to those who perform on a level of excellence. And you never know who might be noticing! Like Tony Danza and Mary Kay Place, the notice you get for doing an unrelated job well can lead directly to an acting career.

THE LUCK OF THE DRAW

I honestly believe that luck is *not random.* I think it **happens to** those who have a lucky awareness. Lucky people are alert. They pay attention, observe and use the information to create opportunities. They have a positive mental outlook. They believe in themselves. They make decisions. And they back up their plans with concerted effort. They are *dreamers* who *take action.*

Sometimes the Shortest Distance Between Two Points Is Not a Straight Line!

Not every situation you will find yourself in will have a giant sign with "Opportunity" written in gold letters. Often an opportunity, a lucky break, will arise in the most unsuspecting places. It did for me.

Luck is when preparation meets opportunity.

—Oprah Winfrey, TALK-SHOW HOST
AND ACADEMY AWARD NOMINEE for
The Color Purple

Almost everyone in this business—actor or other professional—has a good-luck story. So do I. I came to Hollywood to get into TV and movies as a director and writer. I had quite a bit of experience directing theater in New York and was looking for my career to expand. When the opportunity to work in the casting department of Embassy Television came along, I was reluctant. But I had long admired Embassy's creative head, Norman Lear, and the type of product the company turned out. I decided to take the job as a clerk, at least for a short time, because it was a good way to gain some experience and meet some people. I got "lucky." On the second day of my job, the casting director for whom I worked quit and I was asked to take her place. What most people call lucky is really the fact that I was willing to take a chance and I was ready to handle it. It might very well have turned out that my boss didn't quit and I would be a clerk for a time until another lucky break occurred. I was ready and willing. Somehow luck found me. And the truth is *I wanted to get lucky.* Out of this career in casting, I'm now producing and writing and have continued directing.

I was eager to give every opportunity a fair chance. Sometimes I see actors turn down offers because it's not exactly what they want. I don't think you should do that. If an actor limits himself by saying he'll only do theater, for example, the actor is rejecting possibilities that could lead to fantastic things. A lot of performers snub the idea of working small parts, or extra work. But when you're first starting out, these smaller roles and extra jobs not only provide some source of income, but also afford you the advantage of a ringside seat to watch how movies and TV shows are done. Sure, as your career advances, you may need to limit the kinds of jobs that are appropriate to your career development. (We'll be discussing just such career judgments in later chapters.) Until that time, put false pride aside and get out there and seize every opportunity to learn about this business and to meet people.

I never could have guessed that the clerk job would be my lucky break. But I was convinced that somehow, someway, I would break into this business and be a success. I'd be a liar if I told you I never had doubts. Of course I did! But I believed— and still believe—that if you work hard enough, if you pay attention to the opportunities under your very nose, eventually you will get your shot at success. You get lucky.

This business abounds with such stories. Tony Adams, the well-known producer of many of Blake Edwards' films, such as *The Pink Panther* series, *S.O.B.*, *Victor/Victoria* and *A Fine Mess,* began his career as Edwards' chauffeur! John Badham, the director of such entertaining films as *Saturday Night Fever, Blue Thunder, Wargames* and *Short Circuit,* was a television casting director at Universal. Fascinated with direction, John spent many hours observing on the set. Finally, he was given a chance to direct . . . and the rest is history.

JACK NICHOLSON'S LUCKY BREAK

Poor Jack Nicholson. That's what his agent, Sandy Bresler, used to think about his client and close friend who couldn't seem to get his acting career off the ground. Bresler and Nicholson had become friends when they were both in the service. When they were discharged, Bresler became an agent and Nicholson was one of his clients. From 1961 to 1966, Bresler worked on getting acting jobs for his pal, but hard as they both tried, their efforts weren't greatly rewarded. Most of Nicholson's jobs were in low-budget horror films like those he did for producer Roger Corman. Finally, there came one year when Nicholson didn't work at all. To Bresler, it seemed hopeless. Only a miracle could open things up for this actor and there were none in sight. Bresler suggested that Nicholson should get out of the business—that considering another profession seemed in order. Though his prospects looked bleak, Nicholson refused to give up. He continued working whatever acting gigs came his way. Then, one day, Bresler got a call from his actor friend saying that he was leaving for the desert to act in a film being done by some guys he knew. It was a last-minute job. Originally, Rip Torn was booked to play the role of a conservative salesman who hooks up with two dope-smoking hippies and decides to travel with them across country. At the last minute, Torn pulled out to do a play and the producer/actors, Peter Fonda and Dennis Hopper, asked Nicholson if he would step in. Bresler told Nicholson to have fun, not realizing at the time that it would be this film, *Easy Rider,* that would turn his pal into a star!

Overnight success? Well, yes, in a way. Before the success of *Easy Rider,* Jack had problems getting his career going though he had been plugging away for many years. But once he found his lucky break, he took off to become one of the film industry's megastars!

Every Situation Has Within it an Opportunity, No Matter How Oblique It May Appear at the Time!

Whatever you are doing, whether directly related to your primary goal or not, each situation holds potential for you. Time and time again, I have heard stories about people getting lucky breaks in situations that were seemingly totally unrelated to their goals. I have a friend who had always wanted to write who got her big break while helping some elderly people in front of a New York City apartment house. She began talking to another woman who was also helping these senior citizens, and the two women hit it off instantly. But the big surprise came when my friend discovered that this woman was one of the magazine editors my friend had desperately been trying to meet! So be aware:

Anywhere, at any time, your lucky break can appear!

Even the actor's staple—working as a waiter or waitress—can be a career-making opportunity if you know how to make the most of it. One young woman turned waitressing into several TV guest spots without ever "telling" anyone she was an actress How? By knowing *who* she was, *what* she wanted and *believing* that *everything* she did was leading her to her goal. Her positive attitude and enjoyment of her job was very appealing. She used her personality to win over her customers. One afternoon, she finished her work shift and rushed to an audition for a popular TV show. She walked into the office to read for the director, and who was it but a friendly customer who had been sitting at her station just an hour before. He was surprised ("I didn't know you were an actress"), she was surprised ("I didn't know you were a director") and guess who got the job? She was instantly relaxed with her auditor and easily won the role.

People who don't have a good attitude don't draw good energy. If your attitude is bad, your luck fades away. Time and again, I've observed this direct relationship between luck and attitude. When one's not working out, the other's not working out either. I don't know *why* this is so, only that experience and observation have convinced me that *it is so!*

Perhaps when you have a negative mind-set, you fail to notice potential in any of the opportunities that cross your path. Or perhaps it's as simple as the old cliché "Laugh and the world laughs with you. Cry and you cry alone." No one enjoys being around people who are consistently negative about themselves, their career, their lives or the miserable state of the industry. These kind of people can throw a damper on even the most positive situation. There are many things in "show business" that are unfair, unreasonable and just plain rotten. But to be around someone who continually reminds you that the world is a mean and terrible place can be exceptionally draining. I've met these types. They complain bitterly of the Catch-22's of union membership, auditions, acting school rip-offs, nepotism . . . ad infinitem. Some of their complaints are justified. Still, listening to this litany of negativity could drive Pollyanna to cynicism. Personally I try to avoid being in the company of such people. It's not that I'm trying to pretend that everything is right with the world. I know it isn't. But I'm not interested in focusing on the negative. I'd rather turn my attention to what is good and what can be done to make it better. I refuse to live my life on a day-to-day basis with a continual overcast of doom and gloom hanging over all.

I believe in the inextricable connection between attitude and luck. So if my luck seems to have disappeared, I first take an attitude check and try to regain my positive outlook. I believe that, like a horse and carriage, one is married to the other.

THE UNLUCKY CYCLE

Nothing lasts forever. Luck comes and goes in cycles. Your responsibility is to stay strong when luck disappears and be ready to make the most of lucky opportunities when they reappear.

Only an unrealistic dreamer believes that life is always a joy. The reality is that sometimes life can deal you a dirty blow and knock you down for the count. You get a series of not-so-good things happening. You get fired from a show. You break your leg—literally. Suddenly things just seem to go bad. And you are powerless to correct them. Where's your luck now? Life's gone bad on you not because you aren't trying hard. But just because that's the way life is. You feel tired, drained, de-energized. What happened to the normal productive, positive individual you might ask. And when you're down on your luck, you're down on yourself and you're down on life. What do you do? This is the time when you turn inward. You turn toward your spirit for help, consolation and guidance. Above all, respect your right to be sad. Respect your right to be down. No one— and I repeat, *no one*—doesn't know the agony of tragedy, disappointment and sadness. But this is not the time to give up, to roll over and play dead. This is the time for you to summon the great inner strength all human beings possess. This is the time to seek out whatever will help—whether it's spiritual or psychological counseling, or some other form of guidance. Turn to those that are eager to help. It's a time for family and friends. Allow them to bolster you. When you're going through bad times, don't let it eat you up. You owe it to yourself as an artist and a human being not to suffer. Know in your heart that no tragedy, no pain, lasts forever.

Sorrows come not as single spies, but in battalions.

—William Shakespeare

Bad luck seems to run in streaks. It's usually not just *one* thing that puts a damper on our lives, but a rush of things that rains us out. You're in trouble and you're hurting. And you really feel that life has turned against you. Perhaps, however, life is trying *to help!* If you continually get fired from acting jobs, for example, what does that tell you? Anyone can have a run of plain old bad luck, but often our bad luck comes from something we may be able to control. Perhaps it's time to attend to some area of your life that you've been neglecting or ignoring. Take a look.

THE TORTURED-ARTIST MYTH

We've all read tragic stories of successful performers who had fabulous careers while their lives were cracking at the seams: they refused to attend to that aspect of their lives. Unfortunately, some artists believe that their creativity would be jeopardized if they handled their problems with counseling. It is truly an unfortunate misconception. Creativity is not born out of neuroses, but rather *in spite* of them. Van Gogh did not paint when he was in the throes of psychotic turmoil, but rather when he returned to a state of normalcy. History and myth have painted the image of the artist as tortured, imbalanced, at odds with life and society, suggesting that only in a state of emotional unrest is it possible to create true art. That's simply not true. Most artists *are* affected by life. That's what art *is*—an expression of your experience and observations about life and human existence. Artistic awareness entails experiences that many nonartistic individuals will not experience. It's part of the territory of the profession—just like a surgeon's experiences are not shared with the majority of the nonmedical population.

As an artist, you are mandated to search out and understand various life experiences and reflect that understanding creatively in your work. That doesn't mean you don't have a right to be happy and have a happy life. Don't listen to these silly myths. In fact, the more you are willing to face those difficult areas of your own life, the more you will understand *about* life.

What about you? Is your "bad luck" trying to point out an area of your life and development that you've been disregarding? Is it screaming out to get your attention? Maybe it's time to take inventory. To really investigate the various aspects of your life and relationships. Life is full of problems—some large, some small. But some of the most challenging and major dilemmas, some of the biggest tragedies, can turn into positive experiences. No one wants a tragedy, but when a crisis does occur, allow yourself to use the experience. Look for what might be positive about it. This is where the person who has trained himself to have a positive outlook has the advantage.

One night a few years ago, actress Eileen Brennan had just said goodbye to her close friend, Goldie Hawn. She began to cross the street, when suddenly, out of nowhere, a car ran her down. The accident was devastating. Her career ceased as Brennan lay in a hospital bed trying to recover from this tragedy. Surgery to her body, reconstructive plastic surgery to her face and long months of therapy were necessary to get Brennan on her feet, figuratively and literally. And then she discovered that she had to face therapy to cure her addiction to the once necessary painkillers. There is no way to rationalize such a grave tragedy. It was a terrible misfortune. But the amazing thing about this episode is that Brennan is able to discuss what was *good* about it all. In one recent interview, she discussed discovering her strength to go on. She discovered she wasn't a quitter. She refused to "roll over and die" and, instead, fought her way back into life and back into her career. The accident completely altered the way she looked at life. It changed—and even improved—the relationships in her life with both family and business associates. Her fortitude was an inspiration to all. And when she returned to acting, it was with an entirely new artistic vision. She had been tested to the extreme—and she had made it. There is no doubt that it was an unfortunate, tragic experience that she wished had never happened. But it did. And Eileen Brennan, like so many other strong and sensitive individuals, chose to find the positive. She chose to use this horrible experience to assist her personal growth.

SETBACKS

A serious setback or challenge often helps individuals decipher their truly meaningful priorities. Many times, individuals who have come close to death have gained insight into their own lives, reporting that suddenly they realized which people and things were most important to them. And if you're open and believe in the positive aspect of life challenges, you will use such an experience to add joy, motivation and interest to your life.

"I DO BELIEVE. I DO BELIEVE."

When your career luck is going badly—you can't get an agent, you've choked on your last three auditions, the casting director you've been dying to meet called you while you were on vacation—you have to keep your spirits up. Any way you can. You just have *to know* that it's going to happen for you. When your spirits are down—when you're feeling the lowest—that's when you have to work the hardest at keeping your attitude at its most constructive.

When I feel like life's turned into an uphill battle, I use precisely that mental imagery. I visualize that I'm on the side of a steep mountain. The air is thin, and it takes gargantuan effort to move my legs. I want to sit down and rest, but I know that I have to go on. Turning back is against my belief. It means death on the mountain. Even to stay in one place too long risks a snowslide or possibly losing my footing. Even though it's taking so much time, I have to keep moving up that mountain. And I visualize my journey and triumphing over the difficulties. And reaching the top. Enjoying the air, the view, the triumph of it all!

There are other visualizations. You're swimming between two land masses, and are halfway to the other shore. You're tired and you want to give up. Instead, you take a break. Float on your back as you summon the strength to keep going on. You can't turn back. And if you don't keep moving you'll drown because where you are is nowhere. It's not any good. Being nowhere *is* nowhere. You *have* to take that next stroke. You have to keep kicking your legs. You have to keep swimming.

There are many types of motivational techniques. Find the ones that work for you. When your luck is down, seek out those inspirational stories or sayings that can help you take the next step. Some people go to church or seek spiritual guidance. Others, believing that "what goes around, comes around," concentrate on doing good deeds—volunteering at a hospital or retirement home. Others seek out psychics or therapists. Yet, others find comfort reading biographies of people they admire and analyzing how they handled tough situations. The list is endless. Any or all of these techniques are okay if they keep your spirits up. When you're feeling down, focus on those people, things, places, events, that keep your vitality up. *Know always—*

You Are Blessed, Because Everyone Is.

Everyone really is. Honest. It's hard to feel that blessing when things are tough. Especially when the bad news comes in triplicate! But this is precisely the time that you must seek out your inner strength. It's these times that test your mettle—that make you ultimately the strong, sensitive individual who expresses her/himself through this art called acting.

Take stock now of the inspirational resources that are around you. Look for those resources of inspiration, determination, strength and self-love. Right now—today—where is the love in your life? Where is the strength? In yourself? Family? Friends? How can you improve your life and more directly and effectively face your struggles? Are you making your life strong—and lucky? Take stock—and steps—*now* to fortify yourself.

THIS CAREER IS SOMETHING YOU'VE CHOSEN

No one's forcing you. And no one *owes* you anything. This is a tough business. An actor's life is a continuous series of ups and downs. But when you're down, you have to take action. You have to cast aside your discouragement and get in touch with what you need to feel good again. Call a friend. Read a self-help book or magazine. Memorize a new monologue. There are millions of ways to get your spirits back up. So take that next step. And the next one. Until that smile comes back again. And once more, *luck* is at your side.

The "Who-You-Know" Game: Networking and Nepotism

net·work (net'wurk): The exchange of information
and services among individuals. Anything
resembling a net in concept or form, as by being
dispersed in intersecting lines of communication.

THE saying goes, "It's not *what* you know, but *who* you know, that counts." And in this business, like most others, it's absolutely true. Many actors take this as proof positive that the world is conspiring against them. If they were only someone's son or daughter or cousin or uncle, all their problems would be solved. Sure, nepotism runs rampant in the motion picture and television industry just as it does in the steelworkers' union or the medical profession. The fact is, children often choose the same career field as their parents. But that doesn't mean "outsiders" don't have a chance.

There are advantages and disadvantages to growing up in the business—just as there are advantages and disadvantages to being the first to break in. Whether you're the child of a powerful film executive or the offspring of a hardworking salesman in Des Moines, you will need sharp social skills to form the kind of business relationships needed to succeed. Show business is a social business and has its own etiquette. People work long intense hours with a high degree of stress and anxiety. The "product" they manufacture is the result of creative collaboration, with many egos and millions of dollars on the line. It only makes sense that they would prefer to work with people they already know, respect, like and trust.

Nepotism

To deny that it exists is ridiculous. To not make use of it is also ridiculous. In the strictest definition, nepotism refers to favoritism between family members, for example, Uncle Harry is directing a movie and he gives you a part. It is part of an age-old tradition of one family generation passing the family trade to the next generation.

Originally acting was considered just such a trade. You became an actor if you were born into a theatrical family. The child "lived out of a suitcase" while the family toured. The children learned their craft from their parents. As soon as they were able—which usually meant when they could walk on-stage—the children began to perform. This theatrical tradition was passed down then to the next generation. It was only a rare outsider who tried to infiltrate the trade.

Gradually the theater became more and more acceptable as a career alternative. There were great stars. And dreams of being on Broadway sparked many young talents to try their hand at the profession. When motion pictures were invented, the face of the industry changed completely. For the first time, entertainment was big business and the movies were reaching millions as well as making millions.

Today the entertainment industry spends and earns billions of dollars. The stakes are fantastically high. You become a star, you become a millionaire. The same is true for directors and writers. Thousands upon thousands of individuals struggle continually over many years hoping to get their big break. As critics are all too eager to point out, art and talent sometimes takes a back seat to a good business deal and an assured profit.

Yet for all its money, competition, pressure and glamour, this business is still a cottage industry. The community of working artists, producers, directors and executives is astonishingly small. To survive in this business, you must rely on other people—people you know and can count on. And with competition so incredibly fierce, it only makes sense to utilize those connections that might give *you* an extra edge. And that's what nepotism is all about.

MISCONCEPTIONS ABOUT NEPOTISM

There's this misguided notion that nepotism can make up for talent. It can open the door, give you a break, put you in the position to get noticed. But without talent, you just can't make it. Do you think that Liza Minnelli would be the star that she is just because she is Judy Garland's daughter? Of course not. If Minnelli didn't have her own musical talent, she would have disappeared long ago. Being the daughter of a famous chanteuse certainly gave her opportunities and attention that another talented youngster might not have had. Still, without talent, you simply can't maintain and build any significant career. A break is an opportunity—it isn't your being handed a career on a silver tray. *That* you *always* have to earn!

I'm fascinated when someone tells me that the son/daughter/whatever of a famous actor or director is trying to break into acting. I'm interested in seeing that person and seeing what they can do. Frankly, I'm curious. Could it be possible that the offspring inherited the talent? In many cases they have. Consider the following "second-generation kids":

- Emilio Esetevez and Charlie Sheen—sons of Martin Sheen
- Michael Douglas—son of Kirk Douglas
- Anne Lockhart—daughter of June Lockhart
- Jamie Lee Curtis—daughter of Tony Curtis and Janet Leigh
- Larry Hagman—son of Mary Martin
- Sean and Chris Penn—sons of director Leo Penn
- Tim Hutton—son of Jim Hutton
- Anjelica Huston—daughter of John Huston
- Laura Dern—daughter of Diane Ladd and Bruce Dern

Each one of these actors is the offspring of an acclaimed star, yet each, in his or her own right, is a star because of talent, persona and charisma. Another advantage second-generation performers have is that they generally grew up in the business and thus understand it better than most newcomers. This "secondhand" experience gives them a maturity and professionalism about their work that offers a decided edge. Still, the bottom line is *talent.*

Be a part of the family.

Nepotism and its "first cousin," favoritism, are realities. I see them all the time. The concept of favoritism is really just expanding nepotism to include any close friend or relative. Giving them preference in job situations. Helping and aiding them to build their careers. It's a helping hand. It's having a mentor.

YOUR APPROACH

If you know there's someone in your life that can be helpful, ask them. But don't ask for assistance willy-nilly. One of the most important aspects of "asking well" is understanding exactly what you should ask for. Say you have an uncle who is a producer. He has never seen your work and, outside of rave reviews from your mother, has no idea if you can act better than a stone. To phone him and request a part in his latest movie on the basis of your familial tie is way out of line. You are putting him in an awkward position. Rather, telling him of your interest in acting, possibly asking for a recommendation for an acting teacher, allows your uncle to comfortably participate in your enthusiasm without feeling "on the spot."

Your request should be appropriate.

If, on the other hand, you haven't studied a day in your life and you request an audition for the second lead, your uncle may schedule that. Then you come in, you're terrible, and your uncle is embarrassed. That's when all the negative feelings about nepotism come into play. (Should that happen, mind you, it isn't the end of the world. But I would not ask for another audition unless I were *sure* that this time I could handle it.) If you keep asking for the wrong favors, after a while your contact is going to resent you and perhaps say no or put people between you to shield the requests.

Your next important consideration when looking for assistance is to consider *who* you are asking to help you. It might be that you are asking for a recommendation from someone who doesn't have such a good reputation. In such an instance, getting help from this individual may actually *hurt* you rather than help you. Sometimes actors are so eager—so hungry—that they don't take enough care with this area. If you have several possible sources for assistance, think carefully about who would be the best to contact.

TREAT YOUR CONTACTS WELL

Be respectful—to your family, to your friends. Your friends are part of this association. Tend them as well as you would like them to care for you. Never let your desire for a certain "in" color your ability to treat them well. All the individuals I've known that were the most successful "networkers" have tremendous regard for the close associations in their lives. They do not take advantage. And that is one of the reasons that when they do need some assistance, it is willingly offered. Be respectful—and have dignity. If you keep those two attributes in mind, you will not have to fear stepping over the line of friendship.

No Helping Hand Can Compensate for a Lack of Ability and Hard Work.

We have all seen people who have gotten some terrific jobs unfairly; just because of a strong contact. More often than not, however, a person must prove himself competent in order to stay in his job. This is especially true when talking about performers. You can give parts to someone ad infinitum—if they don't have the talent, they'll never make a long lasting career of it. It's impossible to hide incompetence in this field. If you can't act, there's little anyone can do over a long period of time to keep that information from the public and the rest of the industry. In fact, of all the careers in this industry, being an actor is the one that is least susceptible to unfair nepotism. The public doesn't care *who* someone's mother is—if that actor isn't talented, they won't want to see them.

Twenty or thirty years ago, the idea of favoritism in this business was looked upon with disapproval. Part of the reason for this was simply that the industry was still young and was struggling to gain respectability as a bona fide enterprise. In those days, there were great studio powers with enormous influence. Sometimes they would abuse it, placing truly unqualified people in sought-after positions. They might insist on making a truly inferior talent a star just to prove how powerful they were. No longer. This is a big business. And though there are those with enormous power, their interest is showing success, not proving they can flex their corporate muscle and make a star of a no-talent. Everyone in this industry is only too aware that you have to be good to make a career last as an actor in today's market.

NETWORKING

I don't care if you're the next Laurence Olivier, if no one knows about your talent, *you won't get a job.* That's why networking is so important. It is a process of meeting people, gaining information and getting yourself and your ability known within the industry. It is the process by which you get a job. When you have an agent, he will do a lot of the networking for you. That's an agent's job. But that doesn't mean your networking responsibilities are over. Too often, I hear actors complain about their agents' not sending them out enough on interviews and auditions. But what are *you* doing to get out there and get known?

I admit it can be overwhelming to go to New York, Los Angeles or some other acting center and try to carve out a career. In Los Angeles, the high concrete walls around each studio broadcast a message of exclusivity—of being on the "inside." In New York, agents' offices are locked. Outside there is a printed notice informing any aspiring actors to knock *only* if they have an appointment. Pretty intimidating stuff. Yet, those walls are not as high or those doors as locked as it may appear. Dedication, hard work and a positive attitude can open the door. Remember: *Casting executives, producers, directors—we all want and NEED to find talented actors. WE ARE ON YOUR SIDE.* But we have to know you're out there, and that's why networking is so vital to your career

WHAT IS IT?

Let's be clear right up front: *Networking is NOT hustling.* As we discussed in the previous section, hustling is about using people. It's about opportunism and manipulation. That is *definitely not networking.* Nor does networking require you to be the most popular guest on the Hollywood party circuit; nor your "buttering up" to casting directors by sending them gifts or flowers. I think these common misconceptions are what prevent many actors from learning how to network effectively.

Networking is good common sense. It's about making contact and forming professional working relationships that will help move your career along. Networking is understanding how to get assistance from friends as well as family to accelerate your career. Some people call this nepotism. Nepotism is not an evil; it is a valid form of networking.

Meeting people. Plain and simple. No mystery. No magic formula. Everyone knows how to network. When you asked a friend to recommend a doctor, that's networking. When your buddy gives you a tip on where to get a great haircut, or turns you on to a reasonably priced photographer to do your résumé pictures, that's networking. A blind date is networking. Meeting an alumnus to ask questions about a school you're considering—that's networking. Connections. Introductions. Referrals. Recommendations. These are all elements of networking.

Sometimes it may appear that the "Who You Know" Game is only important in show biz. Not true. If you're working at IBM and you're vying for an important promotion, you won't have a chance unless the "important people" like your boss and other executives know you, like you and respect your work. If they don't know you exist, you haven't got a shot. That's true *everywhere* in life. If you're looking to fall in love, you won't meet the dream of your life staying at home on Saturday nights. Instead, you have to get out of your house and start meeting people. Networking.

It always amuses me when I hear people talk about this industry as being a "people business." Of course, it *is*, but the fact is that *every business* is a people business. Business people have to have solid "people" skills to get ahead.

In this industry this is especially true. People's opinion of your work is an important element. In fact, sometimes in this business the *only* discernible basis for judging someone's credentials is through the opinions of others. Unlike the cabinetmaker who can proudly show his craftsmanship, the creative artist has only himself to show. The artist must, through past work, auditions and referrals, convince the casting director et al. that he's the right one for this role.

The most effective networking is while you're working. You don't need to schmooz with people at parties to form strong contacts. The fact is if you work hard and have a good attitude while you are on the job, you will have a better chance of being hired and rehired by those people and being recommended to their professional friends for future jobs.

—Charles Martin Smith,
*American Graffiti, Never
Cry Wolf, Starman,
The Untouchables*

A NETWORK BEGINS WITH ONE INTRODUCTION

When I came to Los Angeles, I had one name: Kathleen Nolan, an actress and then president of the Screen Actors' Guild (SAG). I had directed a play in New York, and Joan See, the Guild's national secretary, was a member of the cast. She enjoyed my work and supported my dream of becoming involved in television and film. She offered to set up an introduction to

Kathleen. It was a beginning. I met with Kathleen, who introduced me to more people. A network was begun. A network of associations and relationships that would help my career grow and develop.

It's not about getting one specific job, though a network can certainly help there. It is about forming a support system. A resource for assistance, referrals and references. Kathleen Nolan didn't lead me to a job back then. But she did begin "the ball rolling." That's what networking is all about. To begin a network, someone has to help you. Many times, people will offer. Joan See did. It is how careers move.

STATE OF BEING

Every day is a new day. You're out on an audition, you're standing in line to see a film—you meet someone, you start talking . . . It's the beginning of thousands of possibilities. It's the same whether you're the new kid just off the bus or the soap-opera star interested in branching out. Meeting people, becoming known, interacting—this is what networking *is*. If you are open to meeting people, you will be good at networking. If you shun the concept and stay at home, you won't be good at it. Also, remember that networking is a two-way street. Help others when you can. If you only take, eventually you will be considered a "user" and lose your friends as well as your network.

Everyone you meet in this industry is interested in networking. Of course, when you're Tom Selleck you might not network with as much initiative. Basically, people will want to network *with you*. People will seek *you* out. Still, even the biggest star is interested in meeting those people who share their artistic and life concerns. It's human nature.

Networking is a state of being. You always need to know people. People need to know you. You become part of it when you bring two people together or when you help a colleague when the opportunity arises. We are all drawn to people with a little more knowledge, power or experience in the fields that interest us. These people become a source for you. You are a source for others. Getting to know someone who can help you achieve your career and life goals has a positive purpose. That doesn't mean desperately running after someone or using them or lacking dignity. When you help someone else, it gives you a positive image. You become vital and attractive. It creates new contacts. You never know where your contacts will lead you. Networking is a fundamental part of the business. And a fundamental aspect of your development as a careerist and as an artist.

THE NETWORK FOUNDATION

How do you start a career network? Your first "networking" source is your peers. If you are new to a city, start first with those that you naturally come in contact with. Get into an acting class, workshop, showcase, anything that will bring you in contact with other actors. They will form the foundation for your network. You will be there for them as they are for you. These colleagues will help you immeasurably—not only now, but in the years to come. They are very important and can provide the means to an ongoing career. In the old days, the members of radio's Mercury Theatre, led by Orson Welles, were friends and colleagues. Their creative and personal support of each other led to many successful Hollywood careers. Is it just coincidence that Mercury Theatre members like Agnes Moorehead, Joseph Cotton and John Houseman should all succeed? Is it coincidence that the many actors from Second City, like Bill Murray, Dan Ackroyd, Joan Rivers, Harold Ramis, Valerie Harper, Elaine May and Mike Nichols, to name only a few, were able to attain acclaim? Sometimes an entire group will begin to move toward success. Having each other for support, advice and guidance can make the career journey more profitable—and more pleasurable.

John Malkovitch's career was launched when a Chicago theater group, called Steppenwolf, moved its production of Sam Shepard's *True West* to New York. With roles in *Places in the Heart*, *The Killing Fields*, *Eleni* and Broadway's *Death of a Salesman*, Malkovitch's dramatic ability rose to prominence. In addition, the other members of the company are now to be seen everywhere in theater and film. As Malkovitch's career branches into other areas, such as film and stage directing, these same individuals will probably continue to work with him.

To Form a Strong Network Foundation, Develop Peer Relationships.

Sometimes actors make the mistake of thinking that they have to meet industry executives and celebrities in order to network effectively. Though these contacts can be very helpful, it is actually more important to first have a network of *colleagues*—fellow actors who understand the career challenges that must be faced. Actors, as a rule, are among the most generous and constructively helpful individuals in this or any profession. Though competition is fierce, many actors I have met are extremely generous and gracious with their fellow actors. Often it is another actor that approachs me to meet a "talented actor." Actors share information—whether it's about what's casting in town, which class is good or the lowdown on people at the networks and studios. Actors also support each other creatively. In most major cities, there are many actor-organized workshops and career groups that exist solely to support and advance the acting careers of their members. "Rap sessions" deal with fears and stumbling blocks to a career, as well as provide solid information on classes, theaters, etc.

It will be from this foundation that your network will spring and grow. Once you begin to work professionally, your network will continually spread. Referrals, introductions, social meetings—all of these opportunities will help you to become known.

HOW TO NETWORK AT A PARTY

You've been invited to one of the big industry social events. You are sure there will be tons of important people that you can meet. Your best friend, who is the assistant to a powerful executive, is taking you and promises to introduce you around. A golden networking opportunity? You bet! Here are some guidelines on what to do:

- Prepare in advance. Ask your friend who will be there. Then do a little research. Find out what they do and what they've done. You don't want to be chatting with Woody Allen and ask him if he likes comedies!

- Look the part. Look the best *you* there is. Unless you only want to play roles of urban street people, don't wear grungy clothes that make you look like a rumpled sack of potatoes. Dress up. Look well groomed, appealing and attractive. Sometimes actors wanting to look "cool" dress in the most outrageously tattered clothes. If you are a star, you can get away with it. Otherwise, everyone is going to think you didn't have enough money to get your clothes out of the cleaners. Above all, wear something that makes you feel attractive and confident. If you think you look good, you do.

- When you arrive, take a few minutes just to see what is going on. Are there groups of people talking? Or are people spread out in twos and threes? How intimate is the party? How impersonal? Taking some time when you first arrive to get the "feel of the room" is a good way to get acclimated while letting your nerves/excitement subside a bit.

- If there is someone you specifically want to meet, ask your host, or the friend who brought you, if they will introduce you. It's the best way to bridge the gap between two strangers.

- Don't audition or ask to audition or tell them about how wonderfully you audition. I can't tell you how irritating it is to have someone pull you off to a corner to show you ten minutes of their stand-up routine. It's simply not appropriate. Instead, tell the person how happy you are to meet them and that you'd like to contact them soon. (By the way, if you do that, follow up. Write a note expressing your delight at meeting the person and suggest a future meeting. Then, telephone to confirm the plans.)

- Be warm and gracious to everyone you meet. You might think the receptionist from the studio casting office isn't important, but remember, in a few years that individual may be the *head* of the studio!

- Pay attention to whomever you are talking to. There is nothing more annoying than watching someone's eyes strobe the room as they are carrying on a conversation with you. Concentrate on the conversation you are having. You can make it short and move on, but while you're there, give it your full attention.

- Don't gasp and gape at the bigwigs you recognize. You are in the same business as they. Don't act like a tourist clutching a map to the stars' homes! Conversely, don't name-drop. If you think you will impress someone, you're wrong. Besides, you don't want to impress *them*—you want to be impressed!

- When you finally make a good connection, don't monopolize the conversation. It only detracts from your own appeal. And unless you've taken lessons in storytelling from Scheherazade, you run the risk of being a bore. Let the conversation flow and keep it relatively short. Being trapped in a corner for hours isn't going to make any executive think more kindly of you.

- Act confident. You may feel weak in the knees, but hold your head up high and remember you're as good as anyone else.

- Be polite. To everyone. From the bartender to the host and everyone in between, and finally . . . *have fun!*

NETWORKING—A CONCEPT WHOSE TIME IS NOW

The concept of networking has come into its own. Separated from the disparaging favoritism of earlier days, business and society realize how useful "knowing people" can be in a constructive, positive sense. Remember the telephone ads heralding "the best business calls are personal?" Networking. That's what those calls are. Once upon a time, people were born into a class system in this country and that's pretty much where they stayed. You get places now by who you know. You have to be trained, educated, talented and capable, but you will get a break because of someone's help—someone who believes in you, whether friend, family member or executive who sees your work and takes an interest.

Once you remove the onus from the concepts of nepotism and networking and understand instead their most positive and constructive connotations, you will see how much further and faster you will go.

Sex and Your Career 12

Power is an attractive energy.

—Pam Dawber, STAR of
Mork and Mindy, My Sister Sam
and numerous television films

I am absolutely convinced that if a person can't bring their own unique, personal sex appeal to their work, they will never become a star in this business. So when you go to auditions and interviews—when you're hired for an acting job—remember:

Sexual magnetism—don't leave home without it!

A lot of an actor's energy is sensual or sexual energy. Creativity, sensitivity, passion and vitality are part of an actor's makeup. This type of energy often emanates a kind of sexual magnetism. That's why we so easily fall in love with the people we see on stage, television and in the movies. It's a necessary and vital part of an actor's makeup and persona. Without it, you simply can't get past the starting gate. But there's also another side to this subject. Sex, sex appeal and sexuality can be used to seduce, exploit and manipulate. Morality aside, using sex and seduction to get acting jobs is a very risky—and I repeat, very risky—way to pursue your career.

We've all heard the stories about the pretty woman becoming a movie star when a wealthy producer "discovered" her walking at the beach. Or the man who goes to bed with a

homely agent just to get a job. Or the innocent teen proposi-
tioned by a cigar-chomping director. I'd like to tell you that
people only get ahead by their talent, hard work and integrity—but that would be a lie. Some of these outlandish stories
of sexual favors and Machiavellian seduction are absolutely
true. And in some cases, people get ahead and succeed through
such means. But in all my years in this business, I have seen
that the most common outcome for the sexual seducer and
manipulator is to hurt—not help—his or her career. Don't ever
forget: what may give you the temporary edge can very easily
turn on you and backfire miserably. So, *be warned!*

How can you use your sexual appeal to its most positive
benefit? How and why do people use sexuality manipulatively?
How can you be prepared to defend *yourself* against sexual
seduction and exploitation?

Sexual magnetism: what Is it, where you get it and how you use it

Congratulations! You have *sex appeal!* It's part of your birthright
as a human being. It doesn't have anything to do with how
pretty you are, how many muscles are on your body, or how
much you look like Brooke Shields or Robert Redford. Rather,
sex appeal has to do with how fully you realize your own
personality. In other words, how sexy you are depends on how
much you can *be yourself.*

I've met many individuals who have a lack of confidence in
their own attractiveness. It's a terrible shame because they are
overlooking so much that is positive about themselves. Part of
the problem is that in today's society, our definition of sexual
attractiveness, sexuality and being "sexy" is too narrow. Sure,
Marilyn Monroe and Madonna are sexy. They are also part of
the group called "sex symbols." Male counterparts could be
Rob Lowe, Paul Newman, Robert Redford. But there's more—
much more—to the term *sexy.* Robert Duvall is sexy, though I'd

hardly call him a sex symbol. Debra Winger is sexy, though you don't see her modeling on magazine covers with Brooke Shields. Being sexy, having sexual appeal, doesn't necessarily mean being beautiful, having a fantastic body, wearing few clothes and posing for photos of you licking strawberries.

Being sexy has to do with fully realizing and expressing your personality. When you do that, you can't help being attractive, charismatic and, yes, seductive. And I mean that in its most positive connotation. People who demonstrate their personalities in their work use their charisma—their charm, their appeal. And that *is* tied to some sort of sexual vibration. It's the way humans are made. It's not sex. It's a sensual energy. People with great senses of humor are sexy. Just think of Bette Midler and Woody Allen.

People who have a lot of warmth and kindness are sexy like Jimmy Stewart and Matthew Broderick. People who are interested in life are sexy. People who enjoy what they are doing are sexy. It's what you have that makes *your* lifeforce great! So you should be using it. It's what makes you a great performer. We watch great actors, whether they're Lawrence Olivier or Dustin Hoffman, Meryl Streep or Jessica Tandy, and they captivate us. We watch Barbra Streisand sing, and we fall in love. Not because these performers are or are not "pretty" people but because they have sex appeal, and a unique quality emanating from them that's irresistible. We are seduced by their energy and mystery. So if you are not using your natural sexual energy and magnetism, you are not using your talent. If you go to a casting call and you don't put out *all* of your energy, there's a chance that you won't get noticed. You have to be yourself. *And whatever that is, is sexy.* Remember: the people in this business see pretty people every single day. There's a great demand for "pretty people" in today's media. However, when you see gorgeous models—both male and female—every day, actual beauty becomes commonplace. And frankly, it can become very boring. What you look for in a performer, whether beautiful by today's standards or not, is something exciting, interesting or different. That's what is really sexy. Bill Murray is sexy.

146 / Career-Winning Strategies

Not because of his looks, but because of his humor, his style, his enthusiasm. Paul Newman is sexy. Not because of his looks—terrific though they are—but because of that special something about his personality, his charisma, that distinguishes him from the thousands of handsome men we see modeling in clothing catalogs and magazines.

If you want to enhance your sexual magnetism, start by "seducing" your toughest critic and foe—*yourself*. When you stand in front of the mirror, how many times do you acknowledge and appreciate the finer points of your features? Instead, how many times do you search the mirror for every conceivable flaw? It's pretty hard to believe in your own charm if you continually berate yourself for the ten pounds you have to lose, the lack of muscle, hair, height, color of eyes, shape of nose, or whatever. If you enjoy yourself, others will also. None of us are so perfect that there's nothing that doesn't need work. But continually giving yourself a negative appraisal can make you *crazy* and certainly dissolve your self-confidence. Enjoy yourself. Your good features, the bright, entertaining side of your personality, your wit, sensitivity—everything. I'm not trying to downplay the tremendous pressure to be beautiful and handsome that every performing artist feels in our society. It exists. There's no doubt about it. But if you buy into that ideal, you can ruin your chances of success—and, most certainly, happiness. Instead, learn to like and enjoy yourself—the way you look, walk, talk—those parts of you that add up to a unique whole. I've seen average-looking men and women in a casting session transform themselves before my very eyes into marvelously entrancing people. They get the job. Why? Because they "turned us on." That's right. Their own charisma, their own very primal sensual energy evoked a response. Sometimes you'll hear actors commenting on an audition that went well, saying, "They wanted me" or "They loved me" or even Sally Field's famous line when accepting her Oscar, "You like me!" All of these phrases indicate the necessity for involvement and energy from the performer. For an actor to become a star, an actor needs to develop his own uniqueness.

Just remember:

Who you are includes your attractiveness, your warmth, a captivating
personality—and your sexual magnetism!

So it would be silly to try and "edit" yourself before you go
into a business meeting and/or audition. But there's a big difference between magnetism and seduction—a difference between being appealing and sexually manipulative. Use your
head. It's important to allow every part of yourself to exist in
your work. It's part of demonstrating your personality. Of
allowing your special understanding of life and the world
around you to filter through your work and express itself. It's
that quality and ability that gets you the job.

THE CASTING COUCH: PART MYTH, PART
REALITY

In all my years as a casting director, television executive and,
now, a producer, I have heard very few stories from my colleagues about abuses of the casting process for personal sexual
gratification. On the other hand, I've heard a lot of stories from
actors about overt sexual intimidation, propositions and
harassment during auditions and interviews. What's the truth?
Many of the tales told, on both sides, are exaggerations and
fabrications that have little foundation.

Many times, it's a matter of misinterpretation. At a casting
session, that vital sexual energy can be misconstrued. When an
actor is genuinely alive, fresh and warm, the actor is very
exciting—and very appealing. In this situation, an auditor can
misinterpret the message, mistaking a professional enthusiasm
for a personal one.

Likewise, actors are often wary of the interest and warmth
displayed by a casting director, producer or director. When
you've been sitting in a casting session for hours and suddenly
an actor reads who's truly terrific, it's certainly a turn-on. Since

we are human, we respond by indicating our enthusiasm with praise, warmth, respect, etc. That doesn't mean that the auditors have lost their professional stance. Most professionals are clear about the line between business and personal interaction and are very careful not to cross it. I'm not saying it doesn't happen. But many times professional enthusiasm can be misread and thought to be a personal invitation. It's confusing at best. It's such a people business, depending and thriving on such close interaction, that the cutting edge of professionalism can appear awfully fuzzy at times. And let's face it now: The "casting couch" does exist.

WHAT TO DO IF YOU ARE HARASSED? *SAY NO!*

No actor should ever enter a casting session without bringing along his brains. If someone asks you to perform some sexual act, or in some way or manner makes improper advances toward you, simply get up and leave. You don't need to apologize or explain yourself. Just get out of there. And when you're a safe distance away, report the incident to your agent and/or actors' union. Remember: legitimate casting people need to view your talent—not your body. And don't ever believe that sexual favors are necessary to get ahead. In fact, sexual favors can often work against you and hinder, rather than help, your career.

How can actors protect themselves so that they are not abused, embarrassed or harassed? I think you have to be aware right up front about what is going on. Be cautious. Get out of the situation when you first see it coming. Don't ignore and play "dumb," hoping it will go away. If someone starts coming on to you with dinner invitations, or calls you at home, deal with it kindly and caringly, *but firmly.*

It's just too risky to sleep around. When you're young and just starting out, you don't know the way to behave, the way to be sophisticated. You're not sure of the way it's done. It's hard to see the truth clearly—do I really like this guy or what he does? It's very difficult to be in touch with yourself. Most people don't know themselves, especially when the negative side of their nature is revealed. It's near impossible to admit to one's ulterior motives. The women I know who have tried to sleep their way to the top have wound up on the bottom.

—Pam Dawber

Actors aren't the only ones who find themselves in these types of situations. When I first came to Los Angeles from New York, I was desperately looking for a job. Any job. And it was very discouraging. I talked to everyone I had the slightest connection with. I left my résumés all over the place. And I followed up every lead. It was hard and often discouraging work. In the midst of this massive job hunt, I got a phone call from one producer I'd interviewed with. He called me at home at 11 P.M. to talk about a script. He asked me to come over to his house to discuss my possible involvement. Oh, and he wanted me to know that he had the "champagne cooling and the Jacuzzi going." I politely explained to him that I only see people during business hours and would be happy to arrange a meeting, but I would not be able to meet him that night. I was polite, direct and *got off the phone.*

Now, some other new kid in town might have gotten into her car and gone, hoping that this one night would help her career get off the ground. It's hard when you have no power or influence and you want something so much, and someone is dangling things in front of you. But frankly, a person is a fool if they go. It's stupid. And later on, when the whole thing blows up in their face, it's pretty hard to believe the story that "I didn't understand what he wanted." We all know when someone's interested in us—and why. In a situation like this, the best thing to do is to say no in a very correct way.

THE CASTING COUCH IS A TWO-WAY STREET

The casting-couch or "sleep-for-success" syndrome is most decidedly a *two-way street.* Actors try to "seduce" the people from whom they're trying to get jobs—and sometimes this seduction is carried to its most literal extreme. Let's say an actress is auditioning for a part she dearly wants. Her auditor, the director, is a male. To get attention, she puts out a lot of sexual "vibes." We all know about using charm, beauty and attraction to get someone's interest. The big question is: does an actor have a better chance if he uses his sexuality? That depends. Certainly getting someone to pay attention to you is going to improve your chances. You want to be vital and alive in an audition. But there is a limit, and should you overstep your bounds, the whole effort can backfire miserably and seem rude and greatly inhibit your chances for success. The issue here is a matter of degree. There's a big difference between being charming, deliberately flirting and coming on. Once an actor came to read for a fairly romantic leading role. The part required a certain amount of emotion and sexual tension. I had met a lot of attractive men while in search of the "perfect" guy. This fellow had a good résumé, and the right look—but, most decidedly, the *wrong approach.*

I had a reader in the room to read with the men so that I could concentrate on their audition without being distracted by actually doing the scene with them. My reader is a quite talented actress in her own right and was well prepared to help the auditions. This particular actor came in, prepared and began to read the scene with my reader. Only he never *looked* at her! Instead, he used her voice to get the cues but played the scene staring at me. Needless to say, it was very disconcerting. He was ignoring the actor he was working with and it was apparent that his "flirtatiousness" had less to do with the scene and more to do with trying to butter me up. It didn't take long for me to realize that he was coming on. The deliberateness made me uncomfortable. When the reading was over, he walked over to me, took my glasses off and said, "You really shouldn't wear glasses. You're so much prettier without them." I mean, really! Besides being a come on, it was so corny. I couldn't believe his nerve. After he left, my assistant and I laughed. It was so unbelievable. So silly and rude. He didn't get the job, and I was embarrassed for him. Bad choice and bad move. That kind of deliberate manipulation will never work. It's demeaning—and all wrong. There wasn't the slightest chance that I thought this person was being real. I thought he was acting like a jerk. And I had no interest in ever seeing him audition again.

HOW MUCH CHARM IS TOO MUCH?

It's not so much exactly *what you say or do*. Rather, it's the intention. If you are deliberately trying to manipulate sexually, the odds are that your object of manipulation is going to catch on—and resent it. Someone who is sincere may "come on" in a very direct way but not intend to manipulate. People can get away with the most outrageous flirtation *if* it's part of their personalities.

On one project, we auditioned the men on videotape, which was then sent to the director and producer. Readings were going on for a few days when this terrific fellow came in to read. Like the rest of the candidates, he prepared his scene, and when he was ready, we put his audition on tape. Suddenly, on camera, in the middle of his audition, he said, "I want to go out with you." There were a number of people in the room. We all laughed—myself included. It was just so much a part of his personality. His enthusiasm. His magnetism. It wasn't offensive or manipulative. It was charming, and it was a nice compliment. We all enjoyed him, the audition and his personality. Still, his flirting didn't get him the job. Although I was personally complimented, I was looking for another type for a particular part. But I did remember him. His personality and his straightforwardness did remain in my awareness. I recommended him to a colleague of mine who was looking for a certain look and type. He got that job.

Will an actor get a job because he is attractive, cute and coming on? For the most part, *no*. Not that it *never happens*—of course, it can. But the overwhelming odds are against you. Why? Because first and foremost, this is a *business*—not a dating service. The vast majority of show-biz execs are interested in finding the best possible actor for their projects and are not looking to improve their social or sex lives. There are too many dollars at stake to let a flirtatious nod color your opinion. There have been many instances where I've met performers I've found personally fascinating. And perhaps we might become friends. Yet that doesn't get them jobs. Basically, what I'm saying is that

The "casting couch" is a myth, but . . .

POWER, SEX AND YOUR CAREER

The "casting couch" becomes even more of a factor in an actor's life when you add the element of *power.* There you are, auditioning for the best part of your life, and you notice the director's attracted to you. It's a difficult situation. On one hand, you think, "If I'm nice, maybe that'll help get the job." Or, even more frightening, "If I don't play along, he won't like me and I'll *lose* this part."

The ugly fact of an actor's life is that, for the most part, an actor can exert very little power. (Of course, there are the stars—those very, *very* few who can dictate their own terms.) But more often, you will find yourself dealing with people who simply have more influence and control than you do. Traditionally, this scenario involved young female actors who succumb to powerful male producers and directors to get their careers going. But don't kid yourself: dealing with the sexual invitation is no longer the dilemma of young female starlets. There are lots of stories of men who are approached either by other men or women who are in high executive and creative positions.

So, there you are in the audition and you must make a decision—what do you do? Unfortunately, there are no hard and fast rules to follow here. It's a judgment call that you will have to live with. But my own personal feeling is this:

If you're not truly interested in a personal relationship with this person
. . walk away!

Don't try to use their interest in you to further your career, because it can easily turn on you. If you sense that someone is interested in you romantically and/or sexually, and you try to take advantage of that, you yourself are playing a very risky game of exploitation. There's a fine line here of who's using who. This person is relating to you on another level. If you try to use that attraction as bait, teasing them with the possibility of a romantic liason, chances are, when they finally figure out what you're doing and how you really feel they will feel humiliated, degraded and embarrassed. They won't like you as a person, and that can hurt you as an actor. They might be angry and retaliate by blocking your career. The edge a sexual affair gives you in the short run isn't worth the potential damage it can cause in the long run. And ultimately, the successful actors are the ones that stick around and work over the *long run.* That's what a career is all about. If you're not really interested in someone, walk away from it. I'm not saying playing along won't work. There are people who can handle this kind of situation and get away with it. But more often, it's a no-win situation. Usually the performer played along and got hurt. People look to relationships like Blake Edwards and Julie Andrews or John Cassavetes and Gena Rowlands to prove their ideas of sexual politics, forgetting the fact that it's abundantly clear that these couples are together because they have a life together. That's hardly exploitation. Again: if you aren't really interested in a personal relationship with a person, if you don't have good *personal* intentions, leave it alone. Sexual politics is simply too dangerous an area and why risk playing Russian roulette with your career? We are talking about complicated issues here, dealing with the most personal of emotions and vulnerabilities. There's no right or wrong. Each of you must come to your own decisions based on your own ideas, moral codes, personalities, etc. Don't blindly walk into these situations, *be aware* and *be wary.*

Creating Star Quality— 13
The X Factor

Duse's spell was not confined to the stage, to the actress . . .
Succumbing to her, people at every age or station would drop
everything and follow her, as they would a pied piper or a
prophet.

—William Weaver, BIOGRAPHER of famed
Italian actress, Eleonora Duse

. . . There was no doubt that when John took the stage, all
eyes were on him.

—quoted from WIRED, about John Belushi by his
HIGH SCHOOL DRAMA TEACHER, DAN PAYNE

IT'S known by many names: charisma, star quality, sex appeal.
It can mean many things. An elusive, mysterious attractiveness.
Effervesence, liveliness. Intense brooding, passion. There are
many components. Humor. Mystery. Confidence. Beauty. It
can have all the attributes, or only one. It knows no bounds.
Neither age, gender nor appearance. Anyone can possess it. But
only a few do. It's what draws you to one person though there
are dozens in a room. It makes a leader of one and followers of
the others. Its force can be used for good or evil. It is rare,
powerful, and as an actor in this industry, it can be your greatest asset.

Many people in the trade call this special sparkle the "X"
factor. It is that unknown aspect in an individual that makes
them stand out.

YOUR CHARISMA QUOTIENT

Exactly how charismatic are you? Do you consider yourself a leader, a forerunner of taste, style and opinion? Do you have that special chemistry that draws people to you? Do you feel gifted with a certain talent and/or magnetism that brings people and events into your life? Or are you just a backseater? Are you the kind of person people don't seem to notice? Is what you have to contribute meaningful and worthwhile or rather dull and insignificant? Are you worthy of a great deal of attention and appreciation? Do you enjoy it?

Actors with star quality exude a certain self-confidence and style. it has nothing to do with being shy. In fact, a surprising number of big stars do consider themselves on the timid side. But not *one* of them doesn't think that they have something special. Something that people want to experience. In short, they truly believe that they are worthy of the public's attention.

In the forties, the movie moguls called it "star quality." Marilyn Monroe had it. Though cast in a tiny, one-line part as a gorgeous blonde bimbo in a Marx Brothers flick, Monroe's film appearance created a stir. Why? Certainly Hollywood was full of gorgeous blondes with fantastic figures. Certainly there were many other actresses with more acting ability, better voices, more technique and experience . . . Why then did Monroe get noticed? The only answer: the *X* factor. There was simply something about Marilyn Monroe that drew our attention, interest and devotion. Today, more than twenty years after her death, her mystique is still felt, as the public's continuing fascination with her life attests.

Humphrey Bogart began his acting career playing hoods and heavies. He wasn't considered handsome enough to play leading men. True, he lacked traditional good looks, but, man, did he have charisma! Despite having all the rules against him, Humphrey Bogart became one of the most powerful stars to ever grace the Hollywood firmament. Why? He had star quality—in spades.

Defining the undefinable

The *X* factor defies concise definition. It's a something all right, but what that something is, is an unknown—a sometimes invisible sparkle that makes one individual stand out. It is a light within a person that draws people. Certainly beauty and sexual appeal are part of its components. A stunning figure. A head of golden hair. Beautiful clothes. Something comes through. This man or woman walks into a room and heads turn. But looks alone are not enough and, in many cases, not even important. Beauty will get attention, but only someone with that special star quality can mesmerize. Lauren Bacall's voice. Bette Midler's outrageousness. Jack Nicholson's smile. Lucille Ball's zaniness. What makes them so special and demanding of our attention?

Consider writer Arnold Bennett's account of opening night and the performance of the famous, and infamous, star of the of the thirties and forties, Tallulah Bankhead:

> *What is Tallulah's secret? If she is beautiful, and she is, her beauty is not classical . . . Her voice is not beautiful . . . Her method of delivery is monotonous . . . [But] she has an exuberant, excessive vitality. Life radiated from her as it invariably does.*

> —from her autobiography, *Tallullah*

Star quality? The *X* factor in operation? You bet. As a casting director, I have auditioned hundreds of talented individuals for a part, and then suddenly one comes in with "that certain something" and blows all the others away.

There is something about them that lets you know *who* they are. It's a life force—not just an attitude. It's a way of being that commands your attention. Charisma can be active or passive. It can be like Svengali staring and hypnotizing. It can be charming and outgoing, sweet and sensitive. It can be a quiet strength or dynamic passions. The *X* factor is a certain self-awareness—the knowledge that a person has that he is special.

That specialness doesn't necessarily make a person nice. Or

happy. Or well adjusted, admirable, etc. Just charismatic. Hitler had star quality. His energy, his madness and his passion drew people to him. He was a leader. He had charisma. And charisma, unfortunately, knows no morality. The devil has charisma—or rather, the image of the devil does. It's tantalizing, powerful, mesmerizing. Jesus had charisma. So did Judas.

All of the most influential world leaders had charisma. John Kennedy. Martin Luther King. Winston Churchill. Franklin D. Roosevelt. Mahatma Gandhi. Yet, each was different in his personality, appeal and appearance. (One could hardly consider Churchill movie-star handsome!) In short, the "X" factor can be anything—a single factor, or a combination of attributes. As a matter of fact, it is precisely this difficulty in describing exactly *what* it is that makes it so powerful. It is like love—ultimately indefinable.

WHO HAS IT?

Do you remember high school? Remember the young guy who all the other fellows imitated and looked up to? Whether he was the best example or not, he was the one who set the pace for the rest. He was the "cool kid"—the leader. Maybe he was a jock, or the school cut-up, or the president of his class. No matter. He was the leader. And the rest of the kids gladly followed. Or perhaps, at summer camp, there was that girl who seemed to appeal to one and all. She set the style and attitude for her peers. There was something about her that drew attention, and therefore she had tremendous influence. Both she and our high school hero had charisma—that special star quality. Other examples of this *X* factor at work are found in clubs, committees and most of all in the media.

STARS AND OTHER ACTORS

There is no doubt that when a charismatic actor walks into an audition, everyone immediately knows it. I've seen producers, directors and writers cut their conversation mid-sentence when an actor's energy exudes. It's a turn-on. There are many actors in this country, and a lot of them are talented and well trained.

But it's that *X* factor that will make them a star. They stand out. Even if the audition doesn't come off well, the actor with charisma will be remembered—and called back. As a casting director, there is simply nothing more exciting than meeting one of these artists. And I've seen charismatic talents come in all different shapes, sizes, age ranges and ethnic backgrounds.

Aidan Quinn, known for his roles in such features as *Reckless, Desperately Seeking Susan* and the acclaimed television movie *Early Frost,* was in a large "cattle-call" audition in Chicago when I first saw him. There were over two hundred actors for me to meet at this audition. From the moment Aidan appeared, I knew he was special. There was something so clear and concentrated about him. He seemed totally comfortable with himself, yet projected an open and intense interest in others. The best way to describe it is to say that he glowed. This charisma comes from tapping into the power within. These individuals project *themselves* without being *self-conscious* or *self-preoccupied.*

When the *Facts of Life* producers were researching girls' boarding schools for their series, they met Mindy Cohn.

There was a fun "something" about Mindy—a charisma—the producers found charming. Even though Mindy had no formal acting training, they decided to include her in the show. As "Natalie," Mindy is a tremendous success story—and a clear example of someone with the *X* factor in full operation. Your charisma, a lucky break, a golden opportunity—they can start a career or push you into the limelight, but from there it's up to you.

After seven years on *The Facts of Life,* Mindy was hired for the feature film *The Boy Who Could Fly.* Day after day, on the set, people would recognize her and ask for her autograph. Finally the director, Nick Castle, came up to Mindy and asked her why she was so recognizable. Mindy told him that it was from seven years on the TV show. It turned out that Castle had never *seen* the show. Mindy was surprised. She thought one of the reasons she got the part was because of her TV success with that series. "No," Castle explained, "you got the part because you looked right, and read well . . . and I couldn't imagine anyone else but you doing it." As Mindy explained to me:

I was thrilled when Nick Castle told me that. He was validating my efforts to learn my craft over these years. To be the best me I could. A lucky break, a special look. You can use it to help yourself along, but it's really up to you to work hard to develop yourself to your fullest potential. And ultimately, that's what charisma is really about. Isn't it?

WHERE DOES THAT *X* FACTOR COME FROM?

Charisma used to be something you were born with. The little baby who had a sweet, bright "Gerber" smile. The tough little tyke whose wit and irreverence delights the adults. Babies that just seem so much more aware and alive than your average infant. From the beginning of life, these children are able to draw a lot of attention to themselves. Not by misbehaving or crying, but rather from the bright glow of their budding personalities. These children possess a special awareness of themselves and recognize the influence they have on those around them. They also learn well. As they test their limits, they continue to increase their appeal. When they try something and it gets positive attention, it becomes incorporated into their personality. In this way, gradually and carefully, children learn to develop their natural charisma.

Often people become tremendously charismatic when they fall in love. Why? No mystery here. *They are happy and excited, turned on to the joy of life!* They feel attractive and worthwhile; they feel appreciated by someone who means a lot to them; they are in touch with their *life force.* When we are in love, we think about ourselves in more positive terms. We become more appreciative of our good qualities and more forgiving about our flaws. Of course, lovers aren't the only appealing folk. Anyone—and I *mean* anyone—who is truly aware and enjoys their own aliveness is charismatic. It is how you project your aliveness that determines how charismatic you can be. Passion, desire, positive attitude, commitment—all are tools, avenues if you will, to obtaining that star quality.

Many people believe they've missed the "charisma boat." I believe that charisma can be developed. Everyone has the potential to be appealing. It's developing this potential that counts. Today, with the media explosion and vast amounts of information available, there is no reason that any interested, dedicated actor can't learn how to maximize his natural "star quality."

Politicians have learned this lesson. Since the 1960 Kennedy-Nixon debates, where the younger, attractive senator outshone the professional politician, political leaders and aspirants have realized how vital this charisma quotient is to their careers. Nowadays, the media is so powerful that responsible leadership is sacrificed for media appeal. Our political leaders realize that creating charisma is necessary to win votes. This shift in focus from content to style is not without its drawbacks. As media appeal has increased in importance, politicians have learned to focus on *how* they say things, rather than on *what* they are saying. Unfortunately, the public has made it all too clear that it is sometimes more fascinated with their charisma than with the substance of their political views.

DEVELOPING THE *X* FACTOR

Awareness and application of certain skills and techniques lead to the charismatic style. It's learning to turn on the light within yourself. First, it is necessary for you to be able to recognize who has it. Through this observation you will prepare to emulate. It also means formulating a strong foundation in self-awareness. A foundation that will allow, and actually encourage, charisma.

STEP 1. RECOGNIZING THE *X* FACTOR

Developing your own star quality is like developing anything else about yourself: You need to observe, learn and practice. If you want to learn about charisma, begin by recognizing and observing it in others. It's hard to develop something if you don't understand it. Look for the "X" factor in others. What attributes do they have that attract, fascinate, intrigue you? It

could be something as singular as their smile, particular sen
of humor, or even their hairstyle or fashion sense. Or it can be
something more pervasive in their personality, like optimism or
high energy, that turns you on. You may find that you are
fascinated by movie stars of the past, or perhaps someone you
went to school with. It may be a political figure or a teacher.
It may even be someone in your acting class, a colleague, a good
friend. What is it about these people that stands out? Check it
out. These people will be your guides.

STEP 2. EMULATION

Now that you have identified who has the *X* factor, you are
ready to develop your own *X* factor. One of the ways to
achieve this charisma is by emulation. This does not mean
imitation. Rather, through your admiration, find what works
for your personality and try to equal or surpass the example.
It means adjusting the characteristic you admire to your own
style, which may not be drawing attention now. Because you
like Jack Nicholson, don't buy dark glasses thinking that will
capture his *X* factor. The way that you can pick up on his
appeal is by tuning in to his energy. As an actor, this should
be an exercise in sensitivity. Look beyond the behavior or
fashion itself for the real message. Is it a desire for anonymity,
or exactly the opposite—dark sunglasses flash a certain personality flair? Most importantly, what does his persona communicate to you that you find so enticing? Open yourself up to
possibilities. Then "try out" your perceptions on yourself. And
then if you still want to buy sunglasses, go ahead. Many actresses have tried to imitate Lauren Bacall's deep throaty voice.
Some of the new, young female stars have applied their understanding of Lauren Bacall's appeal to themselves. They may not
sound like Lauren Bacall, which would be artificial, but they
have their own distinctive sound and mystique.

In a way, that's what fashion is all about. Some people set
the style and others find their way into it. When it looks right,
that person has found a style that suits them. Again, if you try
to look exactly like a model in Vogue magazine, chances are

you'll fail. Don't be a copy. Be an original. Adapt the fashion to your height, weight, coloring—in other words, *to you.*

Recently I tried this exercise with an actress, Gracie L. She is a character type who has a comedic sensibility and a love of musical theater. I asked her who she would want to emulate—whose charisma attracts her. Her answer: Barbra Streisand.

> E.B.: What is it about her that you admire? Think now about the person, not just about her specific talents. What is it that draws you? Close your eyes and begin to feel, to sense, Barbra Streisand's energy. Take your time.
>
> G.L.: It's her style. The way she seems so confident about how she looks, even though she's not a typical beauty. There's an elegance to the way she does things. It all seems to go together—her nose, her voice, her figure, her clothes. She's fluid. It's like her energy and talents flow through and around her. It's odd: To me, even when she's being goofy and funny, or intense and dramatic, it all seems so well connected and flowing. And ultimately, she just seems so strong and certain—about herself and about what she wants.
>
> E.B.: Get more specific.
>
> G.L.: She's strong, while looking like a sweet girl.
>
> E.B.: Can you now interpret that for yourself and your own style.
>
> G.L.: Sure.
>
> E.B.: How?
>
> G.L.: Work on my self-confidence. I'd take a song or play and do it with her assurance. I'd like my haircut to be softer. And start focusing on my clothes—more fashionable, a bit freer, more creative. Maybe even try wearing things I haven't tried before.
>
> E.B.: That's good. It's exactly the process. Physicalizing can help spark the energy. If this doesn't work, keep trying. Investigate the magic and apply it to yourself. Soon your own *X* factor will emerge.

And it will. Just the process alone will turn on your self-awareness. Spending time on yourself in this way will spotlight your own potential. It's a form of self-love and care. There is a transformation of energy when we are turned on. Paying attention to ourselves in positive ways is a great activator.

STEP 3. SELF-AWARENESS

Self-awareness is a mind-set. When I feel the most turned on, the most alive, I'm usually at my most charismatic. I know that the X factor is working. I feel appealing. I feel people notice me. I actually feel fascinating. On days like these, it feels like nothing can go wrong. The whole world is my audience and I am aware of everyone and everything. Sound familiar? I'm sure you remember such days. I call this sensation self-awareness.

Being aware is the ability to be conscious, to realize and to know. It's being *awake.* Too often, we go through our days in a state of semi-consciousness. We interact, think and feel, but never really *notice* what's going on. Ever had the experience of driving along a highway or riding a train and suddenly realizing that miles have passed and you haven't noticed, that you've been on "automatic pilot"? This is a common experience for everyone. As an actor, it is necessary to be conscious, more conscious, in fact, than the average person. Know that paying attention is a vital tool. When you are aware of yourself and pay attention to others and your surroundings, you are creating a magnet. How much you see is how much you'll be seen.

A lot of this has to do with the eyes. The person I notice the most is the one looking at me the most. A person's eyes are "the mirror of the soul." The power they have will draw attention to you. Remember:

How Much You See is How Much You'll Be Seen.

The proof of this is that if someone notices you, you notice them. It's about contact and communication. *And you have to be awake for this to happen—you have to be self-aware.* This may sound simple, and indeed it is, but too often actors behave as if they were half-conscious. This is not a value judgment. It's an insight that I think can help.

Look—and Really See.

It's powerful.

Try this exercise: See how many people you can draw to you

without utilizing a lot of verbal energy. It's a bit like flirting. Allow your natural attractive abilities to emerge. People are drawn to actors who have that awareness. It's not unlike falling in love. Allow this exercise to lead you into greater levels of self-awareness.

Some people practice this instinctively. Models call it "working the camera"—using the power of their eyes to communicate. Practicing exercises like the above will help you to bring this power into your daily awareness. It's like any other habit—practice, and it becomes second nature. It's ironic that actors, continually seeking the "answer" to success in their career, overlook the talents and abilities that they already have and take for granted. Be awake, be aware and empower yourself.

When an actor is aware of who he is, the world becomes interested in them. The actor's persona, the vibration if you will, becomes strong and enticing. He projects who he is as he draws you in. You can, too.

The Confident Style 14

Exploring confidence

What is it? The word *confidence* dates back to the fifteenth century. A descendant from the latin verb *confidere*, meaning to trust intensively, confidence means a feeling of *assurance or certainty, especially concerning oneself.* It's having trust in yourself and your abilities. Having faith in yourself doesn't mean being boastful, conceited or stuck up. Confidence can be silent. It is inviting—not arrogant, pompous or prideful. It is poise, not cocksureness.

Can charisma make you confident in your work? For some actors, their charisma is their confidence. Recognizing their own appeal, they have developed assurance. But for most actors, having charisma does not ensure that they also have confidence. Actually, having a confident working style is something entirely different. Charisma is soft, less tangible, appealing to others in a more mysterious manner. Confidence is bold—not brash. It is strong and vital and creates a sense of power. I know some actors who are loaded with charisma but still cannot get their careers off the ground. I've seen beautiful, energetic women whose appeal could stop traffic. Yet, when they approach a career situation, they crumble. The problem is a lack of self-confidence.

Without confidence in your work, your talent and what you have to offer, advancing your career and winning meaty roles is next to impossible. Performers with a confident style have the best shot at going the full distance with their careers. They know *who* they are and *what* they have to offer. At auditions, they are professional, engaging and assured. At meetings, they exude independence and trust. Many of the great stars are not only charismatic, but also carry with them an air of great confidence. In fact, their personalities stand by themselves, and these stars are often viewed as archetypes and leaders in society.

This does not mean that performers with a confident work style are necessarily confident in other areas of their lives. In their personal lives, they may have great areas of self-doubt. Confidence is no guarantee that you will be happy or that insecurities will vanish. If you look at the biographies of many successful, famous actors, you will see they have had troubled and unhappy personal lives—multiple marriages, drug abuse, etc.—yet they continue to elicit our belief in them as confident performers. Even though Elizabeth Taylor and Cher have lives fraught with public drama, they have carried themselves with dignity and assurance in spite of their human frailties. They are surely examples of the confident style. Obviously, celebrities are in a unique category and are hard to identify with, but I use them as examples. However, when a young actor without any notoriety walks into my casting office and displays strength, sureness, conviction about who he is and what he wants, I notice. This person has the kind of confidence I'm talking about.

ACTING IS ABOUT CONFIDENCE

The very art of acting involves confidence. You, the actor, must believe in your character. If you believe, then we, the audience, believe. We watch the actor transform the character in the imaginary circumstance into reality by the sheer creative force of his confident conviction. This confidence is absolutely essential to transport the audience fully into the creative, emotional experience. When directing, I've often watched actors suddenly take off in a scene. It comes alive. It's convincing, real and emotionally effective. As you watch, you can't help but be drawn in. You believe. Later, these actors discuss the feelings they had while performing. Descriptions like "I felt like I was sailing along—flying" or "It really happened between me and the other characters" or "It felt so real, so honest, so true." They were acting *with confidence.* Acting theories aside, these actors made you believe because they believed. That's when the work is at its creative best. Ultimately, actors must be the master of illusion. They must perform their art with a sense of assurance in order to win us over, to transform us into the heart of the experience, whether we are watching them perform on stage, television or film.

THE CONFIDENT STYLE IN YOUR CAREER

Offstage, I have observed very talented, *confident artists* turn into *unsure, doubting careerists.* As a matter of fact, the single most common lament I hear from actors is how bad they are at auditions and interviews. All their ability and talent is obliterated by their nervousness. This nervousness then translates into global self-doubt, and quickly a very shaky, unconfident individual enters the audition room. These actors fail to realize that the same artistry and techniques they employ onstage can be used offstage—at interviews, auditions, etc. In your career, there are going to be times when you don't feel okay about a situation (it's a big audition, you're intimidated by your competition, or by the auditors, or both!), nevertheless it is your *job* to *become* confident. I'm not saying to fake it. I am saying you should tap into the strength and conviction you have artistically as an actor. Commit to your belief in your talent, your technique, your "okayness" as a professional. You will be tested often. But remember: All you need do is tap into your true conviction about your ability. And then, *fly!*

I know of one actor who "chats" with himself when he gets nervous in auditions. He reminds himself that though he's scared and doubting, he's got a job to do—and that he needs to be assured to do it well. He promises his "scared side" that it can have a turn—later. But for the next fifteen minutes, he's going to shut off all the messages the "scared side" is sending. For fifteen minutes, he's going to concentrate on only his confident side. It works. George Clooney, the young star of *Facts of Life* is one of the most confident actors I've seen. I asked him once what he felt made someone a star. "Confidence," he replied, and I could see he understood it. When he first came to audition, his commitment to his choice was so strong. He came dressed in character. It was an extreme interpretation, but he took the risk and stuck to it. He believed it. We believed it. And he got the part.

Confidence isn't deception. It's putting aside the negative and replacing it with a focus on the positive.

IF YOU DON'T FEEL IT, ACT IT

Actors who have the talent and ability to transform a character into believable reality are well equipped to do that as careerists. The actor simply must have confidence in order to get work. If you find yourself in a situation where your natural confidence flees, don't quit on yourself. Do what you do best—*act it.* You know how.

Confidence draws attention. It is the mark of the professional. To build confidence, you need experience. Each time you experience an audition, a meeting or a performance you will begin to sort out what works and what doesn't. When you talk to professional actors who have been working over many years, they will tell you that experience taught them about their confidence. In the beginning, you may feel that you lack this important quality, but as you test yourself, you will begin to believe in yourself.

I've seen some very talented actors who lacked confidence when they first entered the professional arena. They had youth, charm, talent and sweet innocence—but no confidence. Although I was certain of their talent, it is hard to hire an actor without that strength. Then I meet them a couple of years later, and they are transformed! Experience and hard work have added a confident style to their other abilities. It's so powerful and appealing. You see them in a way you've never seen them before. They look terrific, and they have a way of carrying themselves that lets you know you can rely on them to do a professional and creative job. It's fabulous.

Remember, confidence is an *acquired attribute.* It can be generated. It takes practice. When auditioning, I've sometimes seen actors who are loaded with talent and charisma but lack the kind of self-confidence in their art to really put the audition across. Perhaps they are truly novices. Or perhaps they are seasoned pros who are going through a difficult time in their lives and/or careers. In any case, when I see such an actor, the first thing I, and other executives, directors and producers, will try to do is help build up a little confidence. Sometimes the actor may have confidence and belief in himself but under the stress and pressure of the situation is unable to tap into that wellspring. To get to that source, I'll begin by helping the person calm down. Usually within minutes, you can see the actor visibly begin to relax and reclaim that part of his psyche that believes in itself. With the confidence level boosted, the actor can experience commitment and freedom.

Most casting professionals, directors and producers are willing to work with actors and their nerves. But you can't count on that. One of the purposes of this book is to put *YOU* in control of your career.

BELIEVING IN YOURSELF GIVES YOU POWER

Take responsibility. You don't have to rely on someone else to make you confident. When you are in situations that are stressful, like auditions and meetings, be aware of what's happening to your self-confidence. If you notice that your auditors are trying to build you up, be grateful—and take note. They are trying to help you tap into that confident style. Most executives are very willing to help actors in this way. But I don't want you to depend on luck. Here and now, you have an opportunity to develop this awareness, this strength. Start today. And soon, you'll have a confident style.

CONFIDENCE BUILDERS

There are ways to help boost your confidence quotient. Like many other areas of personal development, confidence is strengthened through continuing awareness, effort and practice. Here are some techniques to help you improve your confident style.

VISUALIZATION

If there are certain situations that put your confidence on the skids, you can help prepare yourself by using visualization. Picture the situation—a business party, an audition—and go through the entire process. Picture yourself acting confidently. Try and be as detailed as you can. If you are meeting someone specific, picture talking to that person. In other words, rehearse the entire event in your mind. Play out different options, different scenarios. See yourself acting with assurance and competence.

FOCUS ON THE POSITIVE

This is so simple, yet it is amazing how often we overlook it. Sometimes we are so intent on correcting the aspects of ourselves that *aren't working,* we tend to neglect noticing the things that are. On a daily basis, put some time aside to just *focus on the positive aspects of your work and your life.* You'll be surprised how much confidence you will begin to acquire. We all need those pats on the back. You must learn to give them to yourself each and every day. Even in the midst of the worst periods, there will still be some positive things happening. Don't overlook them. They are the sources of joy and strength that will help you through more challenging situations and circumstances.

EVERYBODY LOVES ME

If you're seeking love and approval, you put an awful lot of pressure on yourself and others. Why not proceed with your career under the assumption that people really like and appreciate you. Ridiculous, you say? Unrealistic? Well, no more so than the kind of continual worries and doubts about being liked that most of us have. It's a matter of a glass filled halfway with water—is it half-full or half-empty? It depends on your viewpoint. The fact is that most people are likable. So why not start with that as a base rather than worrying about the opposite. I know actors who "prep" themselves before important business functions by talking themselves into believing that everyone in the room loves them. It helps to get you in touch with that natural source of self-confidence.

Performers who aren't constantly worried about getting personal approval can focus on the pleasure *they get* from acting and doing the job well. Look, it's tough. You have to win over people in this industry in order to get jobs. That's a fact. But when winning "them" becomes more important than your own sense of satisfaction and enjoyment, it's time for a little re-thinking. If *all* your focus is on watching and waiting for approval, you'll have little left to actually *be good.* Give yourself a break. Bolster your confidence by focusing on what is *good* about you and your work. And that starts with believing in your basic bottom-line likableness.

BE OKAY WITH THE RISK

People who are consistently self-confident aren't afraid of making a mistake, taking a risk or looking foolish. They understand and accept that no one is perfect. And that everyone makes errors. The difference between them and those lacking confidence is that they are willing to take risks—to get out there and try.

I had a friend who was always so hard on herself whenever she made a mistake. She was constantly checking things and fearful that she would err at some task at work. When she did, she felt terrible. Really terrible. The upshot was that she would rarely take any chances. She always wanted to wait until she was *certain* her choice of action was correct. Boy, did it slow her down! An extremely bright and creative woman, she was so tied up by her fear that she only got a tenth of the things done that she planned. She finally decided to seek therapy. Her therapist promptly gave her an exercise to do: each day, she was to do one thing incorrectly. It could even be a very little thing, but she had to do it incorrectly *deliberately.* Like many of us, she found the assignment very hard to do. She became very aware of what "making a mistake" meant to her. And the fact was, making a mistake wasn't the end of the world! We all know this, yet too often we have real trouble putting our intellectual understanding into practice. Psychological studies have shown that we are our own worst critics. We are often so afraid of looking foolish or failing that we do nothing and never take a risk.

How are you at taking a risk, allowing yourself to feel foolish or make a mistake? Try your own little experiment. Each day, take *one risk.* It doesn't need to be very big. But it definitely should be *a risk.* Take one risk every day, and you'll be amazed at how quickly your confidence in yourself will grow. It doesn't matter if your risk turns out well or not, just taking action *in spite of your fears* will give you increased freedom and confidence.

BEWARE THE CONFIDENCE KILLER:

SELF-CONSCIOUSNESS

You can't open yourself up and work creatively if all your attention is focused back on yourself. Your attention, whether in an audition, performance, at a social business party or screening, must be on others. If you're worried about how your hair looks, or uncomfortable because your suit is tight since you've gained weight, you will have little chance of projecting confidence and drawing attention.

Self-conscious people are constantly taking inventory of themselves, carefully noticing and trying to compensate for their perceived inadequacies. They are so busy with this continual inventory that they have no energy, attention or awareness for what is really happening around them. It's a very self-centered state of mind. All information and feelings are processed from a "How-do-I-feel,-how-should-I-react?" point of view. Trying to do the right thing, to say the right thing and to think the right things, self-conscious people are so preoccupied with themselves that they simply are overloaded. The result: a not-very-interesting person, a non-spontaneous bore. That's what self-consciousness does for you. It's anathema for the actor.

The next time you are in a situation and you suddenly notice those self-conscious feelings erupting, deliberately put your attention on someone or something *outside* of yourself. Perhaps you're at a party where you don't know many people. You're sitting off by yourself and feeling rather awkward. Get up, look around the room and focus on something or someone. If you feel too shy to initiate a conversation, then put your attention on something else, such as watching some other people, looking at the food or decorations, anything. Allow yourself the luxury of really paying attention to whatever you have chosen. The same is true in a business meeting or audition. When you feel self-conscious, that's your cue to place your attention outside yourself. Concentrate on the person you're talking to. Really look at them. Focus on what they are saying, or how they are saying it. Notice their mannerisms. Listen to the message of their communication. In other words, allow yourself to just "be," and place your focus outside. It works. It really does.

One thing I've found to get over self-consciousness in a meeting or interview is to set myself a task. It can be as simple as learning more about the person

I'm talking with or taking the time to notice the office and how it's decorated or learning more about the script or character I'm to play. Whatever it is I put all my focus and energy in that direction. That way I don't have time to think about how I look, etc. My thoughts are caught up with my task and not on me.

> —Betty Garrett, star of
> such famous MGM musicals
> as *On the Town* and *Take Me
> Out to the Ballgame,*
> Broadway plays *My Sister
> Eileen* and *Spoon River,*
> and TV's *All in the Family*
> and *Laverne and Shirley*

The one thing you *should not do* is be upset that you are feeling self-conscious. We all are self-conscious at various times. It's natural. But that doesn't mean it has to cripple you and hinder your career. Self-consciousness can be tamed. Use it as a cue to focus attention on others. Allow your self-consciousness to become self-awareness.

Confidence - Belief:
If You Believe, I Believe

It's never too late to develop your confidence. Or change it. I'm speaking now to those actors who have been working professionally for some time. You may have developed a certain confidence in your earlier professional years that is no longer working for you now. Perhaps your "type" has changed or you've been through some tough times. The result can sometimes be that the confident style you started out with is no longer making you feel so confident. It's time to take stock. Is your confidence based on how you truly feel now about yourself and your work, or is it a relic of your past feelings? Confidence grows out of belief and experience. Yet sometimes your past experiences and beliefs about yourself may no longer be as valid as they once were. For example, I know an extremely talented character actor who discovered his career slipping as he grew older. Part of the cause was simply the gray in his hair that was moving him from one age category to another. In addition, he found that when he tried during auditions to use the things that always "worked" in the past, he was hitting a dead end. His confidence took a sharp dive, and a downward spiral was set in motion. It was time for an adjustment. What this actor needed to do was rethink his strong points. He needed to reassess his appeal, abilities, charisma. (Remember the goals and personality inventory in the first section.) Rather than relying on his past "tricks," this actor discovered new areas of ability and confidence in himself. These areas—many of which were based on his life experience—gave him a new base on which to depend. His confidence grew and changed as he grew and changed. His confidence was up-to-date with his developing talents and life experience.

Men and women who have always relied on their youth and beauty as a source of confidence are usually called upon to make some adjustments as they grow older. There is nothing sadder than to see a fifty-year-old pretending to be the "cute ingenue." Relying on physical beauty as your source of charisma and confidence is dangerous to begin with. But as the years pass, it can actually begin to be a liability. Those actors that have developed a confident style from a strong foundation of belief in themselves as human beings and artists find the transition a lot easier to handle. There are probably no more stunning examples than Katherine Hepburn and Lauren Bacall. Although both were known in their younger days for exquisite looks and charisma, neither woman depended solely on the transitory nature of youthful beauty as their source of confidence. Hepburn and Bacall are amazing examples of women whose confidence has carried them through every stage of their professional life. Instead of being held back by fading youth and hiding from the public, these women have gone forward, challenging the public's conception of female beauty, fighting agism and enlarging our awareness of the exquisite elegance of a woman's later years. Nowhere is a confident style more strongly evident than in these two women.

CONFIDENCE IS FUN!

A confident style will add a lot of *fun* to your work. And I mean that in its most innocent sense. Most performers dreamed of being actors as little children. Why? Because it's fun to play make-believe. As they grew older, acting became a "profession" rather than a game. I know quite a few actors who don't have any fun when they work. Instead it's all about struggle and trying to create art. All of that may be true, but the actual truth of the matter is that it's *fun to act—to be creatively expressive.* When you develop your confidence, one of the wonderful side-benefits is that your sense of acting as *fun* will increase. Confident performers enjoy themselves. Free from the stress, doubts and anxieties of their less-confident counterparts, these artists really enjoy their careers. In fact, one of the things that's so captivating about confident performers is their obvious enjoyment of what they are doing. This book isn't just about working and succeeding. It's also about enjoying yourself and this career. This is your life path, your career choice, and you owe it to yourself to get the most enjoyment and satisfaction that there is. Go for it!

And if you really want to get an edge on confidence, take Betty Garrett's advice:

> *You want to know how to have confidence as an actor? Be prepared. Sharpen your acting tools, work on your craft, your body, your voice. I've never stopped studying or working in workshops. If your voice and your body does what you want it to—well, that's the whole basis of confidence. If you are not prepared—not just for one particular part, but as a craftsman—how can you expect to feel confident, to instill confidence. I certainly wouldn't want a surgeon who hasn't been practicing to operate on me! I think it's the same for actors.*

Making the Most of Your Looks 15

IT'S no secret that movies and TV love "beautiful" people. For some, their looks are their fortune, and talent is only a secondary consideration. These people take excellent care of themselves with diet, exercise and good nutrition. But even if your face isn't your fortune, your physical appearance and well-being are important elements in your career. *You are your product*—and it should be in the healthiest and most appealing condition possible.

Some people were brought up with the notion that you shouldn't try to improve on nature—that it's not good to change. I don't agree. I think it is your inalienable right as a living, breathing, *thinking* human to do whatever it takes to make yourself feel and look the best you can. Every time a man shaves, every time a woman applies some lipstick, we are "improving on nature." True, some styles and fashions may seem ridiculous. What you change isn't nearly as important as *why* you do it and *how* you feel about it.

BEAUTY IS A STATE OF MIND

That may sound like hokum, but it's true—*absolutely true*. I've seen stunning men and women who don't think they are beautiful. And I've also seen rather plain-looking people who carry themselves with such self-appreciation and respect that they become very attractive. If you don't feel good about yourself, no amount of makeup, surgery or hairstyling will make you beautiful. The very first step to making the most of your looks is to appreciate *who you are*. Remember: Your attractiveness comes out of your uniqueness. To strive to look like someone else or, worse, a conglomeration of artificially combined features, is to miss the point. Having Liz Taylor's eyes and Linda Evan's cheekbones isn't as important as having *your own unique attractiveness*.

Though the pressure to be pretty in this industry is more intense for women than for men, it is nonetheless there. Some male actors diet vigorously and nearly kill themselves working with weights to acquire the macho physique of Arnold Schwarzenegger or Sylvestor Stallone. Here again, these individuals are trying to be *someone else*.

KNOWING WHAT, WHEN AND WHY

Who are you physically? By that I mean, what is it about your looks or your physique that you would like to change, improve, enhance or alter? Begin by taking an assessment of your physical characteristics:

- How old are you?

- How much do you weigh? Are you overweight or underweight? How much?

- What is your best feature? How can it be accentuated or developed?

- What feature is your worst? How can you de-emphasize it or change it through makeup, surgery, diet or exercise?

- What are your most prominent physical characteristics? How do they contribute to your "uniqueness"?

- How much of your physical appearance do you accept and how much do you want to change?

- What aspects cannot be changed?

- What kind of image emerges in the way you dress, talk, etc.? How does it match your personality, your charisma?

- What kind of reactions do you get? Are they the ones you want? If so, why? Or why not?

Be specific. Really take a look. Before you make *any* changes, it is imperative that you think things through and that you know *what you want to accomplish.*

Take into consideration the feedback you get from your friends, family, peers and others in the industry. If everyone tells you you'd be beautiful if you lost fifty pounds, then you have to take a look at that and do something. On the other hand, if altering your nose might damage a wonderful singing voice, you have to weigh the consequences.

DON'T OVERLOOK THE YOU *YOU* WERE MEANT TO BE

Sometimes people make the mistake of thinking that they have to fit into some sort of mold—"cookie-cutter" beauty, if you will. Like so many assembly-line parts, these folks sacrifice their individuality in order to conform to a stereotyped version of attractiveness. You want to get in touch with what makes you more appealing, not what makes you look more like everybody else. If Day-Glo hair works for you, stick with it! Sometimes it is precisely the unique or *irregular* feature that becomes your fortune, the feature that identifies *you,* like Streisand's nose.

Don't be afraid to be a little different from the rest. Dare to really be yourself—an individual. Look at who you are. What kind of image do you want to project? Looks that are clean, healthy and vital are necessary in your work. Remember: your style (dress, physique, overall appearance) sends off information at auditions, meetings and social occasions. What do you need to work on to enhance the most appealing aspects of your look, without losing your individuality?

When I was first starting out, I had some doubts on what I should change. I was prematurely bald and didn't know what effect that would have on getting jobs. I didn't know whether I should keep my name or change it to something simpler. Then one day my acting teacher, Frank Corsaro, recommended me to an agent. It was my first crack at representation. The agent's office, bedecked with photos and posters of his well-known clients, was very intimidating. To mask my own insecurity, I copped a tough guy "Brando-like" stance of self-importance—a pop attitude in those days. After a few minutes of conversation, the agent explained there wasn't much he could do for me until I got a hairpiece, changed my name, and filled in the gap between my two front teeth (I never even thought about changing my teeth). I was shocked—an uptown kind of guy doesn't go capping his teeth. I told the agent I would change nothing. I walked out of the office with a new confidence in my physical appearance and my own self-worth.

—Hector Elizondo

WHY?

Once you've taken an in-depth assessment—you know *what* you want—look at the *why*. As in the goal-setting in the very first chapter, understanding *why* you want what you want can be very helpful. Why are you making these changes—for yourself, your career, neither, both?

What do these changes reflect? Are they a reflection of poor self-esteem? If you believe that alterations are going to save your career, you're likely to be disappointed. You should improve yourself for *yourself* and not to "fit in" with someone else's expectations. Making the most of your appearance will not save a failing career, any more than it'll save a failing marriage. You must want to improve and change yourself for *your life,* not just a career. Sure, it may help, but you can't count on physical changes to get you work.

HOW TO MAKE CHANGES

Okay, so you've made a list of all the things you want to improve or change. You vow you're going to lose weight, start going to the gym every day, grow your hair, get a nose job, get a toupee, take speech lessons, and overhaul your wardrobe. Terrific. But if you try to institute all these "improvements" at once, it's likely that your self-improvement program will fizzle inside of a week. You simply can't stand up to a massive self-demolition and overhaul. You can't do it physically *or* psychologically. We are all creatures of habit, and we need time to adjust to changes. If you want to remodel yourself, do it one step at a time. One *little* step at a time. In the long run, your changes will be more effective, more satisfying and longer lasting.

First things first. Start with the most obvious changes and make a priority list. What is the most important change or improvement? It might be losing weight or improving your skin. Whatever—order your goals.

Experiment. Try new styles and then get feedback from friends and professionals. Use all your resources. Many people don't ask for advice and opinions and so are never open enough to trying new things. Give yourself time to adjust before deciding what you think. When you make a change in your appearance, it sometimes takes time to get used to the change before you'll know if you like it or not. Be flexible and withhold judgment for a bit.

Most importantly, allow yourself to change your mind. Some of your experiments may not be that successful. It's only natural. But if you are so afraid of making a mistake, you may very well pass up some interesting and fabulous ideas.

A final note: You will *always* be in the process of making changes. You don't just overhaul yourself and then stay that way for the rest of your life. There are new styles, new fashions, new ideas. And your needs will change. What appeals to you today, may not tomorrow. Self-improvement is a lifelong task. And it can be a fun one, at that.

RESEARCH

When it comes to physical appearance, this culture *abounds* with ideas, advice and news on fashion and trends. Do your research to glean all possible ideas. Look at magazines. Seek out professionals and consult with them. In your local bookstore or library, there are loads of books on how to do everything from "dressing for success" to altering the timbre and tone of your voice. Before you make any decisions, be sure you've gathered all the pertinent information.

YOUR IMAGE

Unless you can carry off an eccentric look, you're better to stay away from it. Cher's show-stopping looks have really worked for her, but for most of us a more conservative approach is probably advisable. Eccentric looks set certain limitations on how casting people and directors will think of you. If you dress like Cyndi Lauper, don't be surprised if you don't get a lot of calls to play the girl-next-door. In addition, if you're not comfortable with an outrageous style, you run the risk of looking foolish.

This doesn't mean you shouldn't take chances. You absolutely should! If eccentricity works, use it. If it doesn't, let it go. For most people, a more subtle approach that still reflects an individual personality is the route to take.

The way you appear is in part how you are defined. A tight sexy dress and a deep cleavage sends a message. Is this the message *you want to send?* In our culture, people are often defined by their appearance. It may not be fair, but it is reality. People who are well groomed and look good are generally treated well.

Deciding on the right image for you should be based on a number of different considerations. What kind of image are you striving for professionally: leads, glamour roles, character parts? In general, I think you should try to look the best you can look, with an image that is possible for you to maintain.

MAKEUP AND HAIR

Start with what you have—and enhance it. That sounds like simple advice, but I'm amazed how many actors—mostly female—feel the need to look like someone else, whether it's a current star or the cover girl on a fashion magazine. Allow yourself to look like you. Truly stunning women understand that. Take a look at your best features. How can they be enhanced? Is your hair "hiding" you or does it enhance your face like a beautiful frame does a painting?

Attention, men: many male actors give no thought whatsoever to their haircuts. If that's how it was when they were five, that's how it probably has stayed. If it's something you haven't thought about, maybe you should try some experimenting. There isn't anything wrong with working to make yourself as appealing as possible. Hopefully, your career will involve *lots* of photography. Start now to try out some different looks.

There are quite a few truly excellent hair and makeup books on the market. Browse through them. Also look around for a professional who can advise you. Photographers usually know of good hair and makeup professionals. Experiment. Be a little brave. You may make some mistakes, but that's what successful experimentation is about. Try not to judge a look too soon after you try it on. Sometimes it takes a bit of getting used to. See how others respond—not only those people who see you a lot, but new people.

DIET AND NUTRITION

The camera adds about ten pounds. Bad news for most of us. If you are interested in a professional career, you will probably have to deal with this issue sooner or later. There are simply more parts for actors of normal weight than there are for those that are overweight.

If you are going to diet, do it with a healthful plan, please. Ultimately, how you diet will have a lot to do with how successfully you will keep off the weight. Fad diets not only don't work in the long run, but they also can make you look bad. You need proper nutrition to make your skin glow, to keep your eyes shining and to avoid unsightly bags and wrinkles. You may lose all your weight, but if you look like a prisoner of war, it's not going to help your career very much.

Check with your doctor. Eating disorders and chemical dependence are unfortunately all too common for those who struggle to maintain a trim figure. Do yourself a favor. Get counseling and a steady support system to help you look your best. If food is a big problem, consider joining a Weight Watchers or similar group, or possibly becoming part of Overeaters Anonymous, an organization based on the principles of Alcoholics Anonymous. These are all low-cost, or free, plans and organizations that will help you accomplish your weight goals without sacrificing your health.

COSMETIC SURGERY

If there is something about your looks that is driving you crazy and undermining your sense of confidence, perhaps you should consider cosmetic surgery. It's a big step, but it can make a big difference in how you feel about yourself. However, remember it is expensive and has its risks.

The most important step to take when considering this type of procedure is to *consult a qualified expert.* Every state has a listing of licensed doctors specializing in the field of cosmetic surgery. Be sure the doctor you consult is reputable and qualified. And get more than one opinion. The money you spend in consultation fees will be money well spent if it helps to find you the best care available.

A note of caution: Having plastic surgery will not make the world fall at your feet! Sometimes people believe that if they just fix this one thing, every dream will be fulfilled. If you hope your nose job is going to make you look like Elizabeth Taylor or James Dean, you may be setting yourself up for disappointment. Be realistic. Your goal should be the best *you* possible, not a carbon copy of some celebrity.

DRESS FOR SUCCESS

Looks count. That's a fact. The clothes you wear say a lot about you. I'm not recommending that a certain style of dress will make you a star. That's silly. But you can start now to develop your own personal look. Whether it's figuring out what colors look good on you or what style of clothes suits you best, you should pay a lot of attention to the clothes in your closet. Many actors have what they call "audition clothes." These are outfits ranging from very casual to more dressy that they can wear for meetings and auditions. These "audition clothes" are chosen not only for the fine figure they will help you cut, but also because they are comfortable and, most importantly, make you feel good. When you feel comfortable and confident, you'll carry the look to success.

Where to find specialists? Look at current magazines for ideas. Then take a trip to a few department stores and try on some different looks. You don't have to buy anything at first. Just try on different clothes and see what hits you. Take along a friend whose clothes style you admire. Anyone can become a fashionable dresser. It just takes an open mind, some observation and research and some experimentation. Try it on. It will become you.

YOUR NAME (SHOULD YOU CHANGE IT?)

Years ago, if you had an ethnic name, the studio would make you change it. Thus, Mary Gumm became Judy Garland, Archibald Leach became Cary Grant and Anna Italiana became Anne Bancroft. Names were changed without a blink of an eye. But times have changed. Now ethnic names like Robert DeNiro or Al Pacino indicate a pride in their heritage. Difficult names like Meryl Streep are not discarded because they may take some time to learn. It isn't necessary to change your name unless *you* want to.

If you don't like your name, then change it. It's really that simple. Like any other of these changes, try it out for a while. Your friends and family may object at first, but hang in there. Introduce yourself with your "new" name at a party. See how people react. Your name is yours. If the one you were born with doesn't feel right, try something else. If you like your name, if it makes you feel "right," go for it.

BECOMING YOU

In the midst of all this talk about changes, I would just like you to remember that making the most of your looks is about maximizing what you have. It is not about wishing you were someone else. I've met a lot of actors who waste their time focusing on their appearance flaws—they're too short, too fat, not blond enough, not pretty enough. It's a waste of time. Instead, focus on what you have that makes you uniquely you. Start with what is truly yours and work from there.

Knowing *who* you are and using that power is good career sense. Striving to alter yourself beyond recognition is an empty goal and one that can easily backfire.

The Ultimate Strategy: Self-Appreciation 16

*Actors: Bruce Willis, Michael J. Fox, Don Ameche.
Actors? Actors are men who are terrified that a five-year-old
might get more attention than they can.*

—Russell Baker, in the "Sunday
Observer," New York Times Magazine

AH, yes—the traditional image of actors, both male and female: totally self-absorbed, always "on" and only interested in
themselves. There's the joke about an actor talking with someone at a party. After monopolozing the conversation for hours,
with chatter about himself, he finally looked sheepishly at the
other guest and said, "Enough about me. Let's talk about you.
What do *you* think about *me?*" It's an exaggerated image surely,
yet we all know there's more than just a hint of truth there.
Actors are exceptionally self-absorbed, and you know what?
They have to be—that's their job!

An actor has to spend a lot of time being self-involved. It
goes with the territory. The actor must constantly pay attention
to personal and professional development, must constantly
work to improve and overcome obstacles, must constantly reinforce all positive ideas, thoughts and "feelings." An actor is not
a social worker or schoolteacher or philanthropist. The actor's
focus must be back on him/herself, rather than out there on the
world. As a matter of fact, I have a pet theory that actors love
doing work for charities—benefits, telethons, as fund-raisers
and volunteer help—precisely because it gives them a respite

from the necessary self-observation their careers demand. It gives them a chance to round out their life experiences by focusing on things, situations and people *outside* of themselves—and outside the necessary concentration on their careers and this business. Actors are expansive people: they like to learn, grow and give back their understanding in their art. Their generosity comes out of the intense type of self-awareness and self-appreciation their careers demand.

BEING CONCERNED WITH THE SELF ISN'T SELFISH

Being self-involved does not mean being selfish or inconsiderate. It simply means *concentrating on improving, developing and refining your product—YOU.* A virtuoso violinist makes sure that his instrument is well attended and given all the care and maintenance necessary for him to practice his art brilliantly. Dancers exercise and train daily to insure their bodies are in good physical condition. Any artist, actually any *professional,* tends carefully and thoroughly to the tools necessary to produce his work and further his career. For the actor, the instrument, the tools and the product are the very actor himself. And of course, it isn't *just* your body or your voice or muscles or intellect or emotions or philosophical awareness or observational skills—it is *everything that you are, were and believe you will be.* It is the *totality* of yourself that you are selling. If that isn't a good reason to pay a lot of attention to yourself, I don't know what is! And now we come to *the ultimate career strategy for the actor:*

Care For, Love and Appreciate Yourself.

Sounds simple, yet all too many actors do their best to tear themselves down. They may treat themselves terribly through either neglect or an overly critical perspective. Part of the problem is semantics—like the kind we investigated with opportunity. Self-involved is confused with selfish; self-aware, mistaken for self-absorption; self-love, thought to be extreme egotism. The result: Actors are *afraid* to focus on themselves and treat themselves *well,* and thus cut themselves off from the most powerful and charismatic asset they have—*themselves.*

When You're Down On Yourself, You Can't Be Up On Anything Else.

If you want to climb the ladder of success, the first rung is learning to like and appreciate yourself. People who belittle themselves, who treat themselves sloppily or shoddily, rarely are liked and appreciated by others. If you don't care, why should we? It's absolutely *mandatory* for you to like yourself if you desire success and happiness from your career.

YOU CAN NEVER LIKE YOURSELF TOO MUCH

If I had a magic formula that would make each of us love and appreciate ourselves as much as we should, I could probably put the entire roster of psychiatrists and psychologists out of business! Most of us need to "learn" to like and appreciate ourselves. Life is a continual process of learning, altering, re-defining, changing and appreciating ourselves and those around us. Too often, however, we spend a lot less time appreciating ourselves than we do our friends.

The more you invest in you, the more interest there will be in you.

—Lotus Weinstock, COMEDIENNE

Self-appreciation is not self-adulation. It isn't blind acceptance of everything you do. Rather, it is the *positive basis from which you can begin to develop yourself.* It allows you to enjoy those aspects of your personality and your body that you like, and to take a close look at those aspects you don't, not for condemnation, but rather to change, grow and develop. People who have a basic appreciation of themselves are able to take constructive criticism. Why?

Because they are working from a solid foundation of belief in their fundamental self-worth. They aren't afraid of being imperfect. They accept it as part of the human condition. They are eager for input, eager to develop, eager to be *the best self they can be.* That's self-appreciation!

How do you feel about yourself? How do you express your positive feelings about yourself? What do you do to give yourself the proper love, attention and caring that you deserve?

Do You Treat Yourself Like Somebody You Love?

Stop. Don't just pass over that question. Take a moment and really think about it. How much *haven't you done* for yourself?

Self-Appreciation Exercise

Learning to appreciate yourself more and treat yourself well is a learned skill. Learning to express your appreciation for yourself gives you one of the most powerful tools for success. When the chips are down, when life seems filled with just too many obstacles, it is your self-appreciation that can help you forge ahead. It is the strong foundation material that allows you to build your dreams. It enhances not only your career, but your entire life. Learning to like and care for that special person that is *you* is to take a giant step toward success and happiness.

When you answer these questions, be specific. It may be difficult at first. People usually answer these questions very generally in the beginning. That's fine for a start. But take your time. Mull over your answers. Then try to sharpen the answers by becoming more specific, more detailed, by really getting down to it—the bottom line on expressing your self-love:

1. How do you treat someone you love?

2. How does that differ from the way you treat yourself?

3. List ten positive ways you could show your appreciation for yourself, i.e. getting a massage, eating better.

THE EVIDENCE OF SELF-APPRECIATION

People who like themselves show it. They pay attention to themselves, and you see it in their grooming, their attitude and their interaction with others. Self-appreciative individuals are interested in others—willing to share the "spotlight"—because they don't have to continually prove their worth to themselves or others. There is a simplicity about their self-belief. Whether animated or shy, their personalities nonetheless reflect this self-love. Self-loving people put us at ease, relax us, because we aren't pressed into convincing them of their basic "okayness."

People who respect and appreciate themselves do not allow the world to "chew them up." You must make yourself a priority in your life. I know too many people who allow the demands of others to dictate how and what they should be doing. If you have an early-morning work call, you simply cannot stay out late the night before if you want to be your best on the set. That might mean that you will have to pass up your best friend's birthday bash. It's unfortunate, but you must make yourself a priority in your own life if you want to succeed. All too often, I see actors allowing everyone else to dictate their priorities. Perhaps it's the continual fear performers have of not "pleasing their audience." You have got to learn:

You Cannot Fulfill Everyone's Expectations!

You must learn to say no. And you can. Do it for the one you love—yourself.

Don't Wait Until the World Loves You Before You'll Love Yourself!

Until you get this message, you will have nothing. Even should stardom fall into your lap, without self-appreciation you will still have nothing.

> *The first time I turned down something, I was made to feel so bad, so guilty. It made me realize how much I needed to say no. I am one of those people who likes to do everything in life. But I have to learn to say no for self-preservation.*
>
> —Shelley Duvall, ACTRESS/PRODUCER,
> *The Shining, Popeye, Faerie Tale
> Theatre, Three Women*

I want you to *start today* to develop your appreciation of yourself. If you find obstacles, get help—*now.* Make your life and career better by making a commitment to improving your sense of self-appreciation. Build yourself up, don't tear yourself down. Treat yourself. Pamper yourself the way you would anyone you loved, with your whole heart and soul. Remind yourself daily that you are worthy of being loved by *you*.

LOVING YOURSELF IS YOUR RESPONSIBILITY

I don't care whether you have to buy out the entire self-help section of your local bookstore or have to get into therapy or some other kind of guidance to set yourself on the path of self-appreciation. Whatever *works* is what's important. The simple truth is:

It Is Up To You To Love Yourself!

Get that? It isn't up to your parents, or your friends, or your agents, fans, etc. *It is up to you!* You and only *you* can give yourself the kind of love necessary to face life with joy and enthusiasm. If you aren't treating yourself as well as you should, start today to change that. Make it a priority. Tend to yourself and you will be able to tend to others. Self-appreciation gives you the strength and confidence that you will need to make your mark. It is within your grasp—*grasp it!*

Question-and-Answer Seminar for Section C 17

1. I'm very popular. I'm invited to all the "right" parties and know a lot of people and stars, yet my career isn't really happening. What am I doing wrong?

Being seen in social situations is fine—up to a point. You may be overdoing a good thing. There's the kind of person who is always around, hanging out at all the "in" spots, knowing all the "in" people, going to the right parties, but they aren't taken very seriously when it comes to their career. I call this the "Fate of the Social Butterfly." This kind of individual is loved by the "group" but is considered more of an entertaining "companion" than a colleague. This applies to both men and women. I know of quite a few individuals who are prominent in the Hollywood social scene, but whom I never consider for a job. Part of the reason is that they seem to be specializing in socializing rather than working hard on their craft. These actors hope to get work when their friends get work—a "trickle-down" effect. I also suspect that their identities are based on "who they're with" rather than "who they are." I prefer the professional when I'm casting, and that means someone who really *practices* his art and is respected for more than being "hip" and "in." If you seem to have gained this reputation, you can take steps to change it. Back off a bit on all the social events. Instead, take some classes. Get yourself involved with other actors on your own level. Forming a network of *peers* is an important element in career development. You need some support from actors facing the same challenges as you. After a while, word will get around that you have really been working on your career, and people will see you in a different light.

2. One of my closest friends is a very successful actor. I've asked him a few times for a little help with my career, but he's never done anything. Should I back off?

Perhaps. If your friends don't want to help you, you might ask yourself if you are doing something to turn them off. Are your requests reasonable? Are you constantly asking for things and expecting too much? How would you feel if positions were reversed? If you feel you haven't been overstepping your bounds, you might take a look at the friendship. You should consider the fact that your friend may not want to help you. There could be many reasons. The point is, if your friend isn't on your team, you have to question how much of a friend that person is to you. That may sound harsh, but in actuality people in the same business become friends because of their mutual interests, abilities and respect. That is why friends are so eager to help each other out. They cannot get you a job if you're not right, but they can provide contacts and support. It is also necessary for you to look at the reason you value this friendship. If it is merely for what your friend can do for you, then you shouldn't be surprised at your friend's hesitation.

3. I was invited to a big party that was star-studded with actors, directors, studio executives, etc. I was nervous and began to drink to calm myself down. But instead, I got really smashed and made a fool of myself. Now what do I do? I'm afraid to see any of these people, but I know I must. How should I handle it?

Relax. You're not the first person to lose control. If you offended anyone directly, apologize—certainly to your host.

Find out from your host if you need to make amends elsewhere. Losing dignity is awfully embarrassing, but if it's not a constant problem I wouldn't worry about it. You're probably more concerned than need be. Stop suffering. Most likely it went unnoticed. If this is a regular occurrence, get some help. You may have a serious problem.

4. I'm afraid I don't "fit in" with the other successful actors I know. They seem so comfortable. I'n not.

Feeling uncomfortable with success may occur because you are afraid you don't deserve it. We all have a bit of the "kid dressed up in grown-up clothes" when we are suddenly put in the limelight. You should start finding ways to feel comfortable with the attention you receive, for example, after a good performance. Observe how others you admire handle their success. Emulate them. But most of all, realize that you deserve to be appreciated for the hard work you do. Eventually, you will feel comfortable and wonder how you could ever have felt otherwise.

SECTION D

Staying on Top of Your Career

NOTHING EVER STAYS EXACTLY THE SAME IN LIFE—or in your career. The working actor—and even major stars—has high and low points in his career. Typecasting, overexposure, periods of unemployment and doubts about staying in the profession are common problems for the actor.

It's said there are five stages to any actor's career—even a famous one like Helen Hayes'. The stages are:

1. Who is Helen Hayes?

2. Get me Helen Hayes.

3. Get me a young Helen Hayes.

4. Get me a Helen Hayes type.

5. Who is Helen Hayes?

At first glance, that might look a bit harsh—or even ridiculous, but I assure you it is all too often true. When you choose an acting career, you are actually choosing a lifestyle. It is a life commitment to an art form. The actual working—being hired to play a role—is only a part-time job. No matter how in demand you are, you will *never* work all the time.

Now, there are points in a career when an actor is "hot." For a period of time, the public can't get enough of them. They go from finishing one project to immediately starting another. They can do everything and anything from appearing on the cover of a magazine to TV to films. For a select few, like Meryl Streep or Dustin Hoffman, there might be a steady stream of award-winning films, TV and stage projects. But you can't stay "hot" forever. At some point, and for some reason—public taste or society changes, the performer ages, bad choices are made—the career changes. They're no longer the focal point of the public eye and life begins to challenge them in a new way.

In this section, we'll take a look at these potential trouble spots and find concrete solutions to an actor's career dilemmas. We'll look at the successful stars—those that have lasted over the years—and see how they've managed to keep their careers in the pink.

Most importantly, this section is devoted to the *working actor*—whether a star, a regional "character" man or one of the many wonderful actors that may not be known to the general public, but who have marvelous, lucrative, involving careers. In this section, the *working actor* can get all the information needed to keep a career prospering and to avoid the two biggest career "killers": boredom and idleness.

How to Pay Your Rent

*How to earn money while looking for work is a neat trick.
Anyone who's tried it, recognizes this as Catch-22 through
29. The bottom line is to face this reality with
dignity—something that provides a lifelong challenge for
many of us.*

—Alan Thicke, WRITER,
PRODUCER AND ACTOR in
hit series, *Growing Pains*

LET'S get down to the bare facts: most actors don't make a living at their profession. There are many reasons for this—not enough work; no government endowments, thus low salaries; a tremendous number of actors competing; stereotypes of women and men excluding many talented people; unfair hiring practices; lack of negotiating power—the list goes on and on. . . . Now, you can choose to rail against these facts. You can choose to get out your soap box and campaign for reform. You can be bitter and angry. But that isn't going to move you closer to your goal. The basic reality is that *you will need to find a way to support yourself.*

There are all sorts of ways to do it. You may be lucky and have inherited or personal wealth. Or perhaps your family or spouse is willing to subsidize you until your career is self-sufficient. If so, terrific. And maybe you'll be one of those blessed people who hit it big ten days after you hit town. Fantastic. The likelihood, however, is that the acting jobs won't be enough to support you.

Here's proof. According to 1983 Guild calculations, there were a total of 76,345 members of the Screen Actors' Guild·

ANNUAL EARNINGS	ACTUAL NUMBER OF ACTORS	PERCENTAGE OF SAG MEMBERSHIP
Under $1,000	43,111	56.5%
1,000–1,999	8,472	11.1
2,000–3,499	6,087	8.0
3,500–4,499	3,452	4.5
5,000–7,499	3,558	4.7
7,500–9,999	2,213	2.9
10,000–14,999	2,609	3.4
15,000–24,999	2,511	3.3
25,000–34,999	1,204	1.6
35,000–49,999	1,020	1.3
50,000–74,999	776	1.0
75,000–99,999	382	.5
100,000 and over	950	1.2

Source: SAG-Producers Pension and Health Plans

These are quite depressing statistics, but they reflect a hard-core reality. You should have all the information so you can be prepared for the challenge.

HAVING A JOB UNTIL THE REAL THING COMES ALONG

So, you have to make a living. But how? Should you take jobs such as waitressing, secretarial, messenger? Or should you try to develop a second career—one that will eventually supply you with enough income to live on? The answer lies in your priorities and goals. You must consider your specific needs—money, work schedule, commitment—and what you hope to accomplish. Some actors worked for a few years at a regular job, saving their money so they could devote themselves to their career without worry. For some, this type of plan is ideal, while for others, the need is to get out there now, not in a few years. Again, it's a matter of personal choice.

At various times in your career, "earning a living" will have different meaning. Sometimes "earning a living" will be necessary to subsidize your acting classes and other career needs. In order to get started as an actor, there are many expenses besides the basic needs of food, clothing and shelter. There are classes, answering service, pictures—the expenses you need to invest in yourself. All of this takes money. If you don't have any put aside or at your disposal, you will have to earn it. This can be an enthusiastic, exciting time, like the first day of school—full of possibilities!

If you are at this stage, your focus should be on getting a job that can earn you maximum money but still allow you the time needed to work your career. What you *don't* want to do is get all involved with a job that drains your energy or demands so much responsibility that you can't leave your work at the office.

One of the best sources for job leads will be other actors. Ask them how they're making ends meet. Often, they can give you an idea of what kind of jobs are available. Like all else in your career, you must know *what you want out of this job.* If it's money, then you don't want an interesting occupation that doesn't pay well. Likewise, a well-paying job that requires a tremendous time commitment may also not be the answer. There are all kinds of jobs you can do. Some of the standard jobs are waiter, bartender, temporary office worker, cabdriver, house painter, handyman or telephone salesperson. These jobs have flexible hours, so you can adjust your schedule to your career needs. Also in their favor, you can usually find work without too much difficulty. And finally, none of these jobs is so involving in terms of commitment and responsibility. They will allow you to focus on what is important—getting your career going! It is important not to lose sight of the purpose of your "paying" job:

To Subsidize Your Acting Career Until It Can Become Self Supporting!

As you begin to get work as an actor, you will still need to have another job, since your acting income may be inconsistent. Now is a good time to consider exploring jobs that are more interesting to your personal taste.

It is at this stage that some actors begin to look for jobs that are of special interest even if the pay is lower than their previous non-acting job. For example, there are actors who work in bookstores or art galleries. The pay may not be high, but the work, the environment, fulfills a special need for the performer. It's also during this period that some working actors begin to investigate their other interests and passions. It's a wonderful time to do this. Your career is moving and the extra time you have is there to use as you wish. For example, an actor who supported himself as a carpenter began to design wood furniture as his career began to advance. He did not need the weekly paycheck from his carpentry anymore, since his acting work increased. Yet he still had free time. So he took his carpentry skills a little further and began designing and building furniture pieces.

Finally, another "job" might actually mean looking into a second career to fulfill your needs and talents.

The "make a living" questionnaire

Start now to plan your goals and needs. Having some kind of game plan will help avoid scrambling later on when your career demands a certain shift. If you know you need days off for auditions, then begin to think right now of options for night employment. More likely, you will discover that your career needs will vary. Sometimes you'll need days off, and other times you'll need your evenings. Like any other aspect of your career, planning and preparation will help maximize your chances for success. This questionnaire will help you go over some of the elements you should consider about other jobs.

1. How much money do you need to meet expenses each week or month?

2. How much time do you need to work your career each day? Each week? Each month? (Confer with your career goal list from your daily work plan. Are you taking classes? What are your time commitments?)

3. Do you need days off, nights off? What's the mix? (What will best fit your schedule. For example, if you're planning to do a lot of theater work, you will have to plan to work during the days. Does your present job allow that? Or is your job flexible enough that you can easily change hours? If not, should you consider finding another job, and how long will that take?)

3. Do you work best when you focus on one thing at a time, or are you the type who likes to work on several projects simultaneously?

4. Are your financial needs temporary? If so, how will they *change?*

5. Make a list of possible jobs. Divide them into the following categories:

· JOBS WITH HIGH PAY

· JOBS IN A FIELD THAT INTERESTS ME

· JOBS WITH FLEXIBLE HOURS

· JOBS THAT CAN LEAD TO A SECOND CAREER

(The object of this questionnaire is twofold: first, it will help you ascertain which jobs best fit your present needs. Secondly, it will help you organize your personal interests and, perhaps, the possibility of another career.)

A WORD ABOUT EGO

Taking on outside work to make ends meet is a very common situation. Sometimes actors feel embarrassed by this. They feel that they should be able to make a living from their art alone. I wish that could be more common, but the economics of the situation indicate that many actors will need to supplement their income.

There are two schools of thought as to how you should deal with your other job in terms of your career. One approach is to totally separate your "money" job from your acting career. Some performers like to keep the two separate and choose never to discuss their other "money" job. Another approach is to use your knowledge of the industry to earn an income in some other aspect of the business. I know quite a few actors who earn a living as script readers, or who take on production jobs. In either case, the point is to realize that there is no shame in having to depend on other sources of income to sustain yourself.

Some actors unfortunately see earning a living outside acting as some sort of affront to their self-esteem. This is a dangerous type of ego-trip. It depends on appearances to bolster self-worth and self-respect. If you want to keep your "money" job separate from your career, that is fine. However, do not confuse your economic needs with your self-esteem. You simply must face, and deal with, the realities of this business. You chose to be an actor—and sometimes that might mean obtaining income in another way. It happens. Get out there, earn your living and go forward with your career. Deal with the reality and keep going. Don't procrastinate, hoping for miracles. I've seen some actors who refuse to go out and get a paying job even though their funds are running low. They keep hoping to "score" and keep putting off job-hunting. The result: They become a burden to their friends—both financially and emotionally. Don't be a bum. Take responsibility for yourself and your well-being. The world doesn't owe you a living just because you want to be an actor. It might be an unfortunate situation, but deal with it like a professional and an adult. Do what you must do to keep yourself alive, cared for and respectful of yourself. Your personal dignity will come from being able to support yourself, your life and your career.

ACTORS AND OTHER CAREERS

Actors and odd jobs—they go hand in hand. But what about actors and *other careers?* It's true that beginning actors will need to make their acting careers their first priority. There's a lot to do in organizing a career and getting it underway. It must be the singular focus and the top time priority. But what about the professional actor whose career hasn't yet caught fire and who has a lot of time on his hands? Or the working actor who has a self-supporting career and desires new challenges and a way to spend his non-acting time?

Many professionals, to avoid idleness and boredom, adopt completely different professions. Harrison Ford, star of *Star Wars, Indiana Jones* and *Blade Runner,* is well known for his expert carpentry skills. Wayne Rogers is a real estate developer in his "spare time" as is Arnold Schwarzenegger. The Smothers Brothers are becoming famous for their winery. Jane Fonda has one of the most successful chains of exercise franchises and workout videos. Rod Steiger is a psychological counselor. And the list goes on . . .

Actors do particularly well in entrepreneurial enterprises. Their demanding profession, which combines selling with sensitivity and demands a thick hide to withstand rejection, makes them excellent candidates for self-employment. One of the talented performers in *Five Easy Pieces,* Helena Kallionites, discovered that her ability to bring people together turned into another career. She became the very successful owner of a private club, Helena's, that entertains the very stars she works with:

> *The supper club is an extension of my acting. I get to observe people all the time and it's a continuation of communication. Every night is living theater. You never know who the cast will be and it's always changing. It's the greatest improvisation.*

Over the years, I have met many actors who have a wide range of second careers. Actors seem to excel in such fields as design, fashion, cooking, catering, real estate, modeling, car sales, insurance, psychology, fine arts, music, construction, journalism, the esoteric arts and metaphysics—to name only a few. In fact, some actors use their acting to subsidize their second career. Lisa Freidman's first love is her painting. For her, acting is a way to finance her art with a job that doesn't take all her time and pays well. Another young, talented painter, James Mathers, makes money modeling. It not only pays well but helps to introduce him to people who might be interested in his work. Jason Miller and Sam Shepard are probably as well known for their writing as they are for their acting. And Michael V. Gazzo, the tough Italian hood of *Godfather* fame, is also a well-respected playwright best known for his play *Hatful of Rain*. Ronald Reagan used his acting career as an introduction to a "second career" in politics!

WHEN AND HOW TO HAVE A SECOND CAREER

Is it good for an actor to have a second career? Absolutely. Does it mean you'll have to sacrifice your acting? That depends on *you* and your goals.

In the early stages of your career, you will probably need another source of income to survive. But what about later, as your career begins to develop? All actors, even stars, go through stretches where they are between projects. The actor may or may not need an extra income. But they do need other interests. It is these other interests that can lead you to a second career. These interests can fill, or augment, not only an actor's financial needs but also his creative and emotional ones. I encourage performers to consider second careers, but with the awareness of how it can help, or hurt, their acting career.

ANOTHER CAREER CAN DISTRACT YOU

If you decide you've always wanted to be a lawyer and march off to law school, your acting career is probably going to get short shrift. Some careers simply are so involving that it would be impossible to develop them without giving up your acting career. This is a tough decision to make. However, it doesn't mean you have to run away from it. If another field really interests you, investigate it. Allow yourself the freedom to experiment. You may discover that your second career is really your first love.

Many of the industry's finest executives, lawyers, producers and directors started out as actors. These individuals stayed within the business and switched focus. Others discovered they enjoyed completely unrelated fields more than the entertainment industry. Should you "test your vocation"? *Without a doubt.* I feel sorry for those individuals who refuse to consider other life possibilities because they are *"afraid" they'll want to give up acting.* This is *your life*—not some kind of fairy tale. If you leave this profession, you will never know if you could have become a big star. But staying in it and foregoing another, possibly more rewarding, career to prove your fortitude is positively self-destructive. It's true that a second career can distract you, but that may be the best thing to happen in your life.

Remember: Don't Be Afraid To Let Go.

When your second career begins to take too much time and energy and encroaches on your acting career, it's time to make some decisions. If you want to switch places and make acting your second priority, fine. If not, you have to rethink your goals and readjust your priorities, putting your second career back into perspective. Be aware that there are certain careers that are very compatible with your acting career. These careers allow you to switch priorities in keeping with their demands. Artistic pursuits such as writing, painting and music allow for self-employment and a flexible schedule. The same goes for entrepreneurial or project-oriented careers. Michael Douglas, star of *The China Syndrome* and *Romancing the Stone,* is a perfect example. Known for his acting in both television and feature films, Douglas also has a flourishing career as a producer, of *One Flew Over the Cuckoo's Nest,* for example. Sometimes he chooses to both act in *and* produce a picture, and at other times he takes on one or the other job. Nowadays some of the biggest stars in Hollywood are also producers. Not only does it put the actor in control of his own vehicle but it also gives the actor a full work experience between roles.

Shelley Duvall, film actress and producer, explains it this way:

I think producing was the best career decision I ever made. And really, the first one since the acting profession fell into my lap. I did three films before realizing that acting was even a career. I didn't just decide to produce, I had an idea that evolved from my pre-acting past. I wanted to bring my antique illustrated books to life. It came out of reading. It came out of my imagination. It was fueled by my passion, and my love for chemistry. That's literal—I wanted to be a scientist since my first fourth grade science class. Now I'm a chemist, only working with creative elements. I'm also a combination of everything from my past: reader, dreamer, chemist, cowgirl, thinker, producer . . . actress.

BE IN CONTROL OF YOUR LIFE

The vital point to remember is that success in your life and career depends on your ability to continually evaluate your needs, set goals and adjust priorities.

How to Stay Sane in a Crazy Business 19

The minute you stop trying, you get work. Of course you've got to care and try, but not to the point where you drop dead if you don't get the part. I got pregnant and decided to take a year off. Suddenly, I got five jobs! If they see desperation in your eyes, they'll climb out the window to get away from you. It's like a guy—the minute you don't want him, you've got him for life. When you start putting energy into a well-rounded life, then you'll get energy back!

—Marcia Strassman,
Welcome Back Kotter,
M*A*S*H, and feature films,
The Aviator and *Soup for One*

ONCE the issue of money—of making a living—is set aside, there's the question of how to deal with the constant stress of the acting profession. Every day—365 days a year—an actor looks for acting jobs. Even when you get work, you always wonder where the *next* job will come from—and when. It's part of the career, but it can make you crazy.

This is not a profession known for constancy. Or routine. There is no set route for career advancement. No educational programs that set out your path. No "internship" that leads to guaranteed success. Each actor must find a way to deal with this exciting, yet inconsistent, career.

The most stable actors have ways to keep this constant stress from deteriorating their lives. For example, Elke Sommer is well known for her painting. Diane Keaton, Lauren Hutton and

Candice Bergen are respected photographers. William Shatner and William Devane raise horses while Jack Klugman owns racehorses. Raymond Burr collects orchids. Whether it's painting, carpentry or stamp collecting, actors who have outside interests have a focus that helps ground them during the ups and downs of their careers.

IDLENESS AND BOREDOM

The worst thing you can do to yourself or your career is to allow yourself to become idle and bored. Idleness can insinuate itself into every aspect of your life, tainting all your hard work and eroding your dreams. It can become a self-destructive energy that leads to abuse and depression. We all would love to just sit back, watch TV and wait for something marvelous to happen in our lives. But that doesn't happen. What will happen is you will lose all the initiative and verve that makes for an exciting career. As a professional, it is your responsibility to keep yourself actively participating in both the business and creative sides of this endeavor.

Keep Stimulating the Artistic Side of Your Nature.

You are an artist. You must continually be developing your craft, your artistic sensibility and your artistic understanding of the world around you. There should never be a time when you have nothing to do. There are all sorts of professional acting groups, seminars and classes that you can attend. Two younger actors were rather surprised recently when they attended an acting class where another of the students was Anne Bancroft! Ms. Bancroft certainly understands her craft, as her numerous remarkable portrayals attest. She isn't studying to learn acting but rather to continue learning. She's a professional who knows that art is an organic process that never ends. It must constantly be nurtured, attended to and allowed to develop. That is why she goes back to class—to give herself the opportunity to stretch and grow as an artist. I have met actors who think classes end as soon as you start working. They couldn't be more wrong. Whether it's taking classes, getting back on stage after a movie or performing experimental pieces and exercises, the truly dedicated actor understands that his art will suffer if left unattended. These actors usually complain that there isn't ever *enough* time to work, investigate and experiment as much as they would like.

KEEPING UP PERFORMANCE ENERGY

The fact that I'm not just an actor and that I've been writing and doing music has kept me sane. It's more difficult if you don't have something besides your acting career. The world of acting in Hollywood is removed from reality. For someone who is only an actor living in Los Angeles, it's important to find other input, other sources of energy.

—Chris Guest, *Spinal Tap*,
Saturday Night Live

When you're not working, you still have to keep in shape. Like an athlete, you need to practice. You must find activities that will help keep up your performance energy. Acting workshops and theater groups give you the opportunity to get up on your feet in front of people. If you have a bent toward writing, you can work on your own creations or try writing comedy sketches. Offer your services to writing groups to do readings of their new work. Join an improv group—that will keep you on your toes. If you enjoy singing, try your hand at putting together a nightclub act. These are only a few suggestions. The point is to find an outlet for your performance needs. One actor combined a desire to do volunteer work with her desire to keep performing and organized shows for alcohol- and drug-rehabilitation halfway houses. It kept her very busy and was extremely rewarding. As an added bonus, several newspapers heard about what she was doing and wrote some very flattering articles that helped get her name out in the professional community. It is an excellent example of a motivated artist creating her own way of finding joy in her work.

THE CREATIVE MUSE

You don't always need to be doing things related to acting to stop idleness and invoke the creative muse. Many actors turn to other artistic disciplines to help themselves develop as creative individuals. Sean Penn writes poetry. Judd Hirsch does architectual designing as another creative alternative. Painting, music, writing fiction or poetry, designing, building, creating a beautiful garden, woodworking—almost anything can become a creative outlet if you really care about it. It needn't be as serious as a second career, but simply a means of stimulating and exercising your creative nature. If your passion is sports, play them with enthusiasm. The idea here is to get up and get out. Do things with commitment and enthusiasm. That makes you alive, and being alive makes you creative. Don't drag yourself through the day. When you're not working, things can get tough.

It's precisely at this time that you have to *energize yourself.* Making a living may be necessary, but it is not enough for the creative part of your nature when you're not acting. You need to expand *creatively.*

BEWARE BOREDOM

Boredom is a true danger. Many times it stems out of idleness. It is actually a cover-up for unresolved issues like resentment and anger. When you feel bored, ask yourself why. Be ready to get honest with yourself and deal with the real stuff that's behind the boredom.

You can do something about it. You don't need to wait for something or someone to stimulate you out of your boredom.

Free yourself from that negative ennui. Get up and put yourself out there in the world. It doesn't have to be career-related, only life-related. If you have no enthusiasm, you must find out what the reasons are. People are naturally enthusiastic creatures. Don't let idleness and boredom eat away at your vitality.

KEEPING YOUR HEAD WHEN EVERYONE'S LOSING THEIRS

Working hard on a career should not be confused with overworking your career. You can't be a twenty-four-hour-a-day careerist. It just doesn't work. After a while, it becomes the law of diminishing returns. If you want to stay sane in this business, you must be careful you don't become obsessive about this profession.

Have a Life, Not Just a Career.

Actors should have more than a career. They should have a *life*. A career is only *one* aspect of an actor's total existence. Granted, it's a vital one, but even if you were never to act again you should be able to live a happy, satisfying and useful life. Somehow, we in this country have come to believe the old "starving-artist-in-the-garret" picture of the aspiring actor. True, a serious career often requires sacrifices, especially when you're first starting out. But postponing your life until you "make it" is one of the saddest decisions an actor (or anyone) can make. This is your life—now, right now. *It is not a rehearsal!* And *no* career is worth ruining your entire life.

WHEN TO PUT YOUR LIFE AHEAD OF YOUR CAREER

Once I went out of town just to be rushed back to New York by my agent for an audition. I was to read with Bobby DeNiro for director Herb Ross.

*Straight from the plane, and completely exhausted, I raced to the office.
When I got there, Herb Ross tells me to go home and rest for a bit. While
I was taking my nap, Ross hired another actor. I felt good for the nap, but
terrible for losing the job and ruining my out-of-town trip. Never again will
I drop my life to do something like that. An actor should never lose sight
of his or her own life.*

—Joe Regalbuto,
*The Associates, Missing,
Star Chamber, Honkytonk Man,
Six Weeks, Sicilians*

If you're working your career at the expense of your own life
happiness, it is imperative that you *step back and take a look at your
goals.* Sometimes the momentum of "striving" carries us off in
the wrong direction and becomes counterproductive. Take a
moment to assess your situation, your wants and needs, your
desires. Are you happy? Is your career interfering with some
other important life goal?

Sometimes I see actors shortchanging their personal lives
while waiting for career success. This not only is unnecessary
but often undercuts the performers' chances for recognition.
Why? Because when you are not happy in your *life,* your
unhappiness eventually creeps into your work. The happier
you are as a human being, the more likely you will do your best
work. A person's misery will reflect in his career. It's inevitable.
A cause-and-effect syndrome. When you are down and de-
pressed, your work begins to reflect that—less energy, less
confidence, less joy, less freedom of expression . . . If what
makes you happy is a family and kids, and you're waiting until
you're a star before you allow yourself that, you may actually
be setting up a self-defeating cycle.

THE ACTOR AND A MEANINGFUL RELATIONSHIP

When should you put your personal life on hold? Never! Actors can and deserve to have meaningful relationships. If they

desire a family, they should allow themselves to have them and devote time to them. These are life choices. And sometimes these choices may conflict with career choices. Still, denying yourself your life is *always a bad choice.* I can't find words strong enough to make this clear. It is a desperate tragedy to see a gifted performer who consistently denies personal goals for fear of weakening career ones. Granted, you will find it difficult to raise five children and still find the time to go out on commercial auditions. But if you yearn for those five kids and are still childless, no amount of residual checks will make up for the loss.

My career began to work when I got my personal life together. A good relationship can enhance your career.

—Colleen Camp

Juggling a career and an active family life can be tough. Demands vary and sometimes conflict. Again, this is where priority setting is a must. Sometimes it's simply a matter of shifting emphasis for a span of time—while your child is an infant, when your mate needs extra support. Some women performers choose to take time off from their careers to have children and be free to spend time with them during the early years. Others plan on children later, giving these women an opportunity to juggle career and personal demands more easily.

It's a matter of choice. Of knowing how to order your priorities. Oscar winner Sally Field not only made a difficult transition from a typecast TV teen to a feature-film leading lady, but in addition raised two sons of her own. She managed this feat by allowing herself to live her life. She managed it all—not without a lot of effort—because she was dedicated to her goal of being both a leading actress and an active mother.

Women aren't the only ones who need time out for their personal lives. Men are just as concerned about building a family, building a life, as women are. One actor, who was raising his two sons alone, realized that his family took precedence over his career. It was a difficult situation, but he simply had to earn money to support those he loved. He began working odd jobs here and there. He discovered that being a father to his children opened up a whole new creative world to him. He loved acting out stories to thrill and delight them. Eventually, he began to write childrens' plays and finally put all his love, acting expertise and motivation into forming a touring childrens' theater group. He took his troupe to nearby schools, where it was a hit. And gradually, it became his total source of income. His love for his family led him back to his career. An interesting footnote to this story: he got a break on a television series that was about a father raising a child—when he went to read for the part, he had certainly already done the research for the role.

TUNNEL VISION

When you set your sights on only one goal, you run the risk of tunnel vision—an inability to see what is around you. It's a risk all careerists run. You have to be goal-oriented, hardworking and persevere if you hope to succeed in your profession. Yet, you also need to allow life *in*. You need to observe and interact in order to grow. You need that to be a happy individual and a better artist. Actors with tunnel vision spend all their time on their acting. They are "deadly" serious. I put that in quotes because that's what begins to happen to their art—it becomes "deadly." It lacks a kind of vitality because the performer has ceased having real life experiences. Instead, these actors spend all their time perfecting their craft and working their career and spend no time *living*. Unfulfilled personally and uninspired artistically, these individuals are like clocks with worn-out springs—they slowly run down. Their work is flat, imitative, artificial—and so are their lives.

Don't Let Tunnel Vision Ruin Your Life View.

Take the blinders off. Let in the world. You can still keep your goal in sight *and* enjoy your life. Honest. Try it. Get involved with other people, other situations. Participate. Stop focusing only on being a success in your career and start to focus on being a *successful human being.* Analyze your priorities. Have you been giving short shrift to the world and people around you? It's like farming a field. If the farmer plants the same crop on the same field year after year, eventually the soil becomes depleted of the necessary elements for a good yield.

Instead, the farmer alternates crops on the field, which allows the soil to replenish itself. You are your own land—your own territory, if you will. Give yourself the time and the necessary life elements to replenish your life force and your creative drive.

TAKE YOURSELF OUT OF OVERDRIVE

Do you find yourself constantly pushing at your career and not making much headway? You may be in "overdrive." In an almost desperate drive to "make it," some actors begin to push their careers with such frenetic force that they actually begin pushing away the people that can help them. This type of actor is constantly on the lookout for the "break" and is almost angry when he thinks it has gone to someone else. These actors compare their careers with those of their friends and if the comparison indicates they might not be doing so well, they are quick to show their resentment. It is not long before people begin to turn off to such an actor.

If you see that you are overdriving your career, let up. It may be difficult at first, especially if you have been doing it for a while. I've noticed that some of the actors in overdrive are actually the ones who are afraid they are lazy and don't work hard enough. The result: a form of overcompensation that reaps even less benefit. Take it easy. You can still do something for your career each day. Do it quietly. If sitting and talking with other actors about who got the latest job makes you want to tear your hair out, stay away for a time. Relax. You won't get there any sooner if you keep driving everyone away!

Seeing life only through tunnel vision as you "overdrive" your career is simply no way to live. The best actors bring in the world. They experience their lives fully and with courage, rather than trying to run away and hide in a dream.

> *The more we are as people, the more we bring to our acting. If we limit ourselves, our experiences and our thinking, we can only bring the roles we play down to our level.*
>
> *It is easy in this profession to become isolated from the world and to have an unrealistic view of what the world is really like. After all, when you create a role, you are representing life. It's important to participate in the real world.*
>
> —David Morse,
> *Inside Moves, St. Elsewhere*

You must make these life decisions for yourself. What really will make *you happy?* Forget about your parents' expectations, forget about proving yourself to your high-school acting teacher, forget about all those oaths you swore to your childhood friends. They aren't important. *You* and *your happiness* are all that is truly important. Look at your life with an eye to providing that happiness and fulfillment. Look to your career for what it can give you and be realistic about what it *can't give you.* Your career cannot substitute for family, friends, love, security, life satisfaction. It can't and it shouldn't. It is *your career,* not *your life.* Your career is only *one* aspect of your life. Never lose sight of that! Of course you want a successful career with fame and fortune and you have that right. Having a strong goal is terrific. You need it to keep you motivated. But don't ever confuse your career goals for your life.

> *Your Life is Too Precious;*
> *Don't Confuse it With*
> *a Few Fleeting Moments*
> *of Career Glory*

I'm a firm believer in the "you-can-have-it-all" theory. You can be a successful careerist and artist *and* still be an alive, involved and active human being with a meaningful life and close friends and family. You don't have to trade a thing. Just keep it all in perspective and balance. Make choices. Set priorities. Be flexible. If you are, your life will be as abundant as it is meant to be.

It's hard to stay sane when you're juggling school and work and growing up at the same time. I think you have to commit to two things: your career and your personal life—but you can't mix the two or your feelings will get hurt a lot. If you put your all into a project and someone doesn't like it, you have to take it professionally, not personally. When I need time out, I spend time with people who're special to me. But the most important thing that keeps me sane is prayer.

—Kim Fields,
Facts of Life

Why Careers Stop and How to Get Them to Go   20

IF this book were being written for the British actor, there's a good chance this chapter wouldn't even be included. In England it is common to see actors performing on stage, moving to film and television and then back to the stage. British actors have the opportunity of working in all the arenas. It's not uncommon to see an actor go from playing a doctor to a murderer, from performing Shakespeare to Pinter. The public appreciates and accepts the actor as an artist. Unfortunately, this is not prevalent in the United States.

The American entertainment scene, like the American way of life, is loaded with special problems, challenges and obstacles. Some of these challenges and obstacles aren't fair. There's no doubt about it. But the fact is, they exist and a serious actor must face them.

It Takes Consideration, Will and Perseverance.

Whether you are a pro of many years or the newcomer starting out, being aware of these challenges will help you to take *action*—to move your career in the direction you want it to go and help you understand how to handle a "nothing-happening" phase.

MAKING CHOICES

Taking responsibility for yourself, your life, your career—is the only "method" for actors that work.

> —Katherine Helmond,
> *Who's the Boss?, Soap,*
> *Brazil, Shadey*

The first step to making your career move is an attitude check. What kind of choices are you making and how do you feel about them? I've observed that many well-qualified professionals actually *stop* making choices about their own career. Why? Because they've ceased to believe they have any power over their own destiny. Instead, they've allowed themselves to fall into the role of *victim*.

Stop Playing the Victim!

Too many talented, intelligent performers allow themselves to take on this role in their career. They forego control of their own destiny and instead regard themselves as the puppets of those they perceive run the industry—and their lives. It's a "them/us" mentality—with the "them" being an amorphous, nameless group of heartless industry-ites who care nothing for the artistic "us." We've all heard the catch phrases: "I don't know what 'they' want." "I'm not on 'their' A-list, so I don't get any work." " 'They' think I'm only good for TV." " 'They' know nothing about art. 'They' only care about money." Excuses for failure. This self-defeating attitude disempowers you! Give it up. There's no room for it in your career. If you do, you stand the chance of embarking on another fascinating growth period in your profession and your life.

Check out *your* attitude. Is your fear of failure allowing you to slip into the victim role so you'll have someone else to *blame* for your career? Are you really handling your career as fully as you could? Are you in control or are you being controlled? If your career isn't moving, it's time to reevaluate your goals, your plan of action, your commitment. Risk it. Take an honest look at where you are and commit to taking action.

CAREER RED LIGHTS

Even the most stellar careers have ups and downs. There are things that can grind your career to a halt. Some of the more common career snafus that we're going to look at in this chapter are:

1. Typecasting

2. Overexposure

3. Bad career choices

4. Trusting the wrong people

5. Aging

6. The self-saboteur

At some point in your career, you will face one or more of these potential quagmires, but there is something you can do to turn potential obstacles into potential power punches. Once you get into the right mind-set—the right attitude—you're ready to face and deal with these challenges.

1. TYPECASTING

There's one career snag that plagues almost every working actor in this country: typecasting.

Actors are often put into narrow categories based on looks, past work, age or personality. It's one of the reasons you won't see Clint Eastwood frolicking in many comedies. Eastwood is typecast from the "Dirty Harry" flicks and spaghetti westerns as a tough guy. It's okay for Eastwood to play a maverick cop, soldier, prisoner or Western outlaw, but—or so the theory goes—he wouldn't do as well in a romantic and/or comedic Mr. Nice Guy role. Why? Because he would be playing against his popular type. Some actors are so identified with the roles they play, like Carroll O'Connor's "Archie Bunker" from *All in the Family* or Phil Silver's "Sgt. Bilko," that audiences may find it hard to accept them in other parts.

That doesn't mean that an actor shouldn't try. Once again, understanding the evaluation of others doesn't mean you shouldn't try to make it more flexible, and/or change it. Oscar-winning actress Sally Field was typecast from her roles on television in *Gidget* and *The Flying Nun*. Not only did Field wish to change media from television to the selective feature film, she also wanted to drop her limiting image. It was difficult, but Field was determined. Gradually, her work in film, culminating with her Academy Award–winning performance in *Norma Rae,* proved that she had defeated her cutesy TV typecast image.

Whether you're a famous star or a day player who's always stuck with the same character, you have to take into account your typecasting. Is it too limiting to you? How unrealistic are your expectations? I've never met an actor who didn't truly believe he could play dozens of diverse personalities. Though that may be true, the reality of this industry is that you will probably only get work within a certain range. If you're a character actress, it's not likely you're going to be sought out to play Rob Lowe's typical love interest. But just because you are a character actress doesn't mean you have to totally forget all leading-lady roles. What you do have to do is learn how to expand your niche. To expand the way the public and the pros see you. It's necessary that you adjust your attitude. Make it your resolution—you will not be trapped.

Start Identifying With Those
Who Have Beat the System.

Robert Duvall, the well-respected star of *The Godfather, Godfather II, Tender Mercies, True Confession* and *The Stone Boy,* spent many years as a working actor before *The Godfather* made him a star. For over a decade, Duvall played numerous bad-guy parts. That was *his* type—the bad guy. Stardom afforded Duvall the opportunity to stretch out of that villain role and expand his creative horizons, playing the kind of unique leading roles for which he is now famous.

Farrah Fawcett is a key example of an actress who had to buck a typecast image in order to move her career into a more fulfilling and successful place. With the immense fame and notoriety of only one season on the popular television series *Charlie's Angels* Fawcett found herself trapped in a narrow casting image. To make matters worse, she had become a media craze. With shampoo commercials making her golden curls famous, it is no wonder that show-biz execs worried that the public wouldn't accept her in anything but the most glamorous of roles. It wasn't an easy battle. Not only did Fawcett have to combat her TV image and her print and commercial-advertising image, but also all the "newsrag" press about her personal life. She refused to be a victim of the system. It took time—and *loads* of hard work and effort—but finally it began to pay off. Fawcett's moving portrayal of a battered wife in television's *The Burning Bed* surprised audiences and convinced industry leaders that Fawcett could be more than just a pretty face. Next came the stage portrayal of a controversial character in the play *Extremities,* which led to the film version. There's no doubt that this is one lady who broke free from typecast limitations.

Jessica Lange started out as a joke, playing the damsel in distress in Dino DeLaurentis' *King Kong.* She has gone on to a remarkable career. Harry Dean Stanton has finally made it to starring roles after playing losers and misfits for over two decades.

Getting the "perfect role" that catapults you to stardom has a downside, but you can overcome that too. Finding yourself typecast is no reason to roll over and play dead. There *are* ways to remedy the situation. It may mean spending a lot of time doing so.

Today's young actors are aware of the dangers of typecasting. They don't want to get "stuck," so they deliberately pick roles that will help them expand the public's image of them. Sometimes that might mean accepting a role in television or feature films that might not pay as well as other offers or may not be as large as they're accustomed to it. In might also mean switching from film to stage. Successful, young film actors like Demi Moore, Sean Penn and Matthew Broderick are as much at home in an off-Broadway play as they are on the silver screen. These actors realize that stage will often allow them to play the kind of roles that films won't. Often, these stage roles do not pay at all. But for the actor trying to grow and expand, it is the most natural of all workplaces.

Christopher Reeves made a splash as Superman. He was perfect for the part. The film and its sequels were wildly successful. Unfortunately, his other roles have not been well received. It may be a long time before Reeves will be able to free himself from the character. But Chris Reeves continues to grow and explore his art and career as a stage actor. Rather than be stigmatized by his outstanding success, he has used his celebrity to participate in the theater.

Sometimes it's just a matter of time. Sean Connery discovered this when he tried to free himself of his "James Bond" typecasting. Again, like Reeves, Connery seemed to fit his part perfectly—too perfectly. It wasn't until Connery grew a bit older that audiences were willing to accept him in other roles.

BREAKING THE MOLD

Aside from having the right mental attitude, consideration, will and perseverance, here are some practical guidelines.

1. *Discuss the situation with your agent, manager, publicist, etc.* These people are there to help you. If they can't help or are not interested, you have to rethink the association. Listen to what they have to say and truly consider it. Are you being unreasonable in your demand to be seen another way? Sometimes actors lose an objective eye when it's about themselves. If you respect your advisors, listen to their advice. If you still disagree, seek out other support people

who might be on your wavelength. It's like getting a second or third opinion medically. Check around. Get as much input as possible to help you accomplish your goal or perhaps modify the goal.

2. *Formulate a plan to change your image.* You have to commit yourself to the follow-through. Is your image contradicting the type of role you want to play? If you're trying for sophisticated leading roles and showing up at auditions in jeans and cowboy boots, no one is going to take you seriously. Rethink your image. Is it too limiting or even counterproductive to your goals? Do you need to lose weight, restyle your hair, change the look of your clothes? Also, remember not to limit your inventory to just external aspects. What about your manner of speech, vocabulary, tone, pitch, accent—are they helping or hurting you? Once you take inventory, plot out a game plan and begin to make those necessary changes.

3. *Make the change your goal.* If you are trying to "break type," then you must commit to that. Accept acting roles that help move you out of the confining typecasts even if the part isn't large or pays as well as you are used to. This is part of career planning. It will be very difficult for people to take you seriously if you keep accepting the old typecast roles and reinforcing that image.

4. *Say no to the old parts.* This is obviously a judgment call. If you can afford to, say no to the familiar character. Send the word out that you want to do other things and that you are open to all suggestions.

5. *Keep your goal clear in your head—and work hard.*

2. OVEREXPOSURE

If you constantly fear being a flash in the pan, you'll wind up being a flash in the pan.

—Shelley Duvall

Whatever happened to . . . ? That's a question that every actor fears. Sometimes an actor can get very hot in a certain part, and then when the show is over and the public moves on, the actor discovers that he's a "has been." No one cares about him anymore. And all around, from agent to manager to studio exec, the word comes back—overexposure. You've finally arrived. After hard work and classes and auditions and off-off-Broadway plays in places that don't have working plumbing, you've finally hit the "big time." Every major talk show from Johnny Carson to Phil Donahue is clamoring to have you. All your worries are finally over, right? Wrong. You simply can't afford to get overexposed. Learn to pick and choose what you'll do, whether it's interviews, talk shows or charity appearances. If you don't, you run the risk of running out your welcome. Remember—the world is fascinated with you now. But no one can keep the public's attention for long—especially when they can see you every time they flick on the TV.

When you get in the public eye, the pressure will be intense. You'll be hounded by fans, newspapers, gossip columnists. They'll print everything you say and a lot of things you never said. That's all part of becoming famous. Some actors find the pressure infuriating. They might strike out in anger at those writers who follow them day and night. The result: a full-scale campaign about how so-and-so hates the press and is an ungrateful wretch, hates the public, and on and on. Be smart from the outset. Prepare for the pressure. Prepare for the publicity. And know how to handle yourself.

Be Smart, Be Selective and Learn to Say No.

You have to be selective if you hope to survive the heat. This is the time to have people you trust advising you. Listen to their advice, but always be true to yourself. If you want to take a part, go on a talk show, or make a public appearance, do it. Consider all your options and then follow your best instinct. Just remember that the chances are you will have to eliminate some requests. It can be hard. Most actors crave the fame, love and acceptance that being in demand offers. Actors are a generous lot and find it hard to turn people down. But you must—

sometimes. Start now to form a game plan. Look at the career of other actors who were launched into the spotlight. Begin now to gauge what is important, to formulate priorities.

IF YOU'RE YESTERDAY'S FAD, NOW WHAT?

Nothing lasts forever, including an overexposed career. Time is the great equalizer. If you have found yourself being pigeonholed because you've played the same part in the last ten TV shows and your agent says you're overexposed, what do you do? First, take a breath. Relax. Lay low while you formulate a plan. There are many avenues open to you. Sometime the answer is as simple as changing territory for a while. One television actor who found himself overexposed on nighttime television took a year's contract on a popular daytime soap. Because of his recognizable face, his agent was able to negotiate a lucrative contract, and the exposure to the daytime audience helped his recognizability and opened another market to him. After a year, not only did nighttime TV want him back, but many features were eager for his services.

Above all, don't panic. That'll just make it worse. Do some thinking. This might be the time for you to make a major change, perhaps in your physical appearance. Or perhaps it's time for you to go back to the stage, maybe do the regional theater work you've always been eager to try, or experiment with other kinds of characters and creative choices. Maybe it's just time for you to take a break. Take up painting, spend time with your family, travel. Once again, it's a matter of goal-setting and prioritizing.

I knew of one talented actor who for years talked about writing a novel, but he never had the time. Always busy on some acting project or another, he suddenly found the job offers slimming down. He didn't know what to do. He started to "try harder"—a natural enough response, but a completely incorrect one. There was nothing wrong with his auditions. He simply was suffering from a bit too much exposure. Frustrated, he told his wife they were going on vacation. They rented a little cottage out of town on a lake, and he started to write his novel. It drained some of their savings, but eight weeks later when he returned, the acting calls began coming again. And in addition, he now had an outline of his novel and some sample chapters to start peddling to agents and publishers.

The best way to handle overexposure is to prepare for it if it happens. As your career takes off and offers come in, discuss overexposure with your agent and/or manager. What parts should you accept because they show diversity? Is there a special project? Which ones should you turn down? And if you find yourself suddenly on the talk-show circuit, be selective. Look at your career from the long view. If you want your career to last a lifetime, you have to think in terms of long-range goals and objectives, as well as the more immediate goals and choices. Don't be afraid to make choices. Some will be good, some bad. But none, irreversible.

3. BAD CAREER CHOICES

The only power an actor has is the ability to say no. You've got to hold on to that and not make choices based on money, or they own you.

—Kathleen Turner

An integral part of creating a solid career is acquiring the ability to make effective, positive choices. Whether you are just starting out or are a major star, the success of your career will depend on your ability to make effective choices.

NEVER SAY NEVER

Making choices does not mean making ultimatums. Newcomers to the profession sometimes confuse "choosing" with narrowing down their options. So many times I have heard performers declare they will *never* do television, or commercials, or stage, or whatever. This isn't choosing. This is putting career blinders on! This is narrowing down your professional possibilities. This is foolish.

When you let it be known that you have eliminated different types of work, you begin to create an image of not being accessible, and gradually people will immediately pass you by for consideration of these things. You won't have to say no, because no one will even ask you. In essence, you've limited your options, your offers, and have unnecessarily limited yourself. Let's say you've declared that you will not do television, but only features. You tell your agent, manager, publicist. You discourage even discussion of these possibilities, and soon you're not even considered. Meanwhile, although your feature career is advancing well, you feel slightly limited by the studios' idea of you. You may be known for light drama or comedy but passed over for something strictly dramatic. It's a struggle, and one you are not winning. Then, one evening, you turn on the television and see a TV movie with a lead character that is just *perfect* for you. The role is dramatic and seems written just for your greatest acting strengths. This could have been the part that would have let everyone see your range, but . . . You got it. When you call your agent, he tells you that you were never even approached because everyone *knows* you don't do TV. Who's to blame? You and no one else. If you limit your options, you won't have to worry about making choices—you won't have any to make.

MAKING CHOICES: CALCULATING YOUR RISKS

Making choices in a career is about weighing the benefits between different options offered at a specific time and place in your career. Doing a stage play for no money in an off-off-Broadway theater may be a better career move than two weeks on a soap opera at a fantastic salary. It all depends on what factors are involved, what's to be gained and what your particular needs are at the time. Making career choices is about learning to take *calculated career risks.*

What is a "calculated risk"? When should you pass and when should you say yes? Obviously, there are myriad factors involved. Here are some of the more common ones to consider:

- *The role.* Start with the work. Is this the kind of role you have always wanted to play, or is it a character you have done a lot? How challenging is the part? How exciting?

- *Look for the challenging part.* As your career moves forward, you will begin to be offered more and more work with bigger and bigger roles. Terrific? Sure, but there is a danger. It is very likely that you find yourself being offered work that is no longer challenging. It doesn't matter if these parts are going to be surefire hits, if you continue to do unchallenging roles your career will eventually come to a stop. It's only logical: human beings only like so much repetition before it becomes boring. So for a while you may be all the rage, but if you don't take creative and artistic risks you'll be as in demand as last year's fad. Start now. Look for the challenge. In the long run, challenge is the only choice that consistently pays off.

- *Who will you be working with?* Are these professionals you like and respect? Have you been looking forward to working with this director, writer, producer or one of the other actors? Do you know them already or have you always wanted to work with them? Doing a small role in a Woody Allen flick may be ultimately more important to your career than playing a major role in a low-budget exploitation film.

What is the foreseeable impact this job will have on your career? If this is your first feature role, it might be your chance to break into that medium and begin to make contacts with those professionals. Perhaps this role can be used to interest producers, networks and studios in you as a different type than you've been seen as. Maybe it's just a matter of exposure—of doing a TV job so that your face will be more familiar to the public. Perhaps doing this one job can aid in establishing your reputation as a more accomplished actor. (Some actors make a point of going off to do Shakespeare and other classical plays to help round out the industry and the public's image of their ability as craftsmen.)

- *Listen to your inner voice.* What is it telling you about your offers? Will you be happy working on this piece? Is it something you *want* to do as opposed to something you feel you *must* or *should* do? Sometimes when we do things because we feel that it is the "right" thing to do and our heart isn't in it, we don't do as well as we would like. If you really don't want to do a certain piece of work, do yourself a favor and politely take a pass. No one wants you there if you don't really want yourself there. It won't be held against you. In fact, most professionals respect those individuals who have enough respect for themselves to accept a job only if they are sure they can truly commit to it.

- *Do you believe in it?* You must do work that you believe in. It's imperative. Never accept anything else. Even if the project fails, the movie's a bomb, if you believe in it, you can always still be proud of your choice. Time and again, there have been films that were not box office hits but were considered artistic hits. No one criticizes Martin Sheen because *Apocalypse Now* wasn't a box office smash. It still was a fantastic career choice, an artistic success and some of Sheen's most dazzling work.

- *The money.* The amount of money you will make is obviously a very important element. I've listed it last to emphasize that it is never the most important element. Of course, your agent and business manager are interested in your being financially successful, but when shaping a career they should and will make it clear that going "for the bucks" early may actually hurt you in the long run. It's a basic reality. If you *need* the money to support yourself and your family, then making money will have to become a top priority. But I try to encourage actors to organize themselves in such a way that this priority isn't so strong that it overrides everything else. Try to save some money so you're not always working hand-to-mouth. If you have a good year, invest it—don't spend it. And try to keep your lifestyle within reason so it doesn't become a noose around your neck. Still, with all the best advice, planning and control, the ups and downs may mean that for a while you will have to focus on earning money. If that's true for you, then go for it. But as you do, consider what steps you can take to lessen this burden.

Take all of these elements into account, along with any other factors that might be specific to you. For example, a certain role, shooting on location, would take you away from your family at an inappropriate time while another offer would mean you can stay close to them. Make a list outlining the pros and the cons. Consult with those you've hired to help you with these kind of career decisions. This is precisely the reason you have an agent and/or manager, a publicist and so on. Canvass opinion. Then weigh the evidence and decide. No one makes *all* the right choices. Even Steven Spielberg makes mistakes. But it is your responsibility as a *careerist* to take the responsibility seriously. You are the captain of your ship. You can be advised, but ultimately the decision is yours and yours alone.

EVERYONE MAKES BAD CHOICES—IT'S HUMAN

It's been said that John Travolta is the man most responsible for Richard Gere's career. How? It was the film roles that Travolta turned down that made Gere's meteoric rise to prominence possible. Gere's characters in *American Gigolo* and *An Officer and a Gentleman* were both offered to Travolta, who nixed them in favor of films that never scored. It's difficult, if not impossible, for anyone to "know" what the public will like. You have only guidelines: the script, director, producer, co-stars, etc. You weigh the elements and make your choice. Sometimes the choice isn't the right one. Obviously, for Travolta, turning down these roles might not have been the best of decisions.

If you continually make bad choices, you can do great harm to your career. Sometimes being too choosy can backfire. In your attempt to find the "perfect" role, you pass up some terrific opportunities. Conversely, some careers have had to weather the blows dealt by an actor not being choosy enough. Dudley Moore is a talented, charismatic actor. With hits like

Ten and *Arthur,* he clearly established himself in the Hollywood firmament. However, after that he played in a string of rather undistinguished flicks. It looked as if he'd do *any* part offered him. Now, however, Moore has had to become more discerning—to judge roles on their individual merit. It's a difficult balance to achieve, but you must set out now to understand your options.

No matter how carefully you make your choices, there is no guarantee that they will be the right ones. That is why it is so important for you to believe in the projects you do commit to. And ultimately, your work as an actor is judged on far more than the box office receipts. But what if you've made some really bad picks? There are no choices so terrible that they cannot be overcome. Sometimes it's just a matter of waiting it out. Like typecasting, overexposure and other career snags, overcoming bad choices has to do with your own perseverance, flexibility and willingness to learn from your mistakes. If you've made some bad decisions, what have you learned about yourself, the type of material you've been choosing, or the reasons for those ill-advised choices? Is there a pattern here? Perhaps advice from someone more objective could be helpful. If you learn your lessons, you've taken the first step in overcoming your bad choices. Put the mistakes behind you, and go forward. If you need to, reassess your goals and priorities. And then set out with confidence and perserverance.

4. TRUSTING THE WRONG PEOPLE

As soon as your career ignites, you may need a score of people to help you manage yourself. An agent, a business manager (to invest your money), a professional manager, a lawyer, a publicist—these are just a few of the people that you may need to help you manage your affairs and your career. There are stars who travel with a support staff—makeup artist, hair stylist, secretary—a complete retinue. These are the people that the star sees the most of. These are the people that are trusted for advice and guidance. It is therefore imperative that these peo ple are the "right" people. In addition, as your success in creases, you might acquire an entire coterie of people ranging from dear old friends to fans to cloying sycophants. *Who* is around you can make a big difference in your opinions and decisions.

As you move along in your career, take time periodically to look at the people that surround you. What are they like—their values, their goals, their view of the world and the business? Is their world aligned with yours? There is an old saying that you can judge a man by the company he keeps. What company are you keeping? Who are your pals? Are they the kind of people you truly like and respect? Do you trust them? Do you respect their opinions? If not, it's time to make a change.

Sometimes actors like to "hide" behind their support staff. Fearing that they aren't good businesspeople, they will give a lot of decision-making power to an agent or manager. That is fine so long as you acknowledge that *you* are responsible for what that career advisor does. I hear actors disclaim responsibility by saying things like "I would have liked to do this show, but my agent said I shouldn't." Or, "If I had known about this, I would have done it." The fact is that *you* hired *your agent,* not vice versa. If you empowered your representatives to make certain kinds of decisions for you then you must acknowledge that. If they are not making the choices you believe in, you have to correct that situation. If you are at a point in your career where you have a certain amount of success and achievement but still are not getting what you feel you deserve, it may be time to confront your career advisors. As I've mentioned when discussing representation, you are ultimately responsible for your career. Your agent works for you. If he's forgotten about you or misreads who or what you are, it's time to take the matter into hand.

5. AGING

There's something that happens as you get older. You get a little more free. You are a little braver. And you are not so insecure.

—James Garner

It happens to everyone—whether you're Robert Redford, Brooke Shields or Phyllis Diller. We all age. For some actors it poses a particular threat to their careers. For others, a welcome respite from "ingenue" typecasting. Child actors go through an awkward stage before adulthood when they often seem unemployable. Stars known for their youth and beauty—the romantic leads in the business, like a Bette Davis—must switch gears as the years rearrange their physiques. For some, aging is a devastating occurrence—both personally and professionally. It needn't be.

In our culture there are some clearly unpleasant attitudes toward aging. That cannot be denied. Nonetheless, there *are* benefits to aging if dealt with in a positive and creative manner. Aging is inevitable. For those who do not fight or deny the natural process, aging can provide for them an expansion of options in their career.

Gifted character-actor Donnelly Rhodes discovered that aging a bit opened up an entire new range of characters for him to play. With strong features and jet black hair, Rhodes' looks made him perfect casting for the tough mean guy. He worked this type of character a lot and was well respected for it. But it wasn't until he got a little older that he got the opportunity to play more benevolent roles and more sympathetic characters. As he aged, his hair turned gray, significantly softening his looks. Rather than cling to what had worked for him in the past and force nature away by dyeing his hair, Rhodes allowed his natural aging process help diversify and heighten his career.

There are four distinct age ranges professionally for the actor. These are:

1. Child;

2. Ingenue for women; younger leading man for men;

3. Leading lady or man;

4. Character actor.

As an actor ages, he naturally passes into the next category. Sometimes, however, an actor tries to fight this transition, and aging becomes a serious problem. There are some people who do seem to fight the transitions. Cary Grant was a leading man till he died. Elizabeth Taylor will also remain a leading lady due to her larger-than-life image. They are exceptions. But most actors cannot defy this process, and desperately trying to only makes it worse.

Everyone has a pet theory about Marilyn Monroe. Here's mine: she was having a difficult time handling becoming older. Monroe had built an image based on youth and glamorous beauty. Although she struggled to diversify in her acting classes, she was America's sex symbol and was frightened of letting go of that image. As she got older, she began to feel her power eroding. So defined, she was terribly unhappy and finally died escaping the future.

In contrast, look at the career and development of diversified star Angela Lansbury. From a sexy, blond tart in *Notorious* to Mrs. Lovitt in *Sweeney Todd* to her starring role in the TV series *Murder She Wrote,* Lansbury consistently displays a comfort with herself, her age and where she is in her life. It's a joy. Lansbury has done more for women and the subject of agism then all the magazine articles and books discussing the subject. As the years have passed, she has seamlessly moved from one type to another, consistently altering her image to maximize the process.

Because of society's pressure for women to be young and beautiful, some actors have trouble making the adjustment. It is a tragedy to observe a woman unable to make these age transitions with dignity. I have spoken to women professionals who have totally stopped their career because they refuse to face the reality of their age. When you are sixty, trying to look like a leading lady can be limiting and foolish. You won't work because there simply is not that much work for glamorous grandmothers. But take off the makeup and allow your hair to grow out to its natural gray, and it will open up an entire new selection of roles.

Ultimately, it gets down to coming to terms with yourself. If you, like Marilyn Monroe, have hinged your identity on your youth, than aging is going to be a monstrous problem. Through counseling or discussing it over with your professional advisors and friends, you can find a way to make this life transition joyful.

6. THE SELF-SABOTEUR

I've known performers who are fantastically talented yet never work. At first, I simply couldn't understand why these individuals are passed over. Could it really be just a streak of rotten luck? Gradually, however, I began to realize that sometimes it is actually the actor who is sabotaging himself. Whether it's not getting a new picture, or not arriving on time for auditions, self-defeating behavior is often responsible for an actor's lagging career.

Do you sabotage yourself? Almost all of us do from time to time. It's important to become aware of your own peculiar self-sabotage techniques. It is the first step to disarming them.

Your self-sabotage techniques aren't hard to find. Just take a look at what element consistently makes your career stumble. Maybe you need new pictures, but you never get around to making an appointment with a photographer. Or it might be that you are consistently late to appointments. Or perhaps every time you are ready to do some acting work, other things suddenly intrude and divert your attention. These habits aren't hard to find, but they are hard to stop. After all, they are what keeps you from moving ahead into unknown territory. And though failure may be a drag, it is familiar. Stop procrastinating, stop sabotaging yourself and start acting successful.

THE GRASS-IS-ALWAYS-GREENER MENTALITY

Are you undermining your career by undermining your achievements and progress? We all have a tendency to discount what we have and, instead, look to someone else's life and career with a jealous eye. It's good to have ambitions and goals for which you are ever striving. But always wishing you were somewhere else, had something else, is one of the ultimate self-defeating cycles you can get into. Stop it. Where you are *now* is where you should be. Accept that. Be proud of your achievements and progress and work from there. Spending valuable time and energy wishing you had something else is a total waste of time. Everyone's life is different. Each career has its own strengths and weaknesses. If you are constantly looking at others, you will drive yourself right out of the business. You can always find those who are far worse off than you and, of course, those whose careers seem totally blessed. So forget it. Instead, focus on you, your life and your career and get on with living it! Success has its own timetable. Sometimes that can be very frustrating.

Joe Mantegna had a productive and consistent career in theater in Chicago. He then came to Hollywood and, for a number of years, had trouble getting work. He returned to the stage to do *Glengarry, Glen Ross* on Broadway and received a Tony for best actor. Since then, he has claimed a successful film career and is very much in demand. He saw the "slow days" of his career this way:

When things weren't going well, I never ever felt I didn't belong. I never felt I was in the wrong ballpark. I always reminded myself to be patient and to persevere. When things started to go for me, it was a dovetail effect. One thing led to another and the past came around. Paying dues pays off. The work I did in the past was the best thing I ever did because I learned how to become an actor and my peer group came into power. David Mamet and I met back in the early days of my Chicago theater career, and later he gave me my big break. Lots of my pals from then are doing great things—Greg Mosher, Dennis Franz, Meschad Taylor, etc.

KEEPING UP WITH THE EVER-CHANGING EXECUTIVES

One evening, I met a well-respected actor whose work I've admired for many years. He told me he had been thinking of leaving the business. Here was a working actor—a man who had made his lifelong living from his artistic career and he wanted to quit. I was shocked. He told me how embarrassed and angry he had been at a recent audition/interview.

The casting director was all of twenty-six years old and had no idea of any of the work this man had done. Here he was, this professional artist who had twenty years of work behind him, being interviewed by a "child." This casting executive was in the position of deciding whether or not the actor would be seen for a role by the director and producer. The seasoned pro was furious and he let it be known, leaving the casting exec with a none-too-warm impression.

I can understand his frustration, his annoyance. I think it was terrible that this casting person did not take the time to research the actor she was to interview, to become familiar with his work. Yet, what did this actor prove by being indignant? The fact is, the business is constantly changing. New people come each year, and others leave forever. It's the influx of new talent and ideas that keeps this industry ticking. Just because new executives don't have the years of experience that you have doesn't mean they are the enemy. Clearly this actor was mixing pride with business. Surely his reputation should be acknowledged, yet why is he suddenly "above" meeting new people and continuing to win them over? This man was allowing his pride to make him choose *leaving* the work he loves. He wasn't "stroked" by a young newcomer. If that isn't self-defeating, I don't know what is.

Changes are constantly happening. One day, the secretary you once knew becomes the casting director. The gofer around the office, a director. It's the way of this business. It is up to you to continue your relationships with these people and to continue to form new ones. Don't let false pride and bitterness stand in your way.

When to Quit 21

THERE isn't an actor alive who hasn't wanted to give it up. The acting business is tough. And perhaps there will come a time when getting out is the answer—whether temporarily or permanently. Many performers have stayed in long after they ceased to enjoy the profession. Maybe because our culture says it's bad for someone to quit. This is absurd. I think it is better to quit than to be unhappy for the rest of your life. Sometimes, in fact, quitting is exactly what you need to do to *get back on track*. I've seen performers who have left the "business," only to return later. The break gave them a chance to explore themselves and other interests. With newfound confidence and accomplishments, they returned to acting and did well. The big question is *when*—when is it enough, when to call it quits—and *how*.

LETTING GO

From early childhood we are taught that quitting isn't right. As the old saying goes, if at first you don't succeed, try, try again.

Persistence *is* a virtue but not when it is ruining your life. The fact is that persistence alone will never turn the tide in a thwarted career. You can hang around until you're eighty, but if you're not feeling good about the acting profession, you're not going to make it. Sometimes performers refuse to give up on their career because of *pride* rather than drive. They are afraid they'll be seen as failures if they drop out of the acting world. Stubborn pride and the fear of looking like a failure feed their persistence. It's terribly difficult to communicate positive, exciting feelings when you're motivated by such negative ones. It becomes a vicious cycle. The joy for the business is gone and only a type of suffering remains. The actor in this situation feels invalidated. Self-confidence turns to self-pity. Strength turns to anger and sometimes even paranoia with the belief that "everyone's against me." Many actors stop their careers to release themselves from this sort of angst. After years of constant and deliberate focus on their work with no joy, they find themselves at a standstill. They also come to terms with the realization that their temperament does not mix with the workings of this career.

If that's happening to you, maybe it's time to let it go. Set yourself free from suffering. If an acting career was meant to happen, you will return. If not, take what you've learned from this profession and apply it to another. Reorient your life. Believe me, it is no failure to decide to let go. Ask any of the many successful directors, writers, producers and studio executives who began their careers as actors. Directors like Sydney Pollack *(Tootsie* and *Out of Africa)* and Mark Rydell *(On Golden Pond)* abandoned acting to follow careers in directing. Theater and film writer David Mamet studied acting in New York but soon turned to writing, using the skills and insights from his acting classes to create the type of dynamic characters and terse dialogue that is so key in his work. There are many studio executives and producers who were once actors: Robert Evans, former head of Paramount Pictures and producer of many films, including *Chinatown;* Sherry Lansing, former head of 20th Century Fox Studios, and producing partner of Jaffe Lansing Productions; Leslie Moonves, president of network development for Lorimar-Telepictures; and Mary Goldberg, vice president in charge of casting and talent for United Artists and former agent and casting director, who explained:

> *I quit acting because it wasn't something I had to do anymore. I just didn't need to do it. Maybe it was the reason I wanted to be an actor and that reason had changed. I'm glad I realized it and didn't wait till it had become a lifetime commitment.*

These are just a few of the successful careerists who can attest to the fact that letting go of acting was no tragedy. They are fulfilled in their work and are surely glad for what acting taught them. The real tragedy is not allowing yourself to change and grow. Put yourself in an arena where you can feel enthusiasm, appreciation and success again.

WHEN NOT TO QUIT

> *If enough people that I respect told me that I wasn't good, I'd quit. But so far no one has, so I struggle through it all. The truth is I'm not good at anything else, and I love acting. When I feel the most discouraged, that's when I work the hardest. Throwing yourself into the obsession of your creativity gets you away from your depression.*

—Suzanne Kent, *Nuts, Taxi, St. Elsewhere, Mass Appeal*

When things go wrong, we all are inclined to doubt that they'll ever work out, but that doesn't mean you should abandon your goals. Here are some situations when you should *not quit*, though you might want to:

- You've just finished auditioning and you notice the producer, director and execs are laughing hysterically at your rendition of Hamlet.

- The kid in acting class, whose entire talent could fit on the head of a pin, has just gotten the second lead in a feature film.

- Your rent is due, and the landlord hates the theater.

- Your headshots, the ones you've just spent five hundred dollars on, make you look remarkably like a Saint Bernard.

- You haven't had an audition in six months, unlike your roommate, who averages three a week.

- You call your agent only to discover he went out of business two months ago.

- You finally get an audition for a Broadway musical and in your enthusiasm to sing and "move well" you fall off the stage into the orchestra pit.

- The only one who wants to make you a star also wants to give you a back rub in his/her apartment.

Of course, these situations sound funny but they seem like good reasons to quit when you're doubting yourself. All actors get low and feel it isn't worthwhile. However, don't make decisions when you're in the midst of experiencing a setback or a disappointment. Your judgment is affected by your negative emotion. A decision as important as switching career goals should be made as objectively as possible.

I wanted to do it all. So for seven years I tried. Then I realized I couldn't do it all, so I decided to give it all up. I went to a career counselor to find something new. His advice—Stay in show business! I couldn't bear it, so I went to Arizona to work at my uncle's family style restaurant. After my first day in the kitchen, I decided I didn't want to learn Spanish as my first language and wanted out, but my uncle persuaded me to give it a try for a few more weeks. On my second day at work, my agent called with an audition appointment. Over the telephone, I auditioned and got the part. I quickly ended my restaurant career.

—Howard Stevens, ACTOR/
COMEDIAN, HOST of
Friday on Sunset

Sometimes all that is needed is some time and an outlet to blow off some steam before you go back into the fray of battle.

Theater legend has it that when Maureen Stapleton and Eli Wallach were first starting out in New York, they would "make the rounds" of agents and auditions together. Every day they would meet and spend the day looking for work—unsuccessfully. As they walked home together, they would complain about the business and the impossibility of ever getting work and that they might as well just quit. About that time, they would reach the street corner where they would separate and each go to their own apartments. They would stand at the corner for a few seconds, ending the harangue about the hopelessness of the profession, and then, before parting, agree on what time they would meet the next day to go back on the rounds. Find a friend to commiserate with. Sometimes it helps just to know you aren't the only one going through it.

WHEN TO QUIT

Every actor has down times—times when there are no auditions, no work, nothing. It can be very discouraging, but that might not mean you should quit. How, then, will you know when you should move on? Here are some guidelines:

1. *Do you still like the work?* If you don't enjoy the work anymore, you should move on to something else. There are actors who dislike the *work.* Somewhere along the way, the fun went out of acting for them, and now they proceed just because they are afraid to try something else. The money can be a hook, but more often this type of performer doesn't have confidence that there is something else which will make them feel enthusiastic and successful again. This is the most basic criterion for deciding whether to stay or go. If you've lost your love for the art itself, you've lost the most primary of career motivations. Don't stick around for money or fame. They are empty rewards and not the kind on which you should base a life. Ask yourself whether you would enjoy acting even if I were to tell you that you will never make a living at it. Would you still be willing to

volunteer? Is there some other career that captivates you more? Listen to your heart. What does it tell you is your top priority. Don't be the kind of actor who leaves the business out of a childish spite. This person loves the work, loves the art, loves the craft but, angry over feeling shortchanged on the success level, chooses to punish the world and himself by quitting. The actor isn't leaving to go toward something; his intention is only to punish himself and the world for being so unfair.

2. *What is your pattern: Do you usually bail out or do you stick around to the bitter end?* Some people habitually quit too soon. Discouraged by the first failure, they throw in the towel and move on to something else—often, without much more success. On the other hand, there are those who will hang around in a situation long after it could possibly be worthwhile. Which are you? If you generally get scared off by the first disappointment, perhaps you might want to consider the kind of effort and resilience that really is necessary to make something work. For you, devising a long-range plan of action may be necessary. A plan that includes a certain end date and goal to be accomplished before deciding to quit. This is one way to insure that your leaving isn't just a fearful reaction to rejection.

If you are the type who *never* gives up—the one who stands on the baseball diamond waiting to bat when everyone else has gone home—you might want to ask yourself: what is keeping me in these hopeless situations? Could it be that you feel safe in hopeless situations because you are afraid of success? Or maybe you are afraid your leaving would look like desertion or cowardice? Review other similar hopeless circumstances—how were they finally resolved? Perhaps it really is time for you to consider other options.

3. *Analyze the pros and cons of quitting.* You can't make a solid decision without solid facts. Before you take action, sit down and take inventory. Make two lists: one listing all the reasons for leaving and the other listing the reasons for hanging in there. Examine the consequences of quitting.

Then, consider what you might gain/lose if you formulated another long-range plan to continue your acting. Be frank. Ask yourself how much you are getting out of the profession versus how much you are putting in. Is the effort worthwhile? On the other hand, has your effort been rather shabby? Look at the situation and the ramifications from all possible angles and all possible scenarios.

4. *Investigate other options.* It's difficult to leave a profession if you have no idea what you'll do next. Now is the time to take a look at your other options. A lot of actors move away from acting to another area of the business. The transition from actor to writer and/or director is a natural-enough progression. The only drawback of those professions is that they are just as insecure and competitive as trying to formulate an acting career. Yet many actors find the specific demands of these other disciplines easier to cope with. There are also other types of jobs within the industry. Production, script development, administration, even casting—this industry has a plethora of very interesting, lucrative and creative careers. Investigate. Ask questions. Learn all you can about those areas that interest you.

When taking inventory of your options, don't limit yourself to just the entertainment industry. What other interests or hobbies do you have? When you list all your possibilities, let your imagination run wild. You might not know *right this second* what your next career should be. It might take some contemplation, investigation and exploration. Start with allowing yourself to list *all* areas that are interesting to you, even if you can't think of a specific job in that field. One actor really enjoyed programming on his home computer in his spare time. As time went on, he came to realize that he wanted to leave acting but felt he had nowhere to go. At first, he just started looking into the normal type careers in computing, his hobby, but found nothing that he felt he could commit to. Then, suddenly one afternoon, he got the idea to offer his programming skills as a consultant to theaters. The idea took off and branched into all other types of computer-consulting jobs.

5. *Consider feedback from those close to you.* Only you can decide what you should do with your life and career. But sometimes it is difficult for us to get an objective picture of ourselves. Getting feedback from the people whom we trust to give us an honest appraisal can be a tremendous help. Ask your friends, family, anyone that you feel will be straightforward, to give you some feedback on what type of career skills they think you should emphasize. Remember—this is only useful if you ask people you trust and respect. Really *listen* to what they have to say even if it isn't what *you want to hear.* Colleagues can often see aspects of your personality that you take for granted.

6. *Make a decision but give yourself a waiting period before you carry it out.* After you have done all your exploring, etc. and made your decision, *wait.* Giving yourself a waiting period before taking action gives you an opportunity to get used to your new commitment. If it's to give acting another go, then formulate a plan of action that you will evaluate in a month. If it is to leave, don't take drastic action until you've gotten used to what this decision really means.

DON'T QUIT—LET GO

It might be just a matter of semantics, but words like "quitting" or "giving up" conjure up images of failure. I don't think leaving one career for another can ever be considered failure. It's life. You are participating in your life, which means you are flexible enough to make changes when what you have been doing isn't giving you what you want. I like to think of this process as letting go. Letting go of what is not working in your life so you can make room for what will work. If you want to leave acting, let it go—don't quit or give up.

HOW TO LET GO

If you decide to let go of acting, the first thing you must do is *nothing!* That's right. Usually, when performers decide to leave acting, they feel they must make some type of drastic break. This can backfire. Remember:

Do Not Act on Impulse!

Resigning from the acting unions that it took years to gain entrance into is foolish. Dramatic acts of breaking away usually feel good for the first few days. But later on, you leave yourself open for a lot of regrets when the excitement of being a non-actor wears off. Give it some time. If a year or so passes and you still have no intention of returning to acting, then it might be appropriate to go on the inactive list.

Ultimatums are for children, not for the wise careerist. Life is far too complex for you to ever be sure that a decision will remain permanent. Another quirk of life is that you never can be sure when you will need the associations you made while an actor. Therefore, it is imperative you remember this rule:

Don't Burn Your Bridges Behind You.

It isn't necessary to take out an ad in the trade papers announcing your decision to let go of acting. Frankly, no one really cares except you and perhaps your mother. The rest of the world can find out as you go along. If you are intending to make a career shift, start gradually. It's a *big* life change and you shouldn't rush the process. Take it step by step.

Begin by making inquiries into possible alternative careers. This is a time for you to take stock of your goals and priorities. If you've made the decision objectively and rationally, and not on impulse, you already should have some idea what direction you want to go toward. Just as you did in the beginning of this book when you plotted out your goals and priorities as an actor, do this now with your new career goal in mind.

Test the waters. Take time to gauge your reaction. And then proceed. It's a step-at-a-time process. Changing careers can be a marvelously exciting experience, but it won't be carefree. Even if being an actor made you miserable, it *was* familiar, and the familiar is sometimes hard to give up. Be prepared to feel a bit like a fish out of water. It'll take time for you to fully develop all the skills your new career requires. Be patient.

Don't expect your career to take off overnight. It will take the same kind of patience and diligence your acting career required. Be ready for the challenges. You can handle them.

YOU CAN ALWAYS COME BACK

I have seen actors who swore they would never return to acting come back. Sometimes this hiatus can give a performer a new lift. Knowing that you are in control of your life—that you can leave acting when you want to, sometimes renews the strength and resolve needed to keep on plugging forward as an actor. When you've been working very hard on your acting career and getting nowhere, you lose confidence. Then acting becomes more than your profession—it becomes your obsession. Everything turns on this thing and it's not giving you anything back. The obsessive actor is not relaxed, finds no contentment or joy in the profession. Often, you can't sleep or relax. You feel defeated. Disappointed. So, finally, you leave. You try other things. Perhaps you evolve into another career at which you are successful. Then, one day, you feel the urge to act again. To act for the sake of acting. It's no longer the symbol by which you judge your identity, success or failure. It's something you love to do. So you return. And the second go-round is entirely a different experience. A lovely experience. I have known so many actors for whom this has been the experience. They needed that time away to renew and refresh themselves, perhaps just to get a little perspective, make some money and create a little security and self-confidence.

If you want to return, there will always be space for you to start up again. Some actors do much better later on, when they cross into another age category. As we've mentioned earlier, child actors often find a difficult period between childhood and adulthood when there isn't a lot of work for them. This is the time to focus on other things. Then, when you feel the time is right, come back. Take time and devise your plan of action. Use the earlier chapters to focus on a work plan that fits you, and begin. That's all it takes. Intention, commitment and action.

'There's more to life than acting''

Felice Schachter
Facts of Life and *Zapped*

Doesn't it feel good to know that you are in control of your life choices? Once *you* take responsibility for your fate, life has a way of making it all work for the best. Acting is a love affair. If the relationship is unrequited and tearing you apart, you have to let go. But as the saying goes, true love will always find its way back home. Trust in that.

Don't Be Your Own
Worst Enemy 22

JOHN Belushi, Marilyn Monroe, Freddie Prinze, Judy Garland. What did all these performers have in common?

Fame
Money
Talent
Substance Abuse
Death

These incredibly gifted people destroyed their lives, and there are hundreds of other Hollywood tales about drugs and alcohol. Some are casualties. All are tragedies.

There is simply no way that you can continually assault your body and jeopardize your health and well-being and maintain a successful career. It's impossible. One need only listen to the counseling of such diverse celebrities as Sid Caesar, Liza Minelli, Richard Dreyfuss, Stacy Keach, Jr., Jerry Lewis, Richard Pryor, Jason Robards, Rod Steiger, Tony Curtis, Shecky Greene, Grace Slick, Chevy Chase and Elizabeth Taylor to understand the heavy price substance abuse extracts from the individual. There's no soft way to put it—*it will ruin your life, your career, your dreams, your hopes and your happiness.*

It took a while for us to wake up to the fact that this country has a tremendous drug problem that is taking its toll in every school, on every street corner, in the halls of executive suites, among television and film stars, singers, government offices, everywhere . . . Let's face it. For a long time, drugs were chic. It's only now that we see that a price was paid. The entertainment industry, like most other industries and organizations in this country, is waking up to the fact that drugs ruin lives. A college education, a hefty income, a beautiful family, a fabulous career—none of these is strong enough to assuage the damage that drugs can do to a human life. Be aware. Be smart. Don't be fooled.

YOU DON'T HAVE TO DIE TO RUIN A GOOD THING

The untimely death of a great talent is shocking. What is even more shocking are the walking dead—those whose lives and careers crumbled because of their self-destructive behavior. It is insidious.

You're a young actor just beginning to "make it" into the "big time." You're invited to parties. It's social and wild and there's lots of attention. You almost feel immortal.

Life in the fast lane can be very seductive. If your career begins to take off, you will suddenly have to cope with a tremendous increase in emotional stress and with increasing demands on your time and attention. People will notice you. You'll be invited to parties. You'll meet the celebrities you revered as a kid. You'll be "hot," "in"—a star. Money will be available. There will be people who want to wait on you—court you—flatter you. It can be wonderful. And it can also be deadly. I'm no moralist. And I'm not here to debate the ethical reasons for a drug-free life. Frankly, that's for you to decide.

What I am telling you is that from a very *practical* side, *drugs can ruin the good career you've worked so hard to create.* Drugs can, and they will.

There's an actor here in Los Angeles who is a very talented man. A few years back, this fellow met a number of well-known stars. He had access to drugs and quickly became the go-between for stars and their drug deals. He made quite a bit of money and developed a drug habit himself. Everyone in town knew him. Not as an actor, mind you, but as the drug dealer who could get you anything you wanted. Eventually, it all caught up to him. The drugs he supplied to the stars got him in trouble with the law. His own habit was taking a toll on his health. He realized he had to give it all up. He did. It took time but he kicked his own habit. He stopped dealing and got a regular job. Then, he tried to come back to his career. But no go. Although he's shaken his connection to drugs, his reputation is still suffering.

LET THE GOOD TIMES ROLL

Good times? I never had any good times drinking. I wasn't that type of drinker. I would only drink to destroy myself. It was much easier to drink than to commit suicide with a gun or a knife or pills.

—Shecky Greene, COMEDIAN

Drugs may be obvious dream destroyers, but there is another danger that may not always seem so dangerous. In our culture, drinking is a socially acceptable thing to do. In many cases, it even appears the sophisticated and adult thing to do. On television, in movies, in literature, there has always been the romantic image of the soulful, artistic drinker. But I guarantee you that it is a false picture. A lie. Hear the account of any recovering alcoholic, attend any meeting of Alcoholics Anonymous, and you will discover how truly black that picture really is.

Less common is the drug actor, more common is the drunk actor.

Drinking can be a very silent, very secret form of abuse. You can drink in private. It's not terribly expensive and drinking is legal. It's a habit that can sneak up on you and overtake your life. There are all sorts of drunks, not just the fall-down, get-silly, slurry kind. There's the one-drink, but boy-do-I-have-to-have-that-drink, drinker. There's the two-martini lunch exec. The woman for whom booze can bolster her doubtful self-esteem. There's the performer who needs to drink before auditions, or the one who knocks back a couple of shots after the stress of a long show or a hard day.

One inspired comedienne from a popular comedy improvisation group told me of the intense pressure she began to feel before performance. The spontaneity of improvisation made the group popular, but the insecurity of the night's "scripts" was taking a toll. It was common practice for this particular actress to sip a few glasses of wine while putting on her makeup. The group was successful, and this comedienne was well respected for her work, but something was missing. The wine was becoming a habit and a red flag to this actress. Her best friend, and the group's artistic leader, told her they were concerned about this habit of mixing wine and performance, and were worried about where it might lead. She told her talented friend:

It is Better to be a Failure, Sober, Than a Success, Drunk.

This woman recognized the wisdom of these words and promptly cut it out. Now, years later, she is so grateful that a potentially dangerous habit was nipped in the bud. She still performs on stage, and often improvisationally, and she does it straight and with the confidence from her ability and not from a bottle.

THE REPUTATION LIVES A LONG TIME

I've been in casting sessions where an actor's name comes up and instantly, the discussion turns to his reputation for substance abuse. Studio and network executives aren't interested in legislating morality, but they are afraid that performers associated with drugs and drinking simply won't be able to do the job for them. Whether the day-to-day strain of a television series or the enormous strain of millions riding on a feature film, the performer with the problem is a bad risk. Word gets around. So-and-so showed up stoned on the set. So-and-so looks terrible becaue of all the late "party" nights. So-and-so can't memorize lines because their brain is fried from drugs. Once the reputation is created, it is almost impossible to clean it up. It takes only seconds to create the bad rep, but sometimes years to reverse it.

ANOTHER CAREER ASSASSIN: BAD BEHAVIOR

Another thing studio and network executives aren't interested in is an actor's reputation for bad behavior. Offensive, rude, insulting actions and attitudes will eventually not be tolerated. At first, an actor may seem to get away with it. They're "indispensible." But ultimately, no one is.

There are well-known horror stories of stars on the set treating people in the worst way. Abuses of the support staff, flagrant disregard for human feelings, lack of decorum and politeness. Abusive big shots who flaunt and flog people with their celebrity power. Monsters. Their demands exceed all conceivable bounds and they expect people to fulfill all sorts of neurotic emotional needs and sometimes even perform sexual favors. Their indiscretions and inconsiderations fill books and gossip magazines. Their reputations precede them on a set. And what is worse, they get away with it! But not forever. And when their popularity wanes, their past sins come back to haunt them. There are a few once-famous actors whose bad behavior ensured them a place on the unemployment lines once they were no longer popula₁

Be Kind to Those You Meet On the Way Up; They're the Same Ones You'll Meet On the Way Down.

But you don't have to be a major star to gain a reputation for being a jerk and to jeopardize your career. Sometimes actors get the misguided notion that once they are working, they are allowed to be "difficult"—that in some way, the artistic nature of their work allows them to treat people in a rude or mean way. Unfortunately, I have often observed working actors treating crew and support staff on a job with meanness and inconsideration that is simply not allowable—not permissible—under *any* circumstances. No one wants to work with such a person. And it doesn't take long for word to get out about you. You will make enemies. People will resent you. After a while, it will kill your caree₁.

This doesn't mean that you can't speak up for yourself. It doesn't mean that you have to be a doormat, allowing anyone and everyone to walk over you. Sometimes actors get a reputation for being "difficult," but that is a compliment! They are difficult because they demand a lot of themselves. They have high criteria by which they judge themselves and their work. They will not settle for inferior quality, and they expect the same from those around them. Many working actors, not just stars, are respected for their demanding approach to their craft. Other craftsmen feel challenged when working with these dedicated artists. This kind of actor will continue to investigate the character, to invent different interpretations, to question and seek out the best they have within them. Sure, they are difficult and demanding—that is what makes them so good. But they are not *mean* and *rude.* These actors treat those around them, whether the producer or the gofer, whether the harried receptionist or the director's assistant, with the same respect and dignity that any individual deserves.

Talent is Never an Excuse for Bad Behavior.

It is a matter of following the Golden Rule: do unto others as you would have them do unto you. It counts a lot. Actors who are dedicated *and* respectful of others are a joy to work with. And they will continue to get work. While the others—those who inflate themselves with a sense of self-importance that makes them feel above the rest of mankind—will soon discover themselves acting alone, all alone.

WHAT KIND OF HUMAN BEING AM I?

At some point, each of us must come to terms with the human being we've become. How do you fare in your own eyes? I've seen so many people lose themselves in their obsessive drive for fame and fortune. It's not worth it, and it's not necessary. You can be a success without having to sell your soul or turn into an insensitive monster or kill yourself with alcohol and/or drugs. You can have the kind of life you want without all that. What you need first and foremost is your own code of honor to live by. You must decide for yourself who you are and who you want to be. Not by my rules or your next-door neighbor's. Not by what's allowable under the law or by what you can get away with. But by your personal ethics. You must create your own integrity, and ultimately you must answer to it.

Being an actor is a gift. It is a talent, an art, beautiful and impacting. An artist's soul is a delicate commodity. You must tender it well. It is you to whom we look to see life reflected, human emotions displayed, behavior explained. It is on you, the artist, that we depend for your sensitive interpretation of the life around us. To be an actor is a tremendous joy and a tremendous responsibility. As you grow more and more successful in your career, there will be ever-increasing pressures. It *is* a tough business and a difficult profession. Remember, this is a collaborative art, and you are part of the framework. If the part you play is flawed, the entire effort might be ruined for all involved. When you become a successful performer, you are a role model for great numbers of people. There is a great deal of responsibility that comes with it.

You must recognize the seduction of these things. Sure, you are the star so you can yell at the set decorator or the hairdresser and get away with it. But should you? Of course not. Should you pollute your body with dangerous chemicals that alter your perceptions and behavior—that cause you to live a life of delusion and, even worse, could set an example for those who look up to you? Of course not. At some point, you must decide for yourself exactly who and what you are. You can be the biggest success in the world, but if you are a failure as a human being, you have lost everything.

The Working Actor 23

*When Ingrid Bergman told Alfred Hitchcock a scene was
difficult for her to act naturally, he told her, "Fake it." She
said it was the best advice she ever got. He told me in*
Shadow of a Doubt, *when I asked him how to play a
scene: "Don't act. Let the camera do the work." But if
anyone should ask me how to succeed in acting (which they
haven't), I would answer, "Just keep working!" Take any
job you can get that's related to acting. Little theater,
off-Broadway, summer stock, you name it. Me, I'm doing a
soap opera for 20 years and anything anybody offers
me—that's a good part.*

—MacDonald Carey,
*Days of Our Lives, Shadow
of a Doubt, Streets of
Laredo, Dream Girl,
Lady in the Dark,
Anniversary Waltz*

WHEN Beatrice Straight won an Oscar for her wonderful performance in *Network,* she became a star overnight. At least,
that's how the public perceived it: to them, she suddenly appeared on the scene. The fact is, Beatrice Straight enjoyed a
sound career as a working actor for many years before *Network*
and *Poltergeist.*

Working actors may or may not be known to the public. They
are often stage actors from New York, Chicago, Boston or other
regional theaters. They are the "character" performers we see
time and time again in movies and television, playing a wide

variety of roles. These working actors have made a lifelong commitment to their craft and their careers. They support themselves, although the income may vary greatly from year to year. They've learned to invest their money wisely to carry them through lean periods.

In the down time, they might return to theater to keep growing, even though theater traditionally pays less. The splendid Irish actor, Milo O'Shea, known for both his work on stage and in motion pictures, explains:

> *To be a member of a profession you have to serve your time. That is why so many Irish and English actors return to the theater in between sessions in television or film—to find their roots, to get back into training. Coming from a theatrical background is the best possible training and discipline one can have . . . It is not an easy profession. It's not a safe profession. It's a profession where one has to take chances, where one has to sacrifice.*

Often, it is the working actor who is most actively involved in helping other actors. Ed Asner, Patty Duke, Kathleen Nolan, William Schallert and Charlton Heston are some of actors that have served their colleagues as president of the Screen Actors' Guild. They consider their careers both as art forms and as jobs. They are in touch with their own needs, raise families, live in nice neighborhoods and have lives that are remarkably stable for so unstable a profession. Sometimes when we think of being an actor we can conjure up only two images: the struggling, starving performer or the star. Somewhere in the middle is the working actor.

Doris Roberts is an excellent example of just such an actor. She has performed on Broadway and in many regional theaters. She has worked in television and films. Her first "break" into notoriety came when she played the mother in the TV series *Angie*. When the series ended, Doris returned to performing on stage as well as to film and television roles. She began work as the secretary on the popular show *Remington Steele*. There's no two ways about it: Doris Roberts is a professional working actor. Well trained, well respected, hardworking, she is the type of actor that will always work—will always be a pro. She's no fly-by-night fad. Hume Croyn and Jessica Tandy are other examples of the true "working actor." Both have extensive experience both on stage and screen. In addition, Croyn is well respected as a writer. Perhaps their names are not familiar to the general public, but one need only see *The Gin Game* or *Cocoon* to be aware of their tremendous talent and craft.

Though the working actor is the mainstay of the profession, little focus has been given to this particular kind of career. The working actor has specific needs and challenges that differ from either the star or the struggling newcomer.

INVESTING MONEY

There are few actors who make a consistent income year to year. Most actors don't even make enough to support themselves. For the working actor, the income fluctuates greatly. It is important for this actor to realize that he must take financial control of his life. Many actors seem to dislike caring for their finances. Perhaps it's all those lean years when managing the funds is little more than an excursion into depression. In any case, these same actors will continue to ignore their finances as they start to earn decent money. Even when they hire someone to take care of their finances, they are often out of touch with what is being done. This is a mistake. You don't have to "do the books" to be aware of what your money is doing for you or *not* doing for you. As a working career actor, you will have good times and lean times. It is important that you use those moneymaking periods to insure financial security and to begin to build for the future. That means you should be in the driver's seat.

You Are the President of Your Company—Invest Your Assets So They Can Work For You.

Too often, I meet professionals who may have been working on a television series for quite a few years only to learn that they never made any solid investments while the weekly paychecks were coming in. Sure, they paid their bills and had an accountant calculate the best tax breaks, but no one was *counseling* them on how to make their money work for them in the long run! Some don't even know how their salaries were being spent. I think this is a mistake. When an actor begins to work steadily, one of the first concerns should be finding solid financial and investment counseling. And the actor should continue asking questions, looking over the investments, etc. Don't leave it all to someone else. You should always know what is going on. If you don't understand what a financial counselor is suggesting, ask questions. Hire someone to help. A well-respected and honest accountant or business manager. They charge for their services but they are worth it. They will help you with your taxes and investments. No one expects you to be a C.P.A. But it is *your* money and *your* future. Take responsibility and control. Be the leader of your own financial life.

STAGNATION

One of the greatest fears a working actor has to face is the possibility of stagnation—of falling into a rut with his art or career. Is the work you're getting just too routine? Do you still enjoy it? If a career becomes too predictable, boredom can set in. Don't forget—boredom is one of the great destroyers of the artistic sensibility. If this is happening to you, it's time to

Rekindle Your Dream or Create a New One.

Is there a certain professional or personal challenge that eluded you in your days of struggle? Maybe you wanted to do a play? Or write a book? Perhaps now is the time to give it a try. Consider your networking system. Are there new contacts that might help you actualize your dream? You may want to expand your contacts. It is the time to take on a new challenge. It may be a good time to review your career strategies and have a look at Section C.

Be resourceful. Recently I talked with one actor about how

she felt about her distinguished television career. She confided to me that she always dreamed of playing rather outlandish character parts in features, but her career took off in television so she never had the time to try her hand at features. I asked her why she didn't give it a go now that she had such a strong reputation for good character work. She seemed rather surprised at the suggestion and told me she didn't know anyone in films. I told her that there was no better time than now to start making those contacts and that she should talk to her agent about expanding her career interests. She told her agent and hired a publicist.

Once she began to focus on this new goal, it was amazing how quickly she realized that she did have contacts—people she knew from her years in acting who were now in the production end of features, colleagues with contacts, etc. Her enthusiasm for this new challenge ignited her agent and publicist's zeal. She made a list of film directors she admired and sought ways to meet with them. In short, this actress rekindled an old dream and in the process fell in love with her career all over again. In addition, she realized that all her hard work and effort in building her strong working-actor's reputation would now stand as a catapult to assist her in this new mission.

Whether your dream involves the industry, another profession or a personal life goal, finding a new goal that ignites your interest will bring magic back into your life. For some, this is the beginning of their own private comeback, which may lend itself later to a more public reaction.

The working actor may ease from the public eye to a quieter phase of their career. Sometimes it can be discouraging. After years of work and public notice, an actor may find his momentum lacking. Some actors fall back into themselves at this point or become bitter and angry with the industry. Others just seem to hover quietly in the background, taking a play here, a TV show there. But for some, their drive and passion for their art, for their lives, will keep them going. Delineating new goals, taking on new challenges, these actors breathe continuous life into their careers. During a quiet phase, they reevaluate, reconstruct, grow and expand their abilities and their horizons. For some, this leads to another burst of notoriety.

Performers like Bea Arthur, Angela Lansbury, Mickey Rooney, Robert Loggia and George Burns have guided their careers through media stardom and quiet phases back to public limelight and acclaim. Consider the diversity of these careers. Consider the challenges they have faced and overcome.

STARDOM CAN HAPPEN EVEN AFTER TWENTY YEARS IN THE BIZ

Carroll O'Connor, Ted Knight, Jean Stapleton, Ed Asner— these performers hit it big in the business after many, many years of being professional working actors. These performers worked hard while others seem to catch on and move ahead. Then suddenly that one role—that one show—catapults you to stardom. Just because your career hasn't become a media sensation isn't reason to believe it never will! If you still have the passion and the drive, it is amazing how many mountains you can climb.

PERSONAL LIFE GOALS

Sometimes devotion to a career can take so much focus and attention that we suddenly realize our personal lives have gone untended. One successful actor told me of his surprise one afternoon to see a young teenage girl chatting with his wife as she prepared dinner. He stared a moment and then realized that the girl was no stranger, but his own daughter. Of course he knew that his daughter was a teenager now, but somehow his last memory of really interacting with her was when she was still a small girl. He realized in that moment that he had always spent so much of his time, energy and concentration on his career—auditioning for roles, jumping from plays on the East

Coast to television on the West Coast, that somehow the years just slipped by without his even noticing.

It is never too late to set out to achieve a personal goal. Whether it's going back to school or raising a child, there is a way for you to do it if it's what you really want. Don't short-change yourself—ever!

EMOTIONAL AND PHYSICAL DEMANDS

Certain roles have very special emotional, and sometimes physical, demands. In *Raging Bull*, Robert DeNiro gained sixty pounds to play the part of Jake LaMotta. In *The Shining*, Shelly Duvall spent nearly six months playing a crazed woman. These roles drain a performer.

For the working actor—the actor who is constantly taking on various roles of varying degrees—the actual art of acting may be taking its toll. When the roles you play make demands on your physical self or your psyche, you must take whatever steps are necessary to insure your own health and well-being. At times, that may mean structuring some type of support counseling or techniques to help counterbalance the demands of an extremely stressful role.

At times, this may mean choosing to shift away from the type of roles that are producing stress. For example, I know of one actor who always battled a weight problem. With a disciplined diet and exercise plan, she was able to maintain her figure. Then she was offered a marvelous movie role that required her to be considerably overweight. She gained the weight, did the part and it helped her career take off. The only problem was now she was known at this weight. Soon another fat character came and so on . . . After a while, the weight began to take a toll on her health and her head. She was building a career on the kind of role and was not offered parts of women of normal weight. Her agent wanted her to stay heavy. Her doctor, however, was emphatic about her losing the weight for good. It was a difficult decision for her to make, but she realized her health and sanity were more important than an occasional fat role in a film.

Gradually, quietly, she began to lose weight. She continued to play the heavy roles she was known for—and at first, no one noticed she just wasn't as heavy as she used to be. Now, the characters she is offered are not those with forty extra pounds. It was a tough decision and a difficult challenge, but her determination paid off as she moved into another entirely new category and got some of the best roles of her career.

If you have been doing demanding roles that require extreme emotional states, you have to consider what effect they have on your life, your health and your well-being. If you've always played the rough-tough detective who's constantly diving bullets, is it time to request a change. If so, ask your agent to consider pushing you for something else. When you do a part that you know will take a toll, counter it with reinforcement to reinstate your own health. If it comes to a point that you must say no to certain roles, go ahead. Although it may be frightening to quit a good thing, remember there is more to you than one character, one emotion or one look. Be confident and do what you feel is best for you. Discuss your decision and your reasons with your career advisers. Let them help you make the shift.

YOU ARE THE PROFESSION

Being an actor means being a professional and that means being a grown-up, not a child. Frankly, I don't think that it's instinctive; it has to be learned. You have to work on being conscious all the time. You don't stumble into it. To paraphrase Stanislavsky: "If you don't have it in your life, you don't have it in your art."

—Judith Light,
Who's the Boss?

The working actor is the mainstay, the backbone, the foundation, of the acting profession. Revere yourself because you have done what only a few have been able to do. To live and support yourself through your art is a triumph. Do not allow yourself to be complacent or to overlook your past achievements. It should be a testament to your ambition, your courage and your hard work. Allow your career to serve as a source of strength—a source of pride. Your ability to survive the tremendous odds should give you the confidence to look ahead to new challenges, new interests and new goals. Keep building on your career and brave out into new frontiers. You can do it. You already have.

A Daily Work Plan 24

*It's Not Just the Amount of Effort You Put Into a Career That Counts,
But the Quality and Variety of That Effort!*

If you want to be successful, your game plan to achieve your
goals must be solid, varied and able to respond to feedback; to
improve, grow and adapt to your changing needs.

SET UP YOUR GOALS IN PRIORITY ORDER

Get a notebook and a datebook. These are vital tools to help
you organize and structure your career. Have a telephone and
address book also and keep it updated.

Use your notebook to *list your career goals in order of priority.* For
example, you might want to take some classes, or focus on
auditioning for showcases, or concentrate on your singing, etc.
If you're new in town, your first priority is to get yourself set
up and comfortable in your new environment and begin to
make contacts. On the other hand, if you're a seasoned pro
whose career just hasn't caught fire yet, classes and contacts

may be less important than working on some particular type of project, i.e. a one-man showcase, or a stand-up comedy act, or auditioning for more stage work. The point is, you can't formulate a solid plan to support your career if you don't know what your goals are.

Set up a time period in which to accomplish these goals. The importance of this is to give you a sense of order. There's no timeclock to punch each day, and no one to tell you you can't play hooky and go to the beach. You are your own boss. Set goals and deadlines.

The next step is to set up a "to-do" sheet that outlines all the steps necessary to get your goal accomplished. For instance, let's say you need a new headshot and have given yourself two weeks to accomplish this goal. Now, make up the "to-do" list, which would include contacting various photographers, scheduling appointments to see their work, making an appointment for a photography session, getting the proofs, choosing a picture and getting it to the lab for mass printing. This basically covers all the things you "must do" to accomplish your goal, keeping in mind the time period you've allotted. Once you make up this list, you may realize that your time frame is too long or too short.

By establishing a goal with a deadline and a step-by-step plan of action, you take the haphazardness out of your career development. Effective planning is one element of successful career-making.

Take the time now. Write out your list of goals with approximate deadlines, and "to-do" sheets for each goal. Next, organize these goal plans in order of priority and scheduling realities. For example, if there is a specific casting director you've wanted to meet but the executive is in Europe for three months, this goal will naturally have to be listed later on the priority list. On the other hand, you've just heard that a respected repertory theatre is having auditions in your area in one week. The audition requires you to have a prepared scene and monologue. Obviously, with only one week, this goal may supercede others on your list.

STEP BY STEP

Many actors resolve to work on their careers, only to lay out a workplan so ambitious that it is impossible to live up to.

Developing anything good usually takes time. Time and continuous action and effort. That's the secret rule of success. It's like a string of pearls. One pearl alone doesn't mean much, but as you string them side by side in ascending and descending order of size, eventually you've created an exquisite piece of valuable jewelry. Take this philosophy to your career.

DO SOMETHING EVERY DAY FOR YOUR CAREER

It's a simple rule, but a truly effective one. Each day consult your goal list and "to-do" plan of action and get going. If this becomes your habit, you will be amazed at what you can accomplish. You need to be organized to be successful.

SIX WORK AREAS OF AN ACTING CAREER

There are six general work areas to an acting career:

1. *Craft:* This includes classes, reading, lectures, workshops—any and all the things that can help you improve your technique and understand the actual craft of acting. There are natural actors who have succeeded without a class, but most professionals choose to study and strengthen the various areas their profession demands. Attention should also be given to voice and body work. Acting can be a very demanding profession. You will need a strong, well-developed voice if you hope to be heard in a large Broadway house. Studying body movement helps with overall grace and ease on stage.

2. *Image:* This includes your looks, your clothes—all the external aspects of who you are and what kind of physical

impression you hope to create. For most actors, that means regular exercise and a good nutritious diet.

3. *Auditions:* This area covers everything about auditioning, from the material you choose, prepare and update, to the actual process of following up audition leads, casting notices in the trades, etc.

4. *Networking/Contacts:* There's a lot of follow-up work to networking. Sending notes and postcards to casting directors you've met, to phone calls to business pals you want to keep up with.

5. *Promotion:* This area covers your own promotion efforts. Sending out pictures and resumes, postcards, letters, etc.— all this comes under the heading of self-promotion. It differs from networking only in the sense that you are breaking new ground either with new contacts or by getting your name out there to the general public through the media or to the industry through the specialized trades. Initially, actors do not have much to promote. However, getting in the habit of thinking about these areas and noticing how others handle their public relations campaigns will prepare you for later. In addition, you just might be able to seize an opportunity that crosses your path if you know what you're looking for.

6. *Wild Ideas and Crazy Notions:* This is the catch-all section for everything else you can think of to promote and advance your career. If you have a fantastic idea for a one-man show, this is where you should allot that work time. It's exactly what its title connotes—a free work area where you can plan and create either from a careering point of view or an artistic one.

Make one file for each work area. In this file, you will keep any miscellaneous notes, thoughts, ideas, articles or information that will help you develop this area of your career, in addition to your goal sheets with their deadline and "to-do" lists. Let's say you read an insightful article about a director you admire. You might clip this article and store it in the file for

Career Area #4: Networking/Contacts. Or perhaps you've seen a play that has a monologue perfect for you. You might make a note of the play, author and what the monologue is about and file that in #3: Auditions. These files serve a dual purpose: (1) They help you to collect and organize ideas and information that may be helpful to your career; and (2) they become source material for determining future goals. Thus, the article on the interesting director may spark the idea to try and make contact. This article would be a place to start, i.e. you might decide to write to him saying how much you enjoyed the article and how you enjoyed his work.

You can make these files anything you want—all inclusive or just a repository for your "to-do" action plans. It's up to you. The point here is to begin to become aware of the different areas of your career, all of which need attention.

ARRANGING THE SCHEDULE

Ultimately, the point of this work plan is to insure that you will work all areas of your career and not get lost in one particular area to the detriment of the others. The easiest way to do that is to monitor your schedule and make sure that each week you do something in each area of your career.

At the end of the day, review your appointment book and take a survey of what career areas you worked on. As the week progresses, make sure that you spread your work among all six areas. If you notice that one particular area is being ignored, check your priority goal list and see if there might not be a goal in the neglected area that can make it on the priority list. For example, if you notice that your date book is filled with work done on Career Areas 1, 2 and 3, and nothing in 4, 5 and 6, it's time to do some new goal and priority setting in the neglected area. Look through the files of those areas and see if there is a goal just waiting to be given priority. If not, then it's time to do some brainstorming. Concentrate your focus on these areas to get ideas for goals and projects.

At first, your goals may be simple and easy. That's fine. It's important to develop the habit of working your career in this broad-based way. Gradually, as it becomes second nature, you can take on more ambitious goals.

SCHEDULING VACATIONS AND BREAKS

Set aside days when you do not think about your career *at all!* Leave it alone. Walk away. Let your mind play with other concerns. Relax with friends. When you come back to "work," you will be more enthusiastic and energetic. We all need to get away from our jobs. Don't let the unique aspect of your career camouflage your need for rest and relaxation periods. No one can focus on one thing continually without sacrificing too much of life's experiences.

MAKE IT YOUR OWN

This is only one example of a daily plan. Make one that suits your needs. The important element here is that you devise a method that assists you in developing your career. Spending all your time working on only one area is not a good policy. Make it varied and don't avoid those areas that are uncomfortable. If it's a phone call you have to make to a casting director that you're sure you're going to avoid, make the call. Learn to handle things that are unpleasant but necessary. You will become stronger and increase your chances of success.

A Final Note 25

*It can be damaging to the psyche to take yourself too
seriously.*

—Shelley Duvall

"WHY?" Why did I choose this? Why am I the way I am? All
those "whys" we scream out to God and anyone else who'll
listen. It's at these times that you have to remind yourself about
your specialness—the fact that you are different. Life brought
you to this place in this way. You chose this career, and it is
a special one. The artist is a special soul. It's a special calling—
the fact that there's even a glimmer of consciousness about that
gift—that drive to perform, to entertain, to be creative. I want
to remind you that actors are very special. I want to remind you
to stay pure, healthy, happy and joyful. Negativity will kill.
Cynicism will maim. Don't allow that to endanger your pre
cious gifts. Review these pages in a philosophical manner.

Remember how much this career means to you, especially
when you find yourself saying, "Who needs this?" Or when
you see the flaws in your career, this business, your life and and
realize the sacrifices you have had to make. The choice costs
dearly. But you are an artist, a professional artist. You read this
book because you want to succeed. You are special—one of ~
kind. There's no one else like you in this world. And only one
you. Shelley Duvall, Jack Nicholson, Meryl Streep—it is then

specialness that they believe in and are aware of. You may not be the biggest star in the world, but if you have that awareness of your specialness, you will be your own star in your life. If you go into the world with that, you will bring miracles into your life. Miracles cannot happen with negative thoughts, with jealous thoughts, with self-deprecating thoughts.

I understand how difficult this road is. In my own life, I have had to search for a positive awareness to help me rise above obstacles, get out of my own self-absorption, overcome sorrow and seek out joy. Triggering positive thoughts should become a habit. Choose to live in the light. Do not hide in the darkness of fear, ignorance and hatred. Sometimes we fear that if we truly felt good, it might hurt our creativity. It's not true. For too long, we have glorified insane, destructive behavior. Don't be misled—it does not lead to great art. It will not make you a poetic genius. Art will not save your life. Only your desire to really change and grow can move you on.

It takes a lot of positive thinking to realize great ambitions. Wanting to be an actor is a great ambition. Believing in yourself gives you the power to make your dreams come true.

Question-and-Answer Seminar for Section D

26

1. I had an agent for over twenty years, who recently retired. Now I'm not represented by anyone. I feel so awkward about the business side of things. How can I do this myself? What should I do?

Check with your former agent about a referral or a suggestion. Is there anyone else in the agency whom you might connect with or who may be with another agency now? If you come up short, it's time to call all your former and present associates. Fellow actors, producers, directors you've worked with. Ask for assistance. You'd be surprised as to how much they want to help. After twenty active years, you are a respected artist and you must let people know you are in a crisis so they can help. Being too shy and too proud is wrong.

2. I've worked a lot in television and movies. Now my career is falling off and I'm afraid. Is it possible that after you're around for awhile, no one wants you because you're too recognizable and yet not a star?

There is a time even a lesser-known actor is overexposed. Some of it has to do with playing the same role a lot or with just being on too many shows in a short time. When this happens, it is best to consider capitalizing on it by getting career advisors to help. Get a publicist or a manager to help. Or simply try expanding your repertoire and do some theater. Look for a challenging role, one you are not identified with. If you are entering a slower period, relax; it will pass. But you must be active and use this time wisely. Make plans to reactivate areas that have been neglected and consider changes in your image.

4. I took about nine months off from my career to gain back my confidence and lose weight. Here I am sending out pictures and resumes and people are asking what was wrong with me that I took the time off. Should you just be honest with them and say, 'I took time off to clear my head, to lose weight, to gain back my confidence and now I'm ready to go gung-ho?'

Yes.

5. Can it hurt you as an actress to work at another career in a business that excites you and pays the rent? Will people still take you seriously as an actress?

It's best to keep your other business life inconspicuous. It is something you shouldn't emphasize until you are more established and sure of yourself. Being an actress should be your goal. Let it be known that is who you are. I think it will confuse the industry to reveal another career while you are establishing your credibility as an actress.

Reading List

ADDITIONAL BOOKS AND REFERENCE GUIDES FOR THE ACTOR

This is only a *partial listing* of all the books and materials that are available to the actor to assist him in learning more about the craft, history, background and important artists in this business. This list is meant to be a starting point. It covers various areas of interest and hopefully, will assist you in your career and craft growth process.

BACKGROUND AND BIOGRAPHY

Theater

Atkinson, Brooks. *BROADWAY.* Macmillan, 1974.

Clurman, Harold. *THE FERVENT YEARS: The Story of The Group Theatre and The Thirties.* 1945. An account of one of the most vital theater organizations of the period.

Garfield, David. *A PLAYER'S PLACE: The Story of the Actors Studio.* Macmillan, 1980.

Goldman, William. *THE SEASON: A Candid Look at Broadway.* Limelight Editions, 1987.

Hartnoll, Phyllis, ed. *THE CONCISE COMPANION TO THE THEATRE.* Oxford University Press, 1972.

Hartnoll, Phyllis. *THE THEATRE: A Concise History.* Thames and Hudson, 1985.

Sweet, Jeffrey, ed. *SOMETHING WONDERFUL RIGHT AWAY.* Limelight Editions, 1987. Fascinating account through interviews of the creation and development of famed comedy group, Second City.

Film and Television

Arlen, Michael J. *THIRTY SECONDS.* Viking, 1980. A behind-the-scenes look at the production of one thirty-second, million-dollar television commercial.

Dunne, John Gregory. *THE STUDIO.* Limelight Editions, 1985. A behind-the-scenes study of one movie studio. Entertaining as well as enlightening.

Gertner, Richard. *INTERNATIONAL MOTION PICTURE ALMANAC.* Quigley Publishing Company, 1986.

Goldman, William. *ADVENTURES IN THE SCREEN TRADE.* Warner Books, 1983. An entertaining, humorous and insightful look at the film business by an experienced Academy Award winner.

Gregg, Rodman. *WHO'S WHO IN THE MOTION PICTURE INDUSTRY.* Packard Publishing Co., 1987. Up-to-date directory of key individuals in the film business. Excellent reference guide.

Gregg, Rodman. *WHO'S WHO IN TELEVISION.* Packard Publishing, 1987. Up-to-date directory of key individuals in the television industry. Excellent reference guide.

Litwak, Mark. *REEL POWER: The Struggle For Influence and Success in the New Hollywood.* Morrow, 1986. Based on over 200 interviews with industry insiders, it explores the maze of power and politics in today's Hollywood.

Singer, Michael, ed. *FILM DIRECTORS: A Complete Guide—5th Edition.* Lone Eagle, 1987. An extraordinary compilation of directors and their credits. A useful reference guide.

Squire, Jason, ed. *THE MOVIE BUSINESS BOOK.* Simon and Schuster, 1981. The inside story of the creation and making of films by such diverse personalities as Mel Brooks, Sydney Pollack, Robert Evans, etc.

Stine, Whitney. *STARS AND STAR HANDLERS.* Roundtable Publishing, 1985. Book concerns itself with the role of talent agents, press agents and business managers in the industry.

Biography

Allen, Don. *FINALLY TRUFFAUT.* Beaufort Books, 1975.

Brown, Karl. *ADVENTURES WITH D.W. GRIFFITH.* DaCapo, 1976.

Capra, Frank. *THE NAME ABOVE THE TITLE.* Vintage, 1971.

Carney, Raymond. *AMERICAN VISION: The Films of Frank Capra.* Cambridge University Press.

Bosworth, Patricia. *MONTGOMERY CLIFT: A Biography.* Harcourt Brace Jovanovich, 1978.

Cole, Toby and Chinoy, Helen Krich, eds. *ACTORS ON ACTING.* Crown Publishers, 1970.

Courtney, Marguerite. *LAURETTE: The Intimate Biography of Laurette Taylor.* Limelight Editions, 1987.

Curtis, James. *BETWEEN FLOPS: A Biography of Preston Sturges.* Limelight Editions, 1982.

Funke, Lewis. *ACTORS TALK ABOUT THE THEATRE.* The Dramatic Publishing Company 1977.

Hart, Moss. *ACT ONE.* Random House,

Kalter, Joan Marie. *ACTORS ON ACTING.* Sterling Publishing Company, 1981.

Korda, Michael. *CHARMED LIVES.* Avon Books, 1981.

Kurosawa, Akira. *SOMETHING LIKE AN AUTOBIOGRAPHY.* Vintage Books, 1982.

Lawrence, Jerome. *ACTOR: The Life and Times of Paul Muni.* Samuel French Trade, 1986.

Le Gallienne, Eva. *THE MYSTIC IN THE THEATRE: ELEONORA DUSE.* Southern Illinois University Press, 1966.

Olivier, Laurence. *CONFESSIONS.* Simon and Schuster, 1982.

Olivier, Laurence. *ON ACTING.* Simon and Schuster, 1986.

Sher, Antony. *YEAR OF THE KING: An Actor's Diary and Sketchbook.* Limelight Editions, 1987.

Spoto, Donald. *THE ART OF ALFRED HITCHCOCK: Fifty Years of his Motion Pictures.* Doubleday, 1976.

Truffaut, Francois. *THE FILMS IN MY LIFE.* Simon and Schuster, 1975.

Truffaut, Francois. *HITCHCOCK (Revised Edition).* Simon and Schuster, 1983.

Weaver, William. *DUSE: A Biography.* Harcourt, Brace, Jovanovich, 1984.

TECHNIQUE AND THEORY

Note: It is not my intention to advocate any particular course of study in the craft of acting. This sampling of materials is meant to give you some idea of the type of philosophical and practical approaches to the artistry of the acting profession. These books offer a wide range of opinions and ideas. Ultimately, only you can decide which is the best course of study for you and your particular interests and goals.

Ball, David. *BACKWARDS AND FORWARDS: A Technical Manual for Reading Plays.* Southern Illinois University Press, 1983.

Boleslavsky, Richard. *ACTING: The First Six Lessons.* Theatre Arts, 1937.

Brooks, Peter. *THE EMPTY SPACE.* Atheneum, 1984.

Chekov, Michael. *TO THE ACTOR.* Perennial Library, Harper and Row, 1953.

Cole, Toby, compiled by. *ACTING: A Handbook of the Stanislavski Method.* Bonanza Books, 1971.

Hagen, Uta. *RESPECT FOR ACTING.* Macmillan, 1973.

Hethmon, Robert H. *STRASBERG AT THE ACTORS STUDIO.* Viking Press, 1965.

Jones, Robert Edmond. *THE DRAMATIC IMAGINATION.* Theatre Arts Books, 1985.

Lewis, Robert. *METHOD OR MADNESS?.* French, 1958.

Masters, Edgar Lee. *SPOON RIVER ANTHOLOGY.* Macmillan, 1962. This anthology is a series of poetic monologues by 244 former inhabitants (real and imagined) of the small town of Spoon River. It is used by many actors, and many acting teachers, as a source of acting monologues.

Spolin, Viola. *IMPROVISATION FOR THE THEATER.* Northwestern University Press, 1963.

Stanislavski, Constantin, pseud. *MY LIFE IN ART.* 1958.

CAREER GUIDES

Note: Once more, I must point out that these few books represent only a small sampling of what is available. It is meant as a starting place and only that.

Henry, Mari Lyn and Rogers, Lynne. *HOW TO BE A WORKING ACTOR.* M. Evans, 1986. Ms. Henry is Director of Daytime TV Casting at ABC-TV in New York and has valuable and interesting information about finding jobs.

Hunt, Gordon. *HOW TO AUDITION: A Casting Director's Guide for Actors.* The Dramatic Publishing Company, 1977. Concise audition advice from a pro plus interviews with various industry professionals on the subject.

Jaroslaw, Mark. *THE SEATTLE ACTORS HANDBOOK* (1987 Edition). Niche Press, 1987. Comprehensive guide for anyone interested in this rapidly growing theater city.

Mani, Karin, publ. *THE WORKING ACTOR'S GUIDE* (Los Angeles). 1987. New and extensive. It can be quite a help.

Shurtleff, Michael. *AUDITION.* Bantam, 1980. Useful, intelligent and comprehensive guide to making the most of auditions.

RESOURCE GUIDE

Type of Resource	*Los Angeles*	*New York*
Acting Unions	S.A.G. 7065 Hollywood Blvd. Hollywood, CA 90028 213-465-4600	S.A.G. 1700 Broadway 18th Floor New York, NY 10019 212-957-5370
	A.F.T.R.A. 6922 Hollywood Blvd. Los Angeles, CA 90028 213-461-8111	A.F.T.R.A. 1350 Ave. of the Americas New York, NY 10019 212-265-7700

	ACTORS EQUITY 6430 Sunset Blvd. Los Angeles, CA 90028 213-462-2334	ACTORS EQUITY 165 W. 65th St. New York, NY 10036 212-869-8530
Trade Papers	Drama-Logue 1456 N. Gordon St. Hollywood, CA 90028 213-464-5079	Show Business 1501 Broadway 29th Floor New York, NY 10036
	Hollywood Reporter 6715 Sunset Blvd. Box 1431 Hollywood, CA 90078	Backstage 330 W. 42nd St. 16th Floor New York, NY 10036
	Variety (daily) 1400 N. Cahuenga Blvd. Hollywood, CA 90028	Variety (weekly) 154 W. 46th St. New York, NY 10036
Industry Bookstores/ Publishers	SAMUEL FRENCH, INC. 7623 Sunset Blvd. Hollywood, CA 90046 213-876-0570	SAMUEL FRENCH, INC. 45 W. 25th Street New York, NY 10010 212-206-8990
	LARRY EDMUNDS CINEMA BOOKSHOP 6658 Hollywood Blvd. Hollywood, CA 90028 213-463-3273	DRAMATIST PLAY SERVICE 440 Park Ave. South New York, NY 10016 212-683-8960
	THE DRAMA BOOK- SHOP, INC. 723 W. Seventh Ave. New York, NY 10019 212-944-0595	